A COMMUNITY AND ITS UNIVERSITY

D1615582

A COMMUNITY
AND ITS UNIVERSITY

GLAMORGAN 1913-2003

edited by Dai Smith & Meic Stephens

UNIVERSITY OF WALES PRESS
CARDIFF
2003

BRITISH LIBRARY CATALOGUING-IN-PUBLICATION DATA
A catalogue record for this book is available from
the British Library.

ISBN 0–7083–1786–3 paperback
ISBN 0–7083–1787–1 hardback

Published with the financial assistance of the
University of Glamorgan

The Contributors have asserted their rights under
the Copyright, Designs and Patents Act, 1988, to be
identified as Authors of their Contributions to this
work.

Designed and typeset by Andrew Lindesay at the
Golden Cockerel Press Ltd

Printed in Great Britain by J. W. Arrowsmith Ltd.,
Bristol

CONTENTS

FOREWORD

It has been my privilege to serve as Vice-Chancellor of the University of Glamorgan for the first ten years of its existence as a university. It has certainly been a challenging time – the speed of change in higher education has been breathtaking. I am proud of what we have achieved and of the reputation the University has built for itself both on a national and an international level.

It is a truism, oft repeated, that academics owe allegiance to their discipline and thereby acquire an international perspective but identify only marginally with the institution in which they work. By extension, they identify hardly at all with institutional managers – vice-chancellors and their teams (for whom the institution and its success is all)! Trends in British higher education have had paradoxical implications for the way in which allegiances to discipline and institution have developed over recent decades. Increasingly fierce competition for resources (most especially research income) and the struggle to remain solvent have reinforced allegiance to the institution. It is now harder than ever to be a successful and fulfilled academic in a 'failing' university. Yet the precondition of institutions' success is that academics focus ever more narrowly on the kinds of research which will win plaudits from their disciplinary colleagues worldwide. This is the key to that lodestone of modern academic achievement – articles in the 'best' international journals. The 'local' success of a university within the UK therefore depends on academics focusing on knowledge which is generalizable internationally.

The polytechnics – the Polytechnic of Wales included – were pitched into this complex and highly competitive British university system in 1992. They suddenly faced 'mission conflict': they had developed an essentially 'vocational' and 'applied' character, with a strong emphasis on meeting local skill needs and undertaking research which was more likely to be applied than 'basic'. Of course, they were themselves complex organizations and some of their student recruitment was national and international, not merely regional, just as some of their research found its way into international journals. But the 'binary line' between universities and polytechnics undoubtedly represented an underlying difference in history, character and function (just as that between 'ancient' and 'civic' universities once had).

The dilemma facing the 'new' universities of 1992 was nowhere better illustrated than in the Polytechnic of Wales. Its history stretched back to 1913 when forward-thinking mine owners decided to found the South Wales and Monmouthshire School of Mines, financed by a levy on the output of the subscribing collieries. From the outset, the courses were vocational and closely linked to the needs of local industry. Student numbers were 30 full-time and 110 part-time students – a far cry from our current total of over 19,000. The portfolio of courses had broadened to include most academic disciplines bar medicine over the years, but the strongly vocational element and the commitment to the regeneration of the local area had been retained. The task was, somehow, to retain the traditional mission while yet developing that self-respect as a 'real university' which would be essential if staff and students were to be recruited, retained and given the opportunity to flourish.

Personally, I had been facing the same dilemma at the beginning of the 1990s. I was poised between a return to the research academic career at the end of some years in management roles and the vice-chancellor journey into long-term, full-time management. It was towards the very end of a long selection process for the vice-chancellorship of a 'Russell Group' university based in a low-income region of the UK that I began to be troubled: how could a university preoccupied with its foothold in the prestigious world of the 'Russell Group' serve a low-value-added, low-skill economy and potential students who grew up in a culture of educational under-achievement? The self-absorption of the first goal seemed to run completely counter to the second. Could I, if I got the job, reconcile the two? The phone call from Glamorgan came just as I was deciding that one of the 'new universities' might be the challenge which I really sought.

What met me when I visited Pontypridd incognito in jeans and sweater, but officially too as 'a suit', was a sense of moral commitment – to students, generally to teaching as a central commitment and not just as one which got in the way of research, and to the social and economic regeneration of the region. Glamorgan already had what I had been trying to crystallize: the sense of a university with a moral purpose – a university whose 'internal' success was a means to a wider end, not the sole end in itself. A university with a moral vision is one which can go places – especially if that vision has been held lightly and somewhat self-deprecatingly, yet with utter conviction. Such a university can strive to achieve eminence without losing its sense of place, pride in its roots and commitment to the people and communities which it exists to serve. Glamorgan was for me; fortunately, Glamorgan decided I was for it. The rest is our shared and future history – a history of constant striving against a system which professes greatly to value what we stand for as a university while relentlessly measuring us against only one canon of higher education virtue – the prestige of the old, the well established and the well funded. For all our success in the past ten years, it is a struggle which is as hard – if not harder – than ever. The tensions within our complex mission demand constant attention and hard effort.

Resources, at the time, were extremely limited and the fact that the university is now in a very healthy financial position (rated by *The Times* as one of the top five UK institutions for financial soundness five years running) is due to the diligence of governors and senior management. These resources have been invested to good effect in transforming the estate and developing facilities.

Our staff – *all* our staff – have shown an outstanding level of commitment and effort in achieving a standard of excellence throughout this complex mission. This has resulted in:

– an expanding portfolio of courses, responsive to the changing needs of the local and national workforce, and delivered flexibly to suit the needs of students;

– successive cohorts of skilled, adaptable and, above all, employable graduates with transferable skills;

– Quality Assurance Agency (QAA) ratings of teaching excellence in twelve separate areas; and good ratings in most league tables;

– an improved performance in successive research assessment exercises (RAE) with the number of research-active staff doubling over the past few years;

– nationally recognized centres of excellence and expertise at the cutting edge of their disciplines;

– consultancy and technical support for the benefit of local and national industry;

– the successful commercial exploitation of ideas;
– innovation in teaching and learning – particularly in placing us as one of the international front runners in e-learning development;
– international research collaboration;
– a network of collaboration with further education (FE) colleges bringing higher education (HE) within the grasp of students of all abilities in diverse locations.

Our support departments have been proactive in driving up standards in their own areas, gaining national recognition for excellence in human resources – we were the first HE institution in Wales to achieve Investors in People status – and in environmental management and marketing.

We are justly proud of the national and international recognition we have gained for our achievements. However, we remain very conscious of the fundamental contribution we make to the local community. This can be seen in the expertise and facilities which we offer to local business and industry; in the range of facilities and activities we provide for the community – summer schools, master classes for local schools, community education, community regeneration, sports facilities etc. Our award-winning student radio station, GTFM, is one of the UK's first community radio stations.

One of our most important priorities remains that of opening up higher education to those groups which have traditionally been under-represented. There are still many people – of all ages – who, for a variety of reasons, have been excluded from HE. This means we have to change attitudes and provide role models as well as providing the opportunities. We have tried to achieve this by taking activities out into the community; by working with schools and colleges through our student tutoring scheme; and by a willingness to accredit students for prior learning.

Whilst celebrating our history in the pages of this book, it is inevitable that our thoughts should also turn to the future. Where will the University of Glamorgan be in ten, in twenty years' time? In Wales, the National Assembly for Wales's Review of Higher Education has already been the catalyst for change within the sector. For example, we are discussing some exciting possibilities for collaboration with FE and HE (up to and including merger) to extend HE opportunities to a wider community and to develop new curriculum areas.

We have ambitious plans to generate more resources in order to give us the means to be innovative. Not least, we want to build on the success of the experience gained in e-learning through E-College Wales and our significant contribution to UK eUniversities Worldwide for the benefit of both off-campus and on-campus students. Our experience has provided us with many avenues to explore in terms of educational research, product development and student-centred course delivery and we are recognized by institutions in the UK and USA as leaders in this field.

Our continued commitment to widen participation will mean taking a long-term view, first by raising aspirations and empowering people and then by providing ladders of progression for students from a variety of backgrounds.

As I write, we are awaiting the outcome of the White Paper on HE in England. This will undoubtedly have a knock-on effect in Wales and result in more changes and further challenges but I am sure that the University of Glamorgan is in a strong position to meet them confidently and imaginatively. I hope you will enjoy reading about our past and share with me a view of the University of Glamorgan that is well-equipped to face the future.

Sir Adrian Webb
Vice-Chancellor
University of Glamorgan

ACKNOWLEDGEMENTS

The editors and publishers are grateful to the following for permission to reproduce copyright material in this book:

The estate of Alun Lewis for the extract from the early version of 'The Mountain over Aberdare'.

Trevor Griffiths for the extract from his play *Food for Ravens*.

CONTRIBUTORS

Professor David Adamson is Director of the Programme for Community Regeneration at the University of Glamorgan.

Dr Keith Davies is Principal Lecturer in the Centre for Lifelong Learning at the University of Glamorgan.

Dr David Dunkerley is Professor of Sociology and Director of the Centre for Civil Society at the University of Glamorgan.

Dr Peter Harries is Director of the Ashridge Institute for Dyslexia in Swansea.

Dr Lesley Hodgson is a Research Fellow at the Centre for Civil Society at the University of Glamorgan.

Basil Isaac joined the staff of the Glamorgan College of Technology in 1958 and was Principal Lecturer in Geology at the Glamorgan Polytechnic and the Polytechnic of Wales from 1975 until his retirement in 1989.

Professor Dai Smith is Pro-Vice-Chancellor of the University of Glamorgan.

Peter Stead is a writer, broadcaster and External Professor at the University of Glamorgan.

Dr Meic Stephens is Professor of Welsh Writing in English at the University of Glamorgan.

A COMMUNITY AND ITS UNIVERSITY

PONTYPRIDD:
A TOWN with NO HISTORY
BUT ONE HELL of a PAST

Meic Stephens

The writer Gwyn Thomas, a Rhondda man born and bred, once described Pontypridd as 'the hub of sophistication, a town poised genially in an intermediate state of grace'.[1] He was referring, of course, to the town's location in a broad bowl between Llanwynno and Llanfabon, the whale-back mountains and parishes on either side of the Taff Valley, and to its position halfway between the old coal and iron townships of Rhondda, Aberdare and Merthyr and the city of Cardiff, some twelve miles to the south, and with looser links to the leafy villages of the Vale of Glamorgan.

Pontypridd has always been a frontier town, albeit on an internal frontier between Blaenau and Bro Morgannwg, the upland and lowland districts of the old county of Glamorgan. In its first industrial phase during the last years of the eighteenth century and the early decades of the nineteenth, it had, moreover, many of the hallmarks of a town somewhere in the American West, a Klondyke perhaps, growing from a sleepy hamlet into one of the most populous towns in Wales within the span of two or three generations.

The town's geographical location may also have something to do with the sunny, outgoing character and attitudes of its people and the society they have created. In the 1930s, Gwyn Thomas knew a Porth councillor who thought Pontypriddians 'a snobbish lot, full of themselves, proud as Pharaohs', though it must be said this jaundiced view was grounded in the fact that, in those days, Pontypridd had a branch of Woolworths, whereas Porth did not. For their part, not to be outdone in local pride, Pontypridd people tend to look down their noses on the Shoni Hoys of Rhondda (Fawr and Fach), just as they turn them up at the semi-detached outlook of suburban Cardiffians. Indeed, 'The People's Republic of Ponty', as it is affectionately known in some quarters, is in many ways its own place, its people easily distinguishable from those of, say, Trehafod or Abercynon, a mere sheep's walk or engine's shunt to the north, not only by their subtly different mid-Taff accent but also by the extrovert, talkative, gregarious, egalitarian, amiable and altogether hyperbolic quality of their communal personality: they may be properly considered as the Texans of south Wales.

'Pontypridd: Gateway to the Valleys' was the promotional slogan of the railway companies in the days when the region, with the town at its nodal point, was producing most of the coal and iron on which the economy of Britain and its Empire depended. In 1913, at the peak of production, some 57 million tons of steam coal passed through Pontypridd on its way to the docks in Barry and Cardiff, by then the biggest coal-exporting port in the world. Although the town depended largely on the pits and furnaces of upland Glamorgan, especially for as long as coal and iron were required by the British navy and for the building of railways, it was also an important meeting-place, with its famous open-air market, its canal linking it to Merthyr and Cardiff, its railway station (which had the second longest platform in the world, so the Texans say), its bustling streets and a municipal life of its own, and of course its rapidly growing population drawn hither from all parts of Wales and beyond.

Alas, the heyday did not last long. In the years between the two world wars, when in Auden's phrase, 'Glamorgan hid a life grim as a tidal rock-pool's in its glove-shaped valleys',[2] recession, strikes and lockouts (including the General Strike of 1926), mass unemployment and social deprivation left indelible marks on the psyche of the people, just as it scarred both the built and physical environment. Pontypridd took on a new role as the exit-point for hundreds of thousands of workers and their families, perhaps a third of the population, who were leaving Wales in search of employment in the industrial conurbations of England, never to return. According to Gwyn Thomas, whose black humour often matched the grim reality of the inter-war years, valley folk who were about to vacate their homes would put up signs in their windows: 'Not dead, gone to Slough.'

It is the purpose of this opening chapter to suggest that we cannot understand the society of south-east Wales, and of Pontypridd in particular, and will not be able fully to appreciate the significance of the part played by the University of Glamorgan and its antecedents, without reference to what lies over our shoulder. Merthyr Tydfil has to be viewed against what the ironmasters, the Crawshays and the Guests, did at Dowlais; the Rhondda must be seen through the eyes of miners' leaders like William Abraham (Mabon; 1842–1922) and Noah Ablett (1883–1935), just as other valleys – Ebbw, Sirhowy, Rhymni, Cynon and yet others further west – are best understood in terms of the forces which, in times of boom and bust, shaped them into what they are today.

It is as well that a university should understand not only its present-day context but also the historical one, and that its students and academic and administrative staff, and all who come into contact with them, should be aware, if only in outline, of what went into the making of the physical and cultural landscape which lies all about us, but which, all too often in these days of 'globalization', remains largely unobserved and unexplored. It seems an appropriate moment, in a book published to mark the tenth anniversary of the University of Glamorgan, to attempt an overview. The University is making strenuous efforts to engage with local society, and is sure to add cubits to its reputation in this important respect in the years ahead, particularly through the work of its Centre for Modern and Contemporary Wales and its other research groups. Even so, some of us need to be reminded that Pontypridd has not always been the rather nondescript, not to say dilapidated town on which uninformed visitors sometimes comment, but is a place which, with Merthyr, the Rhondda and Aberdare, was one of the great cradles of the industrial revolution. This chapter takes its title from a comment by local playwright Laurence Allan that although Pontypridd, like the University itself, is sometimes said to have no 'history', it has 'one hell of a past'.[3]

Let us try to tease out a few strands from the complex story of Pontypridd. It is often assumed that the town's history began with the building of a bridge in 1756. The reader may be familiar with *The Great Bridge over the Taafe*, the splendid picture by the Welsh painter Richard Wilson (1713–82). He visited the district some ten years after the bridge had been built, at the fourth attempt, by a local stonemason and Dissenting minister named William Edwards.[4] The bridge attracted many visitors by virtue of the aesthetic and architectural excellence of its single arch, a perfect segment of a circle and, with a span of 140 feet, in its day the longest in the world (on that the Texans can be believed). It became so famous that it even helped make south Wales an agreeable alternative to the Grand Tour which young English gentlemen in the eighteenth century were told was part of their education. The Welsh, too, were full of admiration for William Edwards's bridge. It was set as a subject at eisteddfodau and often figured in *englynion* and *tribannau* written by poets of upland Glamorgan.[5]

Yet the bridge, for all its fame, did little to change the rural character of the district. It seems to the present writer that Peter Lord, the distinguished art historian, is not quite right in arguing that Wilson's painting was meant to represent the unsullied landscape of Wild Wales at a moment when the district was already caught up in 'an industrial age based on technology and commerce'.[6] That, as will be shown, did not happen until much later, at least not in the immediate vicinity of the bridge. For all that was made of its beauty by the Romantic imagination, the bridge's origins were quite mundane: it was built to drag not coal, but lime for agricultural purposes, between the estates belonging to Lord Windsor on either side of the Taff. A fine example of the picturesque the painting may well be. Those readers who know Trallwn, the riparine district to the north of the town, will note the drastic relocation of the rocky outcrop of Graig-yr-hesg on the western bank of the river, in the interests of pictorial composition. But, whatever else was going on further upstream in the valleys of Rhondda, Cynon and Taff, coal had not yet been discovered hereabouts. It can be concluded that the dark cloud in the northern sky of Wilson's picture was not meant to suggest industrial pollution in the air over Merthyr, but was inserted by the artist to please the current taste for the deliciously gloomy and foreboding, as epitomized in the cult of Ancient Britain which was then in vogue.

So the bridge was not built to serve the industrial life of the district, nor did it attract industry, for there was none in 1766 or for years thereafter. Even as late as 1803, when Benjamin Heath Malkin (1769–1842) was passing through, the rural calm which had prevailed in these parts since the time of the Silures, 'the small dark people' whose territory once extended throughout southeast Wales, was still everywhere evident. In his book, *The Scenery, Antiquities and Biography of South Wales* (1804), Malkin wrote:

> The appearance of the bridge from the hill on the Llantrisant road has generally been likened to that of a rainbow from the lightness, width and elevation of the arch. Without weighing the exactness of a simile, I may safely say that the effect of such a structure, in such a position between two rocky but well-wooded crags, with a considerable reach of the river and valley seen through the lofty arch, affords an instance scarcely to be paralleled, of art happily introduced among the wildest scenes of nature.

No mention of industry there.

Even so, the small cluster of houses which began to grow on either bank of the Taff at the point where William Edwards's bridge spanned it came to be known as Newbridge. It is worth noting here that the name Pontypridd, officially adopted only in 1856, a hundred years after the bridge was built, was the one which had been preferred among the sparse Welsh-speaking population of the district. The original name is, of course, a contraction of Pont-y-tŷ-pridd (Bridge of the turf house), which is thought to refer to a hut which may have stood near by, though the building in Wilson's picture, on the eastern bank of the river, seems rather more substantial and to be constructed of stone. The island in midstream may be Ynys Angharad (Angharad's island) or Ynys y Cariadon (The lovers' island), later the name of a large house and fine municipal park in the town's centre.[7] However all this may be, the people of Pontypridd are justifiably proud of what is now known as the Old Bridge, notwithstanding the fact that its splendid arch has been obscured by a banausic construction dating from 1857. The present writer will never forget that the badge of Pontypridd Boys' Grammar School was a heraldic version of the Old Bridge and that its motto, *Ymdrech a lwydda* (Perseverance will succeed), was said to be a reference to the dogged determination of its builder. It seems fitting that the University of Glamorgan has adopted a version of the school's motto for its own purposes: 'Success through Endeavour'.

But to return to our story. By the end of the eighteenth century the conditions for the preliminary phase of industrialization in the district of Newbridge were already in the making. The first significant event was the opening of the Glamorgan Canal, from Merthyr to Cardiff, in 1794, a year which now appears to have been something of an *annus mirabilis* in these parts. Up to 1794 Merthyr iron had had to be carried to Cardiff by mule or in waggons over rough tracks along the steep valley sides. The canal, with its numerous locks and horse-drawn barges, flowed through Newbridge on the eastern side of the valley, along a line now followed by the A470; it was still there in the mid-1950s and short stretches can be seen at Melin Griffith in Whitchurch and in the grounds of Cardiff Castle. The canal's importance was that, although it did not link the district with the wider world, since it carried no passengers, it at least facilitated the transport of coal and iron from its hinterland to the coast, thus helping to meet the huge demand for those commodities in many parts of the world, not least during the wars against revolutionary France. As for the transport of passengers, the district in the last decade of the eighteenth century was more or less inaccessible to the mail coach, still the principal means of travel and communication, owing to the hilly terrain and, more especially, because its high and steep-sided bridge, however beautiful, could not be crossed by any large, wheeled vehicle – especially on a wet or windy day.[8]

For evidence of industrial development in the lower reaches of the Taff Valley we must search a little further afield. Iron ore deposits had been exploited near Llanharri and Llantrisant and lead at nearby Mwyndy since Tudor times. There were small driftmines and iron furnaces on the sides of the Garth, the mountain overlooking Pentyrch and Tongwynlais; there was a quarry at Taff's Well and, from 1813, a pottery at Nantgarw, now happily restored, which made fine porcelain china renowned for the delicacy of its designs and colours. But the key development was the discovery of coal, for it encouraged the improvement of the transport infrastructure which, in turn, led to the sinking of collieries in the district, so that it began to change from a rural landscape of farms, fields and woodland akin to those of the Vale of Glamorgan into an industrial area more like the townships to the north. Meanwhile, on the northern side of town and in the lower Rhondda, the exploitation of coal deposits continued apace: the Maritime colliery was opened by John Edmunds in 1841, the Darren Ddu and Hafod pits in 1842, and at Gelliwion the engineer John Calvert introduced the first steam-engine in 1845; this machine has been preserved and now stands proudly near the front lawn of the University of Glamorgan.

One of the satellite villages which began to grow before Newbridge itself was Trefforest, which was in a much more accessible location and which, for a while, looked as if it would outstrip the town in population and importance as an industrial and commercial centre. It acquired, for example, a post office long before one was opened in Newbridge and counted its population in thousands rather than hundreds. So fast was its development that, for perhaps twenty or thirty years, Trefforest enjoyed a greater rate of growth than even the thriving old market town of Llantrisant, which as a hilltop community was beyond the reach of both canal and the tramroads which now began to serve the district. But eventually Trefforest began to lose momentum since it did not have any coal mines in its immediate vicinity. Newbridge, as 'the front door' to the coalfield, caught up with it and soon overtook it in growth and importance. Nor did Trefforest, unlike the town, enjoy the benefits of what might be called benevolent capitalism. None of its works had a school and the condition of its people was sorely neglected, so that the Blue Book commissioners could damn them with characteristically faint praise in their notorious reports of 1847 as 'ignorant and immoral, though not flagrantly so'.[9] Let me illustrate my theme by focusing on Trefforest, the village in which I was born and brought up and where the University of Glamorgan is located today,[10] before returning to Pontypridd.

The growth of Trefforest as an industrial village was due almost entirely to the capital of the Crawshays, 'the iron kings' of Cyfarthfa in Merthyr Tydfil, and of course to the labour of the men and women whom they employed.[11] It was William Crawshay II (1788–1867) who would be involved in the events which led up to the workers' rising of 1831, when the Red Flag was raised for the first time as a symbol of working-class solidarity, and which ended dismally, in the same year, with the execution of Dic Penderyn (Richard Lewis; 1808–31) on the trumped-up charge of wounding one of the Argyll and Sutherland Highlanders who had been sent to quell the insurrection in the town.[12] Hundreds of Trefforest men are thought to have been among the thousands who marched to Merthyr in support of their fellow workers.

The Crawshay name had been first linked with Trefforest in 1794 (again that crucial year), some four decades after the building of the famous bridge. In that year, Richard Crawshay (1739–1810), the son of William Crawshay (1713–66) of Normanton in Yorkshire, the bullish founder of the dynasty, purchased from a man named Christopher James a plot of land at Ynyspenllwch, on the western bank of the Taff opposite Rhydyfelin, on which there stood a small mill for the rolling of tinplate.[13] Fed by pig-iron from the Crawshay works at Hirwaun, about fourteen miles to the north and between Aberdare and Merthyr, the Trefforest enterprise proved an immediate success, for only twelve years later its production was said to exceed that of the large Melin Griffith works in Whitchurch.[14] Even so, the business languished for a while under the shadow of Cyfarthfa, in which William Crawshay I (1764–1834) had invested the family's considerable fortune, and it was against his father's wishes that William II, tired of waiting to inherit, began using his own capital to rejuvenate both the tin-works and the foundries located in Trefforest. Another reason why output fell into temporary decline at the Trefforest works may have been that the cannon which some believe were manu-factured there were no longer required for use against the French.[15] Be that as it may, in 1834, having waited patiently for his father's death, William II came into his own as sole owner of the Cyfarthfa empire.

Shortly afterwards he lost interest in the tinplate works at Trefforest, delegating the completion of the modernizing process to his son, Francis Crawshay (1811–78). Two years later, Fforest was back in full production and the tinworks had become the largest in Britain. Francis Crawshay moved immediately into the large and handsome house known as Tŷ Fforest or Forest House, which had been built for his grandfather. The house stood on the site of a farm, Fforest Isaf (Lower Forest), in the wood called Coed Berthlwyd which still serves as a backdrop to the University of Glamorgan; there is another farm further up the hillside which is known as Fforest Uchaf (Upper Forest). It was Fforest Isaf, farm and house, which gave its name to the Fforest works and, in due course, the works gave its name to the village.[16] The old house, now owned by the University and known as A Block, is a listed building. The grounds of Forest House were extensive: Llantwit Road and its side streets stand today in what were once its orchards.

The Fforest works was managed in conjunction with its coun-terpart at Hirwaun and was on two sites. There was the ironworks situated in the upper grounds of Forest House near what is now the northern gate of the University, close to Brook Street, Oxford Street and King Street, and the tinworks which lay beyond Meadow Street and the Bute embankment, on the village's south-ern flank.[17] The ironworks consisted of a complex of buildings and machinery, including a steam-pump which fed air into the three blast furnaces. In 1873 Francis Crawshay sold the works to a consortium which set up the Trefforest Iron and Steel Company, but kept much of the surrounding land and Forest House as a home for his son, Tudor, who with his brothers owned the lease-hold on many houses in Trefforest until well into the twentieth century. Then there was the tinworks. An inventory made in 1842, by which time it was well-established, shows that it consisted of a refinery for running out fire, four charcoal furnaces, three hollow fires, three balling furnaces, two scaling furnaces, several anneal-ing foundries, three coking ovens and about 2,340 yards of tramway. The initial investment was £4,000 but this figure had increased to £100,000 by 1854 – in today's money, several million pounds, though only a small part of the Crawshay wealth.[18] All the machinery at the ironworks was run by means of eight water-wheels powered at first by Nant-y-Fforest, the stream which comes down off the mountain at the back of the University's main campus, crosses under the road by means of a culvert and then reappears on the other side of the railway line in the field which gives Meadow Street its name. Later, Crawshay would build a weir across the Taff near the Castle Inn bridge, from which to take water to the tinworks.

The tinworks depended on the pig-iron and bar-iron supplied by the Crawshay works at Hirwaun. It was brought down the val-ley via the Aberdare and Glamorgan canals and unloaded at Trefforest near the weighing bridge (also known as the Machine Bridge) which lies under the bridge now bringing traffic off the A470 into Trefforest.[19] The iron was then taken downstream as far as the Crawshay weir and thence along the mill-race, or 'feeder' as it is known locally, which ran behind Long Row and Raymond Terrace, or else by tram across the field on which Meadow Street now stands, and so to the tinworks. The extensive ruins of the derelict works can best be viewed from Llantwit Road or from the summit of the Barry Mountain. Its massive stonework remains an impressive monument to the industry which was once carried on there.[20]

How best to summarize the complicated process of making tinplate? After being cut to size, the pig-iron and bar-iron was heated and passed through the rolling mills to produce flat plates. These plates were then folded in half and rolled again to make thinner sheets known as 'doubles'; this was a dangerous part of the process which required skilled men and often caused hideous accidents, in particular 'doubler's cut' which severed the tendons of workers, whose job it was to fold the plates with the aid of tongs. The process was then repeated, producing 'fours' and 'eights', which of course were even thinner. The sheets were then trimmed, passed through several cleansing and annealing stages and finally coated with a thin, rust-proof layer of tin. The finished tinplate left the works by way of a tramroad, crossing the Julia Bridge into Rhydyfelin and then to the Doctor's Canal [21] which joined the Glamorgan Canal at Dynea; the sheets continued their journey uninterrupted to the Bute Docks at Cardiff, whence they were exported all over the world.

The manufacturing process made for very hot working conditions and gave rise to the distinctive garb of the foundry and tinplate workers. They wore thick, knee-length stockings, long underpants, moleskin trousers, wooden-soled leather clogs and a short-sleeved shirt with no neckband. A sweat-cloth was worn around the neck or as a face-cloth when the men were recharging the furnaces, and, to complete the outfit, a white canvas apron which, as a matter of pride for skilled men, was always spotless at the start of each shift. Women were employed to separate the plates and spent their twelve-hour day with their hands immersed in a bath, or bosh, of warm acid solution used in the pickling process; for this work, in 1842, they were paid 6s 8d a week. At shift's end the workers slaked their thirst at the nearby Dyffryn Arms. [22]

So much for those who were employed in the Trefforest works; what about the man who owned them? The first thing to be said about Francis Crawshay is that he was popular with his mill-hands, among whom he was known as Mr Frank and whom he always paid in cash. [23] The Crawshays were a hard-headed lot who could not afford to be sentimental about conditions prevailing in their works, because for them profit was always more important than the safety and health of their employees. But Francis seems to have had a kinder streak in him and a genuine interest in the welfare of his men and their families. First manager and then sole owner of the Fforest works from 1856, he had what today is called a hands-on approach and was often to be found amid the noise and heat of his foundries. Even so, local tradition has it that whenever he and his wife rode through Trefforest on their white horses, the village children were expected to bow and curtsey as they went by. His stock rose in 1849, at the time of the cholera epidemic in Hirwaun, when he remained in the district until the end, bringing relief to those afflicted by that terrible disease. He also gave financial help to such workers' organizations as the Philanthropic Order of True Ivorites, founded in 1836, which added to the Friendly Societies' usual aims the promotion of the Welsh language and its culture. He was, moreover, the only Crawshay to speak fluent Welsh, albeit, so it was said, the better to curse his largely monoglot workforce in their own language, though how he once came to dislocate his shoulder while wrestling with one of his foremen is no longer remembered.

That Francis Crawshay, as well as being a genial man, was nothing if not eccentric is suggested by the portrait of him in workman's cap and rough overcoat which now hangs in an upper corridor of his old home.[24] It seems that his heart was never wholly in his work and he much preferred shooting rabbits on Barry Island, which he owned long before it became a holiday resort, to running the Fforest works. It was perhaps inevitable that the enterprise would suffer, especially in comparison with the much more profitable Crawshay undertaking at Hirwaun; the actual loss was masked because the accounts always showed Fforest and Hirwaun as a joint venture. Francis Crawshay attributed his lack of success to outdated machinery, but his father, who thought him idle and frivolous, blamed Fforest's substantial losses on Frank's inept management, accusing him of complete indifference to the family motto, 'Perseverance' (that word again, with the stress almost certainly on the second syllable), which is still to be seen inscribed on the parapet of a wall at the tinworks: 'Perseverance. Who is not a fool? If this raise anger in the reader's thought, the pain of anger punishes the fault. W. C. 1835.' This lapidary inscription, doubtless intended to exhort Frank to greater effort after the collapse of the market in cannon, meant little to him. He had a mischievous sense of humour which he was prepared to use from time to time against the authority of his overbearing father. Once, in an after-dinner speech at the family seat of Cyfarthfa in 1846, he caused great embarrassment among the guests by saying he had always tried to live up to his father's motto, 'Live and let live'.

He interpreted this in his own rather louche way. It is said that he had, besides nine children by his wife Laura, who was his first cousin, a large number of illegitimate offspring by Trefforest women, to whom he usually gave a hundred pounds and, to the offspring, a job for life in his works or in his own household. Visitors to Forest House, where he often gave parties and balls, would comment on how amply staffed it seemed, and for years thereafter there were people in the village who were 'the same dap' as Mr Frank. It is said that Laura Crawshay turned a blind eye to his exercise of the *droit de seigneur* and was always expecially kind to the women he had seduced and the children he had fathered. One of Mr Frank's more innocuous hobbies was the erection of monuments and houses of strange design, such as the circular building he put up at Dyffryn: it contained eight dwellings, their doors on the perimeter of the outer wall, and built on four storeys, with a garden entered through a trilithon like those at Stonehenge.[25] The high point of his social life came in 1862, when two of his daughters, Laura and Isabel, married the sons of Rowland Fothergill (1794–1871), a local but lesser industrialist who owned the Taff Vale Ironworks, known as 'Y Gwaith Bach' (The small works), just off the Broadway. The bridal party was led by two works bands, one from Trefforest and the other from Cyfarthfa, and the brides rode with their father in a carriage drawn by four greys, from Forest House, up what is now Llantwit Road, to the church at Llantwit Faerdre. Mr Frank's popularity was attested by the large crowd of tinplate and foundry workers who voluntarily turned out to cheer them on their way.

Five years later, in 1867, having refused a knighthood, Francis Crawshay retired, leaving the Trefforest works to a consortium managed by a local man named William Griffiths. He lived out his last years in comfort at Sevenoaks in Kent, where his main delight was sailing his yacht, *Mamgu* (Grandmother), on the Solent and, growing ever more eccentric, taking great pleasure in annoying his neighbours by striking huge bells which he had put up in the grounds of his home, Bradbourne Hall. After his death in 1878, at the age of sixty-seven, ownership of the Trefforest works passed to his sons, who leased them to a succession of companies. The furnaces had been converted to the Bessemer process in 1875 and continued in production until 1900, when they were 'blown out' and dismantled, a victim of the industry's growing trend away from upland to lowland Glamorgan. The manufacture of tinplate at Trefforest came to an end in 1946 and the site was then occupied by Leiner's gelatine plant until it went bankrupt in about 1980. After the days of the Crawshays, Forest House was owned by a local solicitor named Walter Morgan (1853–1901), who founded the Pontypridd firm of Morgan, Bruce and Nicholas, which did much good work on behalf of the South Wales Miners' Federation; he was a prominent Liberal and, for some years, vice-chairman of Glamorgan County Council. It was from his widow that the house was purchased for the purposes of the South Wales and Monmouthshire School of Mines in 1913.

Today, apart from the ruins of the tinplate works, not much remains of the Crawshay presence in Trefforest, and of the foundries there is no trace. Some of the houses he built for his workers, such as those in Long Row, still stand but most have long been demolished. The Neo-Druidic circle of tall stones which were gathered from various parts of the estate by Henry Crawshay (1812–79) after his brother's death, and which bore the names and dates of the numerous Crawshays, beginning with the first William in 1650, were removed in the mid-1950s to make room for the expansion of the Glamorgan Technical College (as the School of Mines had become) and, much to the chagrin of local residents, the rubble used for the foundations of some of its new buildings. But at least one Trefforest lad remembers the bilingual inscription on the logan-stone:

Duw ni feddaf	I have no God
Haf ni ofalaf	I heed no summer
Gauaf ni theimlaf	I feel no winter
Angau nid ofnaf	I fear not death

The white tips, consisting of waste from Crawshay's foundries, above Duke Street, have been levelled and are now used as football pitches. Of the Glass Tower (also known as the Iron Tower), an iron structure sheathed in glass which Francis Crawshay had built as a hunting lodge on the summit of the Graig, only the base remains, though it can just be made out on the southern approach to Trefforest from the A470.[26] The neo-Egyptian obelisk, a replica of the one erected at Heliopolis by Osortseen, the first Pharaoh, which Francis and Henry Crawshay put up in 1844, can still be glimpsed in a small garden behind a laurel hedge near the Castle Inn bridge.[27] Finally, it is not generally known, even among Trefforest people, that several of the streets in the district are named after members of Francis Crawshay's family: Laura Street (where the singer Tom Jones lived as a boy) after his wife and daughter; De Barri, Owen and Tudor Streets in Rhydyfelin after his sons; the Julia Bridge, linking the tinworks to the Doctor's Canal, after one of his daughters-in-law; Fothergill Street after the father-in-law of his two daughters; Francis Street after himself; and so on. There is not much else by which to remember the egregious Francis Crawshay – the reader is left to choose between the archaic and modern meaning of that epithet – though it may be that the real monument to him is Trefforest itself, and that, as was said of Sir Christopher Wren, the architect of St Paul's Cathedral, '*Si monumentum requiris, circumspice*'.[28]

Let us turn now from Trefforest back to what had been happening in Newbridge or Pontypridd during the long afternoon of Victoria's reign. The second phase of industrialization had begun with the coming of the railway in 1840. This was the Taff Vale Railway, which, like the canal, ran from Merthyr to Cardiff and served the district and town until 1922 when it was taken over by the Great Western Railway.[29] It is an ironic fact of engineering history that when the great Isambard Kingdom Brunel (1806–59) carried out a feasibility study for the proposed railway in 1836 he assumed that its main function would be to carry iron from Merthyr. No one had anticipated the rapid and enormous growth of the Rhondda coal trade which would follow the opening of a level at Gyfeillion, a mile or so up the valley from Newbridge, by Dr Richard Griffiths in 1790 and of another by Walter Coffin (1784–1867) at Dinas in 1807. But, as the extraction of coal got under way in the years following, the town found that it was ideally placed for transporting it to the coast, especially as the railway station, unlike the road and canal, was conveniently situated on the Rhondda side of the valley. Newbridge already had a flourishing chainworks, owned by the cousins Samuel Brown and Samuel Lenox from about 1794, also the year of the Glamorgan Canal's construction; it was the chainworks, built on the land of Ynys Angharad near the canal, which had first brought Brunel to the district. Among its many customers were the

Admiralty, the suspension bridge at Hammersmith, the chain pier at Brighton and Thomas Telford's bridge over the Menai Straits. The firm made chains and anchors for many liners, including the *Lusitania*, the *Mauretania,* the *Queen Elizabeth* and the *Queen Mary*, and for the warships *Rodney* and *Nelson*; when German warships were scuttled at Scapa Flow in 1918, they were found to be equipped with chains and anchors made at the Brown Lenox works in Pontypridd.

But it was Rhondda coal which caused the town of Newbridge to grow apace, outstripping villages like Trefforest, Rhydyfelin, Cilfynydd, Coedpenmaen, Trallwn, Maesycoed, Pwllgwaun and Graigwen, and soon to enfold them within its municipal embrace. The town's new commercial prosperity, based on its function as a market and shopping centre for the communities of Rhondda, Cynon and Taff, but also depending on the coal they produced as well as on its own industries, can be illustrated by a few facts from a process which has been called 'civilizing the urban'.[30] By 1839, the town of Newbridge, a lawless and disease-ridden place in its first phase, had acquired the rudiments of its own police force: a sergeant and six constables. In 1850 it had a Gaslight and Coke Company which was responsible for lighting the main streets. A county court met at the White Hart Hotel in 1851. By 1852 the town had a thousand houses and thirty-three beerhouses. In 1856 the first post office was opened. In the same year the town changed its name from Newbridge to Pontypridd, largely because the postmaster, Charles Bassett, had grown tired of having to deal with mail intended for the many other New Bridges in Britain and Ireland.[31] There had been a market here since the early 1800s, mainly for country folk to sell and barter their wares and for trade in livestock, but in 1860 a new market, at first in its own hall but soon spilling out into the streets, began attracting shoppers from far and wide and became known as 'The Petticoat Lane of the Valleys'. The Pontypridd Workhouse, a primitive form of hospital, opened under the aegis of a Poor Law Union in 1865. Clearly, by that year, the town was becoming a place with its own municipal apparatus and one of some importance: 'a coming place', as Jack Jones noted in one of his novels.[32] Its main problem was the danger of infectious diseases associated with poor housing, inadequate sanitation and the lack of a reliable supply of fresh water.

Nevertheless, the last three decades of the century saw the consolidation of Pontypridd's status as a major urban area. The first church, St Mary's at Glyntaf, had been consecrated in the 1830s and now many more were built, notably St Dyfrig's Catholic church at the lower end of Broadway in 1857 and, in the centre of town, St Catherine's Anglican church, with its famous spire, in 1869. Since 1810, when Carmel Baptist Church was built in Graigwen, there had been a proliferation of Nonconformist chapels where Welsh was the main language of worship, and now similar chapels were built by the Congregationalists, Calvinistic Methodists, Wesleyans and other Protestant denominations. The municipal cemetery, one of the largest in Wales, was opened in 1871 at Glyntaf, 'across the river' as Trefforest people used to say, as if the Taff were the Styx. The first newspaper, the *Pontypridd District Herald*, was established in 1873, followed by the *Pontypridd Chronicle* and, in 1897, the *Pontypridd Observer,* which is still essential reading for the people of the town and district. The Pontypridd Football Club (that is rugby football) was formed in 1875. The first town crier was appointed in 1879. By 1885 there was a horse-drawn tram service between Pontypridd and Porth. The first arcade was opened in 1886. A second railway line to the Barry docks, running through a tunnel and along what is now one of the University's main car parks, was opened in 1889, thus giving its name to the Barry Mountain, the wooded hill which stands behind the University. A new town hall with a seating capacity of 1,700 was built in 1890 at a cost of £5,000, and in the same year a public library, and shortly afterwards the Royal Clarence Theatre (later renamed the New Theatre) opened its doors.

To set the seal on its new-found status, the town played host to the National Eisteddfod of 1893 and, with the help of financial donations made by local colliers, established its own County School in 1896. In the same year the town had a male voice choir and Trefforest had a ladies' choir. The Queen's Jubilee in 1897 was loudly celebrated on Pontypridd Common when Sir Alfred Thomas, MP for the East Glamorgan division (1885–1910) and later Lord Pontypridd, gave a tea party for 20,000 children, who devoured a cake weighing five tons; it was followed by a fireworks show and bonfires on the surrounding hills. The first Workmen's Institute was opened in 1899, in the same year as a branch of the

Young Men's Christian Association. By this time the Pontypridd Urban District Council had been formed and the town's population had grown apace: from 2,200 in 1847, to 5,000 in 1855, to 15,000 in 1861, to 20,000 in 1891 and to 38,000 in 1899. In 1901, the year of Queen Victoria's death, Pontypridd had three woollen factories and mills taking water from the Taff and Rhondda, several breweries, a chemical works, a vinegar works, brickworks and flour mills, as well as shops and offices galore in its busy main thoroughfare, Taff Street. Among the many thousands who had flocked to the district were my grandparents, who settled in Meadow Street, Trefforest, in 1901 after my grandfather had found employment as an electrician with the PUDC, laying cables for the town's new electric trams.[33]

The pace and extent of the growth of Pontypridd in late Victorian and early Edwardian times was breathtaking. A hamlet in a sylvan valley had been transformed within a few generations into one of the most important industrial centres in south Wales. Part of the price it had to pay was that the old rural culture of the Blaenau, or upland Glamorgan, was virtually swamped by the new age of coal, iron, steam, cut-throat capitalism and ruthless exploitation by men for whom profit was the only consideration. True, the Nonconformist chapels remained a bastion of the Welsh language, producing their own poets and musicians and creating a culture centred on the eisteddfod, the male voice choir and what remained of the indigenous literary traditions of the Blaenau. But whereas Welsh had been the language of the majority up to about 1860, by 1891 English – the *lingua franca* of the thousands who had swarmed into the district in search of work – was firmly established as the language of officialdom, certainly in the school, the workplace and public administration; at the census of that year Welsh-speakers living in the town were enumerated as 33 per cent.

The student who attempts to trace the cultural history of Pontypridd in the nineteenth century is advised to bear in mind the dictum that 'culture is the steam off the back of a galloping horse', or perhaps in our context, off the back of a tramload of coal.[34] He or she will find that, apart from the writings of competent amateur historians like the late Don Powell, there are few reliable accounts.[35] In fiction, we had to wait for the novel by Jack Jones, *Some Trust in Chariots* (1948), in which the town figures as 'Pontyglo', and for the later stories of Alun Richards, for an imaginative reworking of its history and society.[36]

But to stay with the histories: we can immediately set aside the most unreliable of them all, the *History of Pontypridd and Rhondda Valleys* written by Owen Morgan (1836?–1921), more generally known as Morien, which was published in Pontypridd and London in 1903. From 1870 to 1899, Morien, a Rhondda man who had settled in Glyntaf at a house known as Ashgrove, was a local correspondent for the *Western Mail*, one of the first in a long line of distinguished literary men who have written for that newspaper. He specialized in the reporting of mining disasters, of which there were many and to which his florid style was well suited. The acme of his career came in 1877 when he reported daily on the week-long attempts to rescue colliers trapped in the flooded galleries of Tŷ Newydd colliery, during which the men had sung the powerful hymn, 'Yn y dyfroedd mawr a thonnau' (In the great waves and waters). The accident was not remarkable as pit disasters go, with only a handful of men killed, but Morien's copy caught the imagination of the public in Wales and far beyond, so that the world's press and many sightseers came to Pontypridd to ascertain what all the excitement was about.[37]

But as a historian Morien left a great deal to be desired. His book, which is now quite a rare collector's item, is described by R. T. Jenkins in the *Dictionary of Welsh Biography* as 'an odd jumble of Druidism, mythology, topography, local history and biography, though not without value for its information on the development of the valleys during the 19th century'. The trouble is that sometimes Morien's fertile imagination took over from sober fact, so that almost everything he wrote seems suspect. The main tenet of his fantasies was that a wholly fanciful version of the derivation of a place-name was always to be preferred to the obvious or straightforward one. Thus Bristol, which is early English for 'Bridge town', is explained as 'Town of the Britons', and Wells, which means just that, is said to be derived from 'Wales'. Glyncoch (The red glen), according to Morien, commemorates a bloody victory of the Silures against the invading Romans. Even more preposterously, he took Craig Evan Leision (The rock of Evan Leyshon) to be a corruption of *Kyrie Eleison*, and so on. The final assault on the reader's patience is the book's chapter on how

Rouget de Lisle (no doubt a Cilfynydd boy like Stuart Burrows and the late Geraint Evans) came to compose *La Marseillaise*.

What did for Morien as a historian was Druidism, or more precisely Neo-Druidism, that feverish belief in the arcane and downright bogus which had been propagated by the wayward genius of Iolo Morganwg (Edward Williams; 1747–1826), a Unitarian stonemason of Flemingston in the Vale of Glamorgan. In 1792 Iolo had invented Gorsedd Beirdd Ynys Prydain, the Assembly of Bards of the Isle of Britain, one of whose first gatherings had taken place on the summit of the Garth. For Iolo, Wales had been the last bastion of the Druids before they were annihilated by the Romans in AD 61 and, in his book, *Cyfrinach Beirdd Ynys Prydain* (1829), Morgannwg or Glamorgan was presented as being at the heart of the Welsh literary tradition. To prove his thesis, he fabricated a large number of fine poems and other texts which he attributed either to Dafydd ap Gwilym, the greatest Welsh poet of the medieval period, or to Glamorgan poets who had never existed, even composing illustrious biographies for some of them. The Gorsedd ceremonies proved popular and since 1858 they have been part of the pageantry of the National Eisteddfod where, every August, they continue to lend colour to the affairs of a people who have been rather starved of indigenous ritual. After Iolo's death, his son Taliesin Williams (1787–1847), a schoolmaster in Merthyr, propagated his father's work among the poets of the Blaenau, presiding over an assembly at the Rocking Stone in September 1834, after which the bards retired to argue on the licensed premises of the New Inn, the home of Gwilym Morganwg (Thomas Williams; 1778–1835), another of Iolo's acolytes. It was not until 1926, when Griffith John Williams published the first fruits of his research into Iolo's papers, that the full extent of his brilliant forgeries was revealed.[38]

The best that can be said for Neo-Druidism is that it was the dream of men who refused to accept the recorded view of the history of their country and who refurbished the past by inventing traditions which mirrored their own aspirations. They sought refuge in the Wales of their imagination at a time when understanding of their country's history, language and literature had been so long neglected that, among a dispossessed people, the main objective was not so much to demonstrate the intrinsic qualities of the Welsh language and its literature as to show that the Welsh people had an honourable place in the British scheme of things – indeed, that they alone should be considered the true Britons.

Iolo's claims for his native and beloved Glamorgan found fertile ground in the minds of Newbridge men and his influence lingered in the district for long after his death in 1826. Although Morien, as a good journalist, was sceptical about his more extreme theories, for example that Druidism was the true religion, he had a soft spot for many of his acolytes, particularly his son, Taliesin Williams, perhaps because the Druids regarded Taliesin, one of the earliest Welsh poets in the sixth century, as the personification of the sun and his name a corruption of the name Jesus. Among Iolo's disciples to be befriended by Morien was Evan Davies (1801–88), generally known by his bardic name, Myfyr Morganwg, which can be rendered in English, regrettably, as 'Student of Glamorgan'. Myfyr had settled in Newbridge as a watchmaker soon after the advent of the railway in 1844. An autodidact, he claimed to have discovered the secret of earthly wisdom which he kept in the shell of an ostrich's egg slung round his neck on a piece of string. It is difficult, without a feeling of dismay and exasperation, to summarize the contorted thinking which went into the making of his credo. In short, he believed that Christianity was but a Semitic form of Druidism, a fantastic theory which he expounded in such books as *Gogoniant Hynafol y Cymry* (The ancient splendour of the Welsh), published at Pontypridd in 1865. Some thought his Druidomania had been caused by his failure to be appointed minister of the Independent chapel known as Sardis, one of the largest in the town. Be that as it may, by 1847, with Taliesin Williams in his grave, Myfyr was claiming to be the true Archdruid of Wales, a delusion which, for the next forty years, at solstice and equinox, he acted out in quasi-religious ceremonies at the Rocking Stone on Pontypridd Common, much to the consternation of the more orthodox among the townspeople.

The Maen Chwyf, as the stone is known in Welsh, is a large boulder of local Pennant sandstone, and is said to be, with the Old Bridge, one of the Seven Wonders of Glamorgan.[39] Later in the century it would be used as a platform by the miners' leader and Liberal MP for the Rhondda, William Abraham (Mabon;

1842–1922), to address the men of Pontypridd, notably during the colliers' strike of 1898, the year in which the South Wales Miners' Federation was formed.[40] But it was Myfyr who made the stone famous. It was he who added the serpent's tail of smaller stones still to be seen near the main boulder which, alas, no longer rocks as much as it once did. For all his outlandish beliefs and behaviour, there was no doubting his sincerity: at his death in 1888 he asked for copies of his books to be placed under his head as a sign that he had written them in sober earnestness and not as a wilful fad, and this last request was duly carried out.

Myfyr Morganwg, though a rank individualist, was one of a circle of poets known as Clic y Bont (The bridge clique).[41] As poets there may not be much to be said for them, and most Welsh-speakers nowadays would be hard put to name them. If their surnames were mainly Evans, Thomas, Davies and Williams, their bardic names are much more memorable: besides Myfyr, there was Dewi Haran (David Evans; 1812–85), Dewi Wyn o Essyllt (Thomas Essile Davies; 1820–91), Carnelian (Coslett Coslett; 1834–1910), Glanffrwd (William Thomas; 1843–90) and Brynfab (Thomas Williams; 1848–1927), to mention only a few of the clique's leading members. They were all men of some substance and not without literary ability. Glanffrwd, an Anglican cleric, wrote a charming history of the parish of Llanwynno, that tract of upland Glamorgan, rich in its traditions, which lies between the Rhondda and Cynon valleys.[42] Brynfab, whose farm, Hendre Prosser, is clearly visible on the hillside opposite the University, wrote a history of the Rhondda before the discovery of coal and was perhaps the most accomplished of the group.[43] Dewi Haran was a local auctioneer. Dewi Wyn's only claim to fame, however, seems to be that, in 1891, he dropped dead in the bar of the Hewitt Arms at Pencoedcae. Of him it was said: 'Even in an age of eisteddfodic zeal, he was considered to have over-indulged his competitive instincts.'[44] His collected works, *Ceinion Essyllt* (1874), run to some 600 pages. It has also been suggested that as poetry editor of the *Western Mail* he was not averse to boosting his own reputation and that of his associates, but let a veil be quickly drawn over that mischievous libel.

The 'Clic' may not have been up to much as individual poets, partly because their work was of only local appeal, though they were all masters of traditional Welsh prosody. Even so, they have some significance as a group. They gave Pontypridd a literary identity at a time when the town was beginning to need one. Still only a random assembly of industrial undertakings of one sort or another, of hastily thrown up and insanitary houses deemed good enough by the coalowners and ironmasters for workers and their families to live in, a place where local government was still embryonic and politics still at a semi-feudal stage of development, the town was nevertheless the regular meeting-place of this small group of writers to discuss and practise their craft.[45] Few townships in the industrial parts of England could claim as much.

Exactly why Pontypridd has produced so many colourful characters, eccentrics even, has for long been debated by historians. It has even been suggested, not altogether jocularly, that there must be something in the air – perhaps a daily whiff of the pungent iron-dust drifting over the town from the Brown Lenox chainworks – which has affected the minds and manners of some of its inhabitants. The town's frontier spirit, in particular its role as a communications centre served by canal, road and railway, and its amalgam of industrious native Welsh people and enterprising English incomers, seem to add up to a more likely explanation. The town marked an interface between the old world and the new and made for a boldness of spirit which put Pontypridd in the vanguard of an emerging industrial Wales.

This view is nowhere better illustrated than in the character of Dr William Price (1800–93), the greatest eccentric of them all. The more lurid, not to say lubricious details of his long career have been vividly presented by several writers, not least by Rhys Davies (1901–78), another Rhondda man, who saw in him the standard-bearer of an older, more vital Wales before the coming of industry and chapel religion, a Silurian version of the Green Man.[46] Dr Price was not a native of Pontypridd, although he was descended from Nicholas Pryce, an ironmaster of Pentyrch. He was a familiar figure in the district, parading through its streets dressed in a white tunic, scarlet waistcoat, green trousers and a fox-skin hat, and carrying the symbols of his Druidic authority, a burning torch and a crescent moon. He too was affected by Druidomania and would perform Neo-Druidic rites on Pontypridd Common.

Dr Price's notoriety was caused by his advocacy of free love, vegetarianism, nudism and moon-worship, and by his fierce denunciation of vaccination, vivisection, orthodox religion and the ironmasters. On his election as leader of the Pontypridd Chartists in 1839 he ended his speech with the words: 'We have tolerated the tyranny of those who oppress us – landlords, coal-owners and the clergy – for too long. We must strike with all our might and strike immediately.' On one occasion, on the run from the police, he fled to France disguised as a woman and, in Paris, became acquainted with the poet Heine. There, in the Louvre, he found a stone, hitherto undeciphered, confirming that he, Dr William Price, was indeed the Archdruid he claimed to be, albeit in rivalry with Myfyr Morganwg. Nevertheless, and for all his weird beliefs, it must be said that the doctor, who had qualified as a member of the Royal College of Surgeons in 1821, did a good deal of work on behalf of the common people. He was among the first medical men to carry out a skin-graft operation, which he performed on a workman horribly injured by molten metal at the Brown Lenox chainworks, to which he was attached as physician. He had a novel attitude to his profession: patients, he argued, should pay doctors only when they were well; when they were ill, the doctors should pay them. He also founded the first co-operative store in Wales, the Pontypridd Provision Company, intended to combat the iniquities of the owners' truck system. His commitment to the Welsh language, which he spoke eloquently, was steadfast: he organized Welsh classes, only to see them broken up by the police who suspected them of being a cover for lessons in the handling of muskets. For Dr Price was nothing if not a 'physical force' Chartist, though his Chartism, a Welsh reworking of the ideas of Tom Paine, was inextricably mixed with his Neo-Druidism.[47]

After the failure of the Chartist march on Newport in 1839 and of the Chartist-inspired strike at Merthyr in 1842, Dr Price's mind fell prey to paraphrenia, a form of schizophrenia, and his fantasies became more and more extreme.[48] Two preposterous examples must suffice: all Greek books, he reckoned, were the work of the early Welsh bards and Homer had been born at Caerffili. From now on he would turn much of his energies to litigation. He had nothing but contempt for English law but was often in court, enjoying every moment of the proceedings and, always the showman, shamelessly playing to the gallery. Even so, he proved an awkward litigant: one case in which he was involved was temporarily halted by his refusal to swear on a Bible because, he argued, he could not vouch for the accuracy of a map of Judea in it. Sometimes he would bring his small daughter, Gwenhiolen, to represent him, addressing her as 'my learned counsel'. But the most memorable of his court appearances took place at the Cardiff Assizes in 1884, when he stood trial for having burned the corpse of his infant son, whom he had named Iesu Grist (Jesus Christ), in a field at Llantrisant. His subsequent acquittal established the legality of cremation and paved the way for the passing of the Cremation Act of 1902. That is why there is a chapel dedicated to the memory of Dr Price at the Glyntaf Crematorium and a somewhat grotesque statue to him on the square at Llantrisant.

Even so, Dr Price's connections with Trefforest seem to require more attention than they have hitherto received. We know that he used to parade through the village in his outlandish dress – as a boy, the present writer knew old people who could remember him doing so. We know, too, that in 1860 he built, or at least designed, the Round Houses at Graig-yr-helfa in Glyntaf, which he intended as the lodge for a sort of Xanadu he wanted to build on the hillside, and that he had a surgery near by. Unfortunately, Lady Llanover, who owned the land and much else besides hereabouts, changed her mind, thus preventing the execution of the doctor's plan, and, to avoid paying the builder who had supplied him with materials, he had to leave the district in a hurry.

More intriguingly still, we know that Dr Price was prepared to make an exception among ironmasters because he was a close associate of Francis Crawshay and his family, whom he served as physician. It is said that the bond between Price and Crawshay came about after the doctor had saved the life of the ironmaster's wife by successfully delivering her of a child by Caesarean section. They also shared unorthodox religious views: although the godless Crawshay paid for the building of several chapels in the district, one of the complexities of his strange personality, he was at heart a pagan who was sympathetic towards the heresies of Dr Price. When, in 1838, Price began collecting funds for the building of a sort of Druidic arts centre or museum on Pontypridd Common, the list of patrons was headed by Francis Crawshay, though

the scheme foundered for lack of support among other industrialists in the area.[49] It may be, too, that Price did not spend the
entire period of his exile in France but, as local tradition has it, was
hidden by Crawshay for a while in the Glass Tower on the Graig.
We are now in the realm of speculation. The secret chamber discovered in 1940 under the floor of what had formerly been Forest
House, and rediscovered every ten years or so since then amid
great excitement, may or may not be the place where Dr Price,
who was often in trouble with the law, was hidden from time to
time. The igloo-like, brick construction, reached through a trap-
door in its crown, may or may not have been the scene of Masonic
or Neo-Druidic rites in which Crawshay and Price both had a
keen interest. The chamber was perhaps constructed for much
more humdrum purposes, but if so we must conclude, rather for-
lornly, and despite the most assiduous enquiries, that we do not
know what they were.

Enough has been said to suggest that Pontypridd in the nineteenth century was a place of great bustle and rapid, fundamental
change. Industrial development went hand-in-hand with municipal growth which, in turn, led to the emergence of an urban,
largely Welsh-speaking culture informed by ferment among
'organic intellectuals', some of whom were highly unorthodox and
subversive of the established order. These men may not have been
entirely typical of their time and place but at least they are distinguishable from the local worthies who gaze out in all their sepia
drabness from the pages of Morien's book; they too are part of
Pontypridd's story. Nevertheless, rather more representative of the
town's cultural history were the composers of '*Hen Wlad Fy
Nhadau*' (The old land of my fathers): in 1856 Evan James (Ieuan
ap Iago; 1809–78) and his son James James (Iago ap Ieuan;
1833–1902) gave their country the words and music of a national
anthem which still lifts the heart of all patriotic Welsh people.[50]
They owned a weaving mill in Mill Street and are commemorated
by Goscombe John's splendid monument in Ynys Angharad Park
and in the name of one of the town's Welsh-medium primary
schools. If this chapter had treated the musical tradition of Pontypridd, the Jameses would have taken pride of place among
composers associated with the district: for example, John Hughes
(1873–1932), a colliery clerk of Ton-teg, the man who wrote the

tune of 'Cwm Rhondda', perhaps the most powerful of all the hymns sung from the chapel pews and rugby terraces of Wales, or Morfydd Llwyn Owen (1891–1918), born and bred in Park Street, Trefforest, who became the first wife of Ernest Jones (1879–1958), the psychoanalyst and biographer of Sigmund Freud, whose premature death robbed us of one of our most promising composers.

But the purpose of this chapter has been to trace the industrial growth of Pontypridd, to show how a period of rapid change produced a number of rebels and eccentrics whose lives were a passionate response to it, and to set the scene for the chapters which follow. We should not, by any means, forget the more abstemious of the townspeople, those generations of men and women who by dint of their hard work made Pontypridd into a thriving, prosperous and progressive community. But let us also remember the rebels and eccentrics, those who chose to swim against the stream and to challenge the bearded orthodoxies of their day. Out of step and out of favour with the society which produced them, and for which they had mostly deep misgivings, they have tended to be marginalized and overlooked in most accounts of Pontypridd's 'official' history. Yet it may be that in a more sympathetic age they will, after all, turn out to be representative figures, or at least figures in whom it is proper to take an interest.

How, then, are we to remember them? The unkindest thing that can be said about men like Francis Crawshay, Iolo Morganwg, Morien, Myfyr Morganwg, 'Clic y Bont' and William Price is that they were loony – literally so in the case of the moonstruck doctor – and had allowed their minds to be distracted and their reason overturned by what had no foundation in historical fact. But there is a more kindly view. It is that their lives, in their various ways, were a reaction against a dislocated, frenzied world, an attempt to make sense and impose some sort of order on a society which was changing too fast and seemed to make no sense at all. Iolo, according to his own lights, was reaffirming his identity as a Welshman by reinventing – forging his country's past, in both senses of that word – so that it would have a place in the sun of the British Empire, which in his day was at its zenith and seemed as if it would never set. More clear-eyed judgements might now prevail, but we should not dismiss him for all that. Nor should we scorn Dr Price, who looked back to an older Wales, before the more baneful effects of Nonconformity possessed our people, and forward to a more egalitarian future in which the working class would no longer be exploited by the capitalist system and have to suffer the harsher aspects of the new industrial age. He too did what he could to bring about a better world. As for Francis Crawshay, the creator of Trefforest as an industrial village of some importance, that old rascal was born into wealth and privilege which he put to good use for the benefit of his workforce as well as for his own; if he was paternalistic and a touch feckless, at least it saved him from the stiff-necked brassiness of his profit-driven father.

Whichever verdict is preferred, it is the present writer's view that these men are certainly worth remembering, and where better than in Pontypridd, the home of the University of Glamorgan, on the very ground that they once trod, should their memory live on? To remember them, and the society which produced them, is to understand more fully where we came from, where we are today and how we might go on from here.

NOTES

1. Gwyn Thomas (1913–81) in his foreword to *Old Pontypridd and District in Photographs* (Barry: Stewart Williams, 1977).
2. W. H. Auden (1907–73), 'Poem', first published in the *New Statesman* on 16 July 1932 and included in *On This Island* in 1937; the poem was dropped from Auden's books after 1950 and does not appear in his *Collected Poems* (London: Faber & Faber, 1976).
3. Laurence Allan, author of *Valley of the Kings* (1991), a 'community play' about Pontypridd, interviewed and quoted by Meic Stephens, 'Ponty's past captured in people's play', *Western Mail* (1 July 1991).
4. There is a plaque commemorating William Edwards (1719–89) in the church at Eglwys Ilan on Mynydd Meio, high above the valley on the eastern side of the Taff; he was a native of the parish and Independent pastor of Groes-wen; the plaque describes him as *Adeiladydd i'r ddeufyd* (A builder for both worlds).
5. The poet Gwilym Harri (1763–1844), also known as William Harry, a Penderyn man, wrote an *englyn* on the bridge for the Eisteddfod held in Cardiff in 1834:

Un darn yn gadarn i gyd – mewn urddas
Mae'n harddu'r gelfyddyd;
Adail gref a saif hefyd
I ddydd barn neu ddiwedd byd.

All of one stout piece in dignity, it embellishes art; a mighty structure which will stand until the day of judgement or the end of the world.

6. Peter Lord, *The Visual Culture of Wales: Industrial Society* (Cardiff: University of Wales Press, 1998).
7. The word *ynys* in Gwentian Welsh can denote not only an island but any low-lying land near a river.
8. An anonymous *triban*, one of the traditional forms of Welsh prosody popular in the uplands of Glamorgan, describes the location of Pontypridd and its bridge thus:

Mae Pontypridd, fel gwyddys,
Mewn hengwm cul, arswydus,
Ac mae y bont sy'n croesi'r pant
Yn meddu cant echrydus.

Pontypridd, as is well-known, lies in a narrow, dreadful valley, and the bridge which crosses the hollow has a terrifying gradient.

9. The government reports known as the Blue Books, which enquired into the state of education in Wales, are discussed in Gwyneth Tyson Roberts, *The Language of the Blue Books: The Perfect Instrument of Empire* (Cardiff: University of Wales Press, 1998).
10. The University of Glamorgan's main campus is at Trefforest while other parts are located at Glyntaf and in Church Village.
11. The most important book on the Crawshays is John P. Addis, *The Crawshay Dynasty, a Study in Industrial Organisation and Development* (Cardiff: University of Wales Press, 1957); see also Margaret Stewart Taylor, *The Crawshays of Cyfarthfa Castle: A Family History* (London: Robert Hale, 1967).
12. For further details of the workers' insurrection in Merthyr Tydfil in 1831, see Gwyn A. Williams, *The Merthyr Rising* (2nd edn, Cardiff: University of Wales Press, 1988).
13. The farmland and mill sold by Christopher James was Rhydfelen; the village is known as Rhydyfelin but local people pronounce the name as Rhidfelan, as in the Gwentian dialect; this accounts for the two names on road signs leading off the A470. The Welsh-language comprehensive school is known as Ysgol Gyfun Rhydfelen.
14. For further details about the tinworks at Melin Griffith see the article by Chris Evans, 'Global commerce and industrial organization in eighteenth-century Welsh enterprise: the Melingriffith Company', *The Welsh History Review*, 20/3 (June 2001).
15. I am indebted to my old friend and amateur historian Billy Mathias of Long Row, Trefforest, for alerting me to the possibility that cannon were

manufactured at Trefforest and for providing me with information which supports his conviction that this was so.

16. Newcomers to the area should note that the first syllable of the village's name is pronounced with a short vowel, not with a long vowel as in 'tree'; the second part of the name is pronounced as in English, 'forest'.

17. The Bute family, sometimes called 'the creators of modern Cardiff' because they built the docks and much else besides, owned land and property in the district of Pontypridd; for a full account see John Davies, *Cardiff and the Marquesses of Bute* (Cardiff: University of Wales Press, 1981).

18. The inventory is included in the minutes of the Assessment Committee held on 13 April 1842.

19. The Machine Bridge was so called because it was the site of a weighing machine which was used to price coal before it was loaded onto barges on the Doctor's Canal and taken to Cardiff.

20. Readers should be warned that entry to the site of the old tinworks, now in the care of the Welsh Development Agency, is prohibited.

21. The Doctor's Canal was so called because it was built for Dr Richard Griffiths (1756–1826), a pioneer of the coal industry in the Rhondda.

22. The best pictorial record of the Trefforest tinworks was made by the artist T. H. Thomas (1839–1915), whose series of twelve watercolours is now housed in the National Museum of Wales; there is also a lithograph by G. F. Bragg after an unknown artist, made *c*.1840, which shows men, women and children at work in the tinworks, and a distant view of the works painted by J. Appleby at about the same time; see Lord, *Visual Culture*.

23. Francis Crawshay appears as a sympathetic, paternalistic character in the novel by Lewis Davies (1836–1951), *Y Geilwad Bach* (Llanelli: James Davies, 1929), which is set mainly in the industrial communities of Hirwaun and Trefforest.

24. There is an anonymous oil portrait of Francis Crawshay, painted *c*.1845, which depicts him rather more conventionally as a young gentleman; see Lord, *Visual Culture*.

25. The Crawshay houses at Dyffryn were demolished in 1938 but photographs of them have survived. For many photographs of the district, particularly of its industrial and social life, see Stewart Williams (ed.), *Old Pontypridd and District in Photographs* (Barry: Stewart Williams, 1977), Simon Eckley (ed.), *Pontypridd* (Stroud: Alan Sutton, 1994) and David James Rees, *Pontypridd South Past and Present* (Risca: Starling Press, 1983).

26. Francis Crawshay also built a similar tower near Hirwaun, after which Tower Colliery, the only deep mine left in south Wales and now owned by its workers, takes its name.

27. The upkeep of the garden, which has an explanatory plaque, is the

responsibility of the Rhondda Cynon Taff Council. It was the council's predecessor, Taff Ely, which restored the village's name from Treforest to its correct Welsh spelling, Trefforest, for all official purposes.

28. 'If you seek a monument, look around you.' The words are attributed to the architect's son, also named Christopher Wren (1675–1747).

29. The foundation stone of the TVR station was laid in 1837 by Lady Charlotte Guest (1812–95), translator of *The Mabinogion* (1846) and wife of Sir John Josiah Guest, the Dowlais ironmaster; see Revel Guest and Angela V. John, *Lady Charlotte* (London: Weidenfeld & Nicolson, 1989). In 1912 the station had seven platforms, in all nearly a third of a mile in length, and was used by some 11,000 passengers daily.

30. My colleague Dr Andy Croll is the author of *Civilizing the Urban* (Cardiff: University of Wales Press, 2000), a study of popular culture and public space in Merthyr Tydfil, *c.*1870–1914.

31. For details of how the town's name was changed from Newbridge to Pontypridd see John Charles, *Pontypridd Historical Handbook* (Pontypridd, *Glamorgan Times*, 1920).

32. The novel by Jack Jones (1884–1970), *Off to Philadelphia in the Morning* (1947), is a fictionalized account of the life and work of Joseph Parry (1841–1903), a Merthyr man, who was a renowned composer and first professor of music at the University College of Wales, Aberystwyth.

33. I have described my grandfather, Charlie Symes (1880–1956), a Londoner who awoke my interest in the history and literature of Wales, in my chapter in Hywel Teifi Edwards (ed.), *Merthyr a Thaf* (Llandysul: Gomer, 2001) and in a memoir, *A Semester in Zion* (Llanrwst: Carreg Gwalch, 2003).

34. Despite the most assiduous search, I have failed to find the exact source of this quotation; it may be in the works of Lenin.

35. Don Powell (1928–2001), was born in Graigwen and brought up in Cilfynydd; during the Second World War he worked as a booking clerk at the GWR station in Pontypridd and was later employed at the Brown Lenox chainworks. As a local historian he was knowledgeable and industrious: he published *Victorian Pontypridd and its Villages* (Whitchurch, Cardiff: Merton Priory Press, 1996), the fullest account of the town's history to date, and *Pontypridd at War: The Second World War at Home* (Whitchurch, Cardiff: Merton Priory Press, 1999), as well as many valuable articles in the *Pontypridd Observer*. A good deal of information about the district's history is usefully summarized in the booklet edited by Huw Williams, *Pontypridd: Essays on the History of an Industrial Community* (Cardiff: Department of Extra-Mural Studies, University College, Cardiff, 1981) and in the *Handbook* of the 57th Annual Conference of the Educational Institute of Design, Craft and Technology which was held at the Polytechnic of Wales in 1982.

36. Alun Richards, born in Pontypridd in 1929, is a short-story writer and

novelist who has taken his native place as the background for much of his work; among his books are a volume of autobiography, *Days of Absence* (London: Michael Joseph, 1986) and his *Selected Stories* (Bridgend: Seren, 1996). Among other writers born in Pontypridd are Elaine Morgan, John Lewis Hughes and Catrin Collier.

37. In the explosion at the Albion Colliery in Cilfynydd in 1894, 276 miners lost their lives; at Senghennydd in 1913, in one of the worst disasters in the annals of British coal mining, 439 were killed.

38. Griffith John Williams (1892–1963) was professor of Welsh at University College, Cardiff, from 1946 to 1957. The book in which he presented his research into the work of Edward Williams was *Iolo Morganwg a Chywyddau'r Ychwanegiad* (Cardiff: University of Wales Press, 1926). Literary forgery was not uncommon in the early phase of the Romantic period; cf. MacPherson's Ossian in Scotland and perhaps the *Barzaz Breiz* in Brittany.

39. Three of the Seven Wonders of Glamorgan are located in or near Pontypridd: the whirlpool in the Taff upriver from the town, the Rocking Stone on the common and the Old Bridge. The other four Wonders are Caerffili Castle, the Dewless Hillock on Margam Mountain, the Nottage Well near Porthcawl and Worm's Head in Gower; see *The Glamorgan County Magazine*, 1/4 (Summer 1949).

40. The history of the South Wales Miners' Federation has been written by David Smith and Hywel Francis, *The Fed* (Cardiff: University of Wales Press, 2nd edn, 1998).

41. There is a chapter on Brynfab by Dafydd Morse in Hywel Teifi Edwards (ed.), *Cwm Rhondda* (Llandysul: Gomer, 1995) and another by Huw Bevan on 'Clic y Bont' in *Merthyr a Thaf* (Llandysul: Gomer, 2001) in the same series, *Cyfres y Cymoedd*.

42. Glanffrwd's *Plwyf Llanwynno* (1888) was reprinted as *Llanwynno*, ed. Henry Lewis (Cardiff: University of Wales Press, 1949) and translated into English by Thomas Evans as *Glanffrwd's History of Llanwynno* (Merthyr Tydfil: H. W. Southey, 1950).

43. Brynfab, *Pan Oedd Rhondda yn Bur* (Aberdare, 1912).

44. T. J. Morgan in *The Dictionary of Welsh Biography* (London: Hon. Soc. of Cymmrodorion, 1959). Most of the people mentioned in the present chapter have entries in the *DWB* and many will also be found in Meic Stephens (ed.), *The New Companion to the Literature of Wales* (Cardiff: University of Wales Press, 2nd edn, 1998).

45. From 1885 to 1918 Pontypridd was included in the East Glamorgan division, for which Sir Alfred Thomas (1840–1927), who was elevated to the peerage as Lord Pontypridd in 1912, was the Liberal MP from 1885 to 1910 and A. Clement Edwards (1869–1938) the Liberal MP from 1910 to 1918. After a reorganization of constituency boundaries in 1918, the Pontypridd, Llantrisant and Cowbridge districts were amalgamated into a

new division and the National Liberal candidate, T. A. Lewis (1881–1923), was elected as Pontypridd's first MP. The constituency has been held by Labour since then: T. I. Mardy Jones (1879–1970) was MP from 1922 to 1931; D. L. Davies (1872–1937) from 1931 to 1937; Arthur Pearson (1897–1980) from 1938 to 1970; Brynmor John (1934–89) from 1970 to 1989; and Kim Howells from 1989 to the present; see Beti Jones, *Etholiadau'r Ganrif: Welsh Elections 1885–1997* (Talybont: Y Lolfa, 1999).

46. See the chapter entitled 'A drop of dew' in Rhys Davies, *Print of a Hare's Foot* (London: Heinemann, 1969; Bridgend: Seren, 1998).

47. For a good account of the doctor see the chapter by Brian Davies, 'Empire and identity: the "case" of Dr William Price', in David Smith (ed.), *A People and a Proletariat: Essays in the History of Wales 1780–1980* (London: Pluto Press in association with Llafur, the Society for the Study of Welsh Labour History, 1980).

48. See David J. V. Jones, *The Last Rising: The Newport Insurrection of 1839* (Oxford: Clarendon Press, 1985).

49. See the chapter by Roy Denning, 'Druidism at Pontypridd', *Glamorgan Historian*, 1 (1963).

50. For a polemic account of the composition of '*Hen Wlad fy Nhadau*' see Harri Webb, *A Militant Muse*, ed. Meic Stephens (Bridgend: Seren, 1998).

The SOUTH WALES and MONMOUTHSHIRE SCHOOL of MINES, 1913–1939

Peter H. G. Harries

The story of the University of Glamorgan in its earliest manifestation as the South Wales and Monmouthshire School of Mines is one of a relentless struggle for survival against several difficulties. This struggle had to overcome the effects of inadequate funding, war, industrial disruption, but above all, the hostility of the Welsh educational establishment. With the steady shift of governance from an aristocratic oligarchy representing only themselves to the freely elected representatives of a full democracy, the tide of history was, after William Forster's Elementary Education Act of 1870, similarly moving against private and charitable educational initiatives and towards a publicly provided system from elementary through to higher education. The Welsh educational establishment, from the end of the nineteenth century, largely comprised a small, tight-knit coterie of politically motivated individuals controlling certain key institutions which collectively wielded enormous power. They felt threatened by the upstart little mining college in Trefforest; threatened because of its independent status and because they could not hope to emulate its success, which was based on the provision of a first-class education for a proven need, rather than simply teaching students what it was believed they ought to know and with scant regard to what their mine-owning employers actually demanded they should know and be able to do.

Although the much discussed (by Welsh labour historians) syndicalists of the Rhondda, who outlined their programme for reform in *The Miners' Next Step*, wanted revolutionary change for society, they only ever represented a minority of public opinion: there was little stomach for this amongst the moderate majority of voters who favoured evolutionary change: a gradual levelling of society. Nonetheless, in the divisive *belle époque* of Edwardian Britain, with the rise of the Labour Party and trade-union militancy, the still all-powerful coal owners were genuinely hated by the majority of Welsh working people for their hitherto exploitative behaviour; so, councillors, local education authorities, committees of university dons, and officials involved in educational policy were happy to forget their differences and combine to see off any threat to the new order of publicly provided and funded education, especially when that purported threat came from a wealthy group as despised as the coal owners.

For more than sixty years before the South Wales and Monmouthshire School of Mines opened at Trefforest, there had been calls for a Welsh school of mines. One of the earliest was that of Samuel Baldwyn Rogers, a metallurgical chemist from Nantyglo who in 1849 petitioned the prime minister, Lord John Russell, for this without any success or encouragement. Rogers was one of the founder members of the South Wales Institute of Engineers which, in 1870, heard another call through its *Proceedings*, this time from T. Coomber, a lecturer in mining at the struggling and soon-to-close Bristol School of Mines. It was later amalgamated into what was to become known as the Merchant Venturers Technical College. It failed in large measure because the coal owners of south Wales refused to send their personnel there for technical training and the Bristol, Somerset and Forest of Dean coalfields which did support it were too small to ensure its continued viability. Most of the managers in these areas had already been trained there. A few years earlier, sometime in the 1860s, Dr Thomas Nicholas, a Nonconformist minister, wrote *Middle and High Schools and a University for Wales* which made a number of demands including that of a technological university to serve Welsh industry, 'properly adapted to the scientific and practical wants of its chief centres of manufacture'.[1] An attempt to establish such an institution had already been made in 1857, at Gnoll House in Neath. Unhappily, the so-called Western University of Great Britain appears to have been something of a scam. The fifty-six members of the local gentry, including C. R. Mansell Talbot, MP for Glamorgan and the county's lord lieutenant, who had each subscribed 100 guineas to the new venture, lost their money. No students were enrolled and Bullock Webster, steward of the 1,400-acre Gnoll estate and the principal promoter of the scheme, was committed to prison. Another call came in 1872 when Lionel Brough, an HM Inspector of Mines, gave evidence to the Devonshire Commission and recommended the siting of a school of mines in Merthyr Tydfil to serve its population of 100,000. This would, he said, 'pay for itself by saving capital lost, both human and production, through pit injuries, accidents, and loss of life'.[2] Nothing having been done, in 1881 George Overton, the coroner of northern Glamorgan – and thus well used to hearing evidence on the cause of mining accidents – proposed a mining school to the Aberdare Committee, again with no official response. Outside Wales, there were also many calls to provide technical education to workers, most notably from Thomas Huxley and his colleagues in the National Association for the Promotion of Technical Education which had been founded in Dean's Yard, Westminster, in 1887.

Huxley's interest in technical education far predated this though. An anatomist, he had been appointed as part-time lecturer in palaeontology in 1854 at what was then known as the School of Mines and of Science Applied to the Arts. This, the earliest school of mines in Britain, had its origins in Henry de la Beche's Museum of Economic Geography, which had been established in 1837, and which in due course became the Royal School of Mines and, ultimately, a key component of the new Imperial College. He had close links with south Wales. His wife, Bessie, was the daughter of a prominent Swansea citizen, Lewis Llewellyn Dillwyn of Hendrefoilan, the owner of the famous Cambrian Pottery. It was de la Beche (1796–1855) who had first mapped out the geological strata of the South Wales Coalfield as part of his function as director general of the Geological Survey to the Chancellor of the Exchequer. The British Association for the Advancement of Science had called for a national depository for the records and documents of mining operations in 1838 and de la Beche's large collection of geological specimens, displayed in a pair of houses in Craig Court at Charing Cross, took on this role the following year. The museum was opened to the public in 1841. A chemical laboratory was added and it started to take on students. The earliest staff appointed included Warrington Smythe, a geologist, and Dr Lyon Playfair (1818–98), who taught chemistry. But it is something of an irony that the incunabula of the Treforest School of Mines was probably the *Report by the Principal concerning the movement for the establishment of a Mining School*, written by the principal of University College, Cardiff, E. H. Griffiths, in 1907.

Brecon-born Ernest Griffiths (1851–1932) was a distinguished Cambridge scientist who had done valuable research into the precise measurement of heat. Although he understood the needs of south Wales's booming industries and sought to cooperate with them in order to make his college central to the local industrialists' educational and training requirements, he was not given the support he deserved by the University's Senate and only £9,000 of an endowment fund could be raised from local industrialists against a target of £50,000. In those days, the University College of South Wales and Monmouthshire, Cardiff, was based at the old Infirmary in the Newport Road, and this was surrounded by a ramshackle collection of temporary huts. There was much over-crowding and the departments of mining and geology, which had been established in 1891 in a very modest way, had to be housed elsewhere. For instance, the mining department, which had few students, was based at the house of the professor, William Gal-loway, for which facility he charged the college £15 per annum. Galloway left Cardiff in 1902 because he had so many outside com-mitments as a mining consultant that they conflicted with his duties as a Cardiff professor. He was replaced by the assistant he had had since 1895, S. Warren Price.

Galloway (1840–1927), who was later to become the external examiner of the Trefforest School of Mines as well as of University College, Cardiff, was a distinguished mining engineer who was noted for his experimental work on the cause of mine explosions which, he proved, were largely caused by floating coal dust. A graduate of Geissen and the famous School of Mines at Freiberg near Dresden in Saxony, he held the chair at Cardiff between 1891 and 1901. He was appointed president of the South Wales Insti-tute of Engineers in 1912. Other honours included a knighthood, a fellowship of the Geological Society, and the receipt of an hon-orary D.Sc. from the University of Wales. He was one of the six appointed central examiners of the Board of Mining Examina-tions which met to grant to mine managers their certificates of competency. He was an enlightened man, and in spite of the widespread public hostility shown towards Germany and all things German during and immediately after the First World War, realized that since a large part of the corpus of technical literature on mining was in German, it was potentially of immense value to British mining students. He told the Haldane Commission meet-ing during 1916/17 that he was opposed to the matriculation requirement that mining students in Cardiff should possess a knowledge of Latin and Greek, and instead sought to substitute a knowledge of French and German. The Senate disagreed, but did subsequently drop the requirement for Greek.

As well as meeting rebuffs from the Coalowners' Association, Griffiths fared no better when the South Wales Miners' Federation was approached. Its minute books show that Cardiff made several attempts to interest it in becoming involved with the proposed new mining school at Cardiff by asking it to have representation on the Joint Committee for Higher Education. It ignored these, but finally passed a minute rejecting any further overtures: 'That a reply be sent to this letter, stating that we think we can do more effective work in our respective localities than by representation on the Joint Committee'.[3] Griffiths's failure to launch a fully fledged school of mines at Cardiff crystallized the position of the Monmouthshire and South Wales Coalowners' Association, or at least many of its leading members, and spurred them into action. They had been lukewarm to Griffiths's approach for funding. The coal owners did not like the way their trainee mine managers and engineers were being taught at Cardiff. They believed the correct way to proceed was to accept that coal mining was a vocational subject, which, although there was an obvious requirement to have a background in the theoretical sciences, could only be deemed successfully taught if, additionally, the students received on-the-job training. This would give a better appreciation of the benefits of applied science as well as those of the theoretical sciences. The English civic universities had already shown the way with the sandwich system. It had been pioneered at the Royal Technical College, Glasgow, around 1880, followed by Sunderland Technical College in 1903, Northampton Polytechnic, London EC1 in 1905 and Sheffield University, which had changed its regulations to permit it. Cardiff resisted this new thinking and did not change its statutes to permit the sandwich system until well after the founding of its own faculty of technology in 1923.

One of the members of the Council of University College, Cardiff, had a foot in both camps as he was also the secretary, treasurer and solicitor to the Monmouthshire and South Wales Coalowners' Association. Oxford-educated Hugh Murray Ingledew (1865–1937) was a truly remarkable man, and one of the main driving forces behind the new venture at Trefforest. He was a partner in the well-established family firm of solicitors, Ingledew and Sons, whose offices were in Bute Docks. He was also involved in numerous other activities in the Cardiff area, both sporting and professional. He was behind the purchase of the Cardiff Arms Park from the marquess of Bute; he was solicitor to the Taff Vale Railway Company: the famous or perhaps notorious judgment he helped secure for them against the Amalgamated Society of Railway Servants in 1901 put back the cause of trade unionism until a later relaxation of the law with the Labour-sponsored Trade Disputes Bill which was introduced in March 1906, shortly after the Liberal landslide in the January general election. Ingledew was to try for a number of years, without success, to bring the mining departments at Cardiff and Trefforest together, in spite of facing many frustrations, which included the often poisonous working relationship between the academic staff of the two departments.

On behalf of some of the larger coal owners who had formed a committee to investigate this matter, Ingledew wrote several letters to interested parties to enquire about the feasibility of a new school of mines. Copies of some of the replies have been preserved in the South Wales Coalfield Archive at Swansea. First, on 11 November 1909 the solicitors to the University College, Cardiff, wrote in a discouraging vein, noting that in all other countries where coal mining flourished, mining schools were either universities in their own right or attached to universities. Mr Gee, of Messrs David and Evans, noted that salaries payable to staff would have to be higher than at a university because there would be less prestige. The proposed school of mines would not be able to contract for any of the academic staff in Cardiff. They cited the legal precedent of the Normal College at Bangor which had been halted by the ruling given by Lord Justice Vaughan Williams, Sir Brynmor Jones KG and Sir Isambard Owen in its decision to employ some of the teaching staff of the University College of North Wales: 'No such lectures delivered in a separate school could in any way be recognised.'[4] The next reply received was from Charles Kirton, assistant secretary of the Wigan and District Technical College which was encouraging and gave helpful costings. The department of coal and metalliferous mining there would probably not have been so helpful had they realized that the south Wales coal owners would promptly poach their best staff, including the head of department, to teach in their own school. Next came the reply from William Thomas, technical adviser to the Cornish Consolidated Tin Mines Limited, at the behest of Principal Berenger of the famous Camborne School of Mines in Cornwall, offering his services to conduct a feasibility study. This task was in fact given to Professor Louis of Armstrong College, Newcastle.

Having taken the decision to proceed with the venture in a meeting dated 26 November 1910, subject to support from other coal owners – the prime movers included Sir Clifford Cory Bt, chairman of Cory Brothers & Co. Ltd, William Jenkins and Thomas Evans of the Ocean Company, Joseph Shaw, KC, chairman of Powell Duffryn and E. M. Hann, director, T. Vivian Rees and W. W. Hood of the Glamorgan Company, W. North Lewis of Insoles, D. A. Thomas (later Viscount Rhondda) together with W. Leonard Llewellyn (later Sir), and David Hannah of the Cambrian Combine, representing some of the largest mining companies – a circular letter was sent to all the members of the Monmouthshire and South Wales Coalowners' Association. The replies being positive, with most of the major firms, who collectively represented an annual tonnage raised of more than 12,500,000 (more than a quarter of the total south Wales output) backing the idea, the coal owners agreed to acquire Fforest House, Trefforest, with the Board of Management confirming the action in a further meeting dated 6 July 1912. Fforest House (sometimes referred to as Trefforest House) had until recently had been the home of the late Alderman Walter Morgan, the founder of the prominent Cardiff-based firm of solicitors now known as Morgan Cole and a former vice-chairman of Glamorgan County Council. The house was acquired from his widow who had continued to reside there after her husband's death with her two daughters. The constitution of the school was established under a deed of trust with the earl of Plymouth, at the time lord lieutenant of Glamorgan, Lord Merthyr and David Davies (later Lord Davies) as the three trustees.

The advertisement for the post of principal to the new school attracted some thirty applicants. George Knox (1869–1950) was selected from a shortlist of seven. He had been born to poor parents in Patna, Ayrshire, and, like most other young lads from working-class families in the late nineteenth century, started work at thirteen without the chance of a secondary school education. Such schools were almost always exclusively fee-paying, with scholarships both rare and inadequate, and thus out of the reach of most people. He chose coal mining as his career and so became a pit boy. Knox attended day-release classes at Glasgow Technical College and went on several summer school courses at the Royal School of Mines in London. His precocious brilliance was noticed by Sir Clement Le Neve Foster who encouraged him and, at the age of 23, Knox was appointed lecturer in mining to Ayrshire County Council. Eleven years later he took over Professor George Winstanley's lecturing programme at Victoria University, Manchester, for two terms following Winstanley's appointment as an HM Inspector of Mines. He then secured the post as head of the department of coal and metalliferous mining at the Wigan and District Technical College where he stayed for ten years before taking up the post of principal at Trefforest. He was awarded the title 'Professor' which, because of his undoubted ability, was deserved; he was a very active researcher and produced numerous papers showing great insight into the problems faced by the mining of coal. The title was awarded in spite of his lack of a degree and the fact that the South Wales and Monmouthshire School of Mines was not categorized as a university or, at that time, a polytechnic institution.

Once appointed, Professor Knox and Hugh Ingledew attempted to obtain credibility for the new mining school by gaining an endorsement from the South Wales Miners' Federation. The minutes of the Fed duly noted on 28 June 1913: 'That a deputation from the Directors of this School be allowed to attend a Council Meeting.' Knox and Ingledew attended the meeting held on 29 September 1913. They did not ask for 'financial support other than any support that may be decided upon for individual students' but instead asked that the Fed should give its 'sympathy and support'. After this meeting, but before consideration could be given to this request, tragedy struck the south Wales mining communities with the Senghennydd disaster. On 14 November, in the immediate aftermath, attitudes had hardened. The Fed minutes record:

> That this Council does not feel itself able to associate itself with the Treforest School of Mines, and further, calls upon the Public Authorities in South Wales to promote under Public Control, facilities for giving instruction in Mining in places easily available to Workmen.[5]

In spite of this snub from the representatives of the mine workers, the new Trefforest School of Mines, from the first, co-operated with the departments of mining and geology at University College, Cardiff, for the basic training of their managerial and supervisory grade employees. They sent students for the first year of their four-year full-time diploma course and the first two years of the part-time courses to learn the theoretical sciences. The professor of geology, Thomas Franklin Sibly, later complained to the Haldane Commission of the misuse of his abilities:

> To illustrate how unsatisfactory the arrangement is . . . I teach them elementary geology. They then go up to Treforest . . . they are taught their advanced geology by men who are not geologists, but mainly mining teachers.'[6]

Sibly was subsequently appointed as the first principal of University College, Swansea, which opened its doors as a mainly technological university in 1920. There is a certain irony in this as, according to the College's historian David Dykes, he had opposed its establishment until offered the job of principal.[7] Part of the purpose of the Haldane Commission (Lord Haldane, a Scot, was a lawyer and a politician who had been Lord Chancellor in 1912–15 and again in the first Labour government of 1924) was to see to what extent the new school of mines – which had successfully established itself, quickly building up a worldwide reputation for excellence – would destroy or otherwise affect the viability of the proposed university college at Swansea which was on the drawing board and only waiting for the First World War to come to an end before receiving the green light.

As one of his first acts, Sibly attempted to launch a school of mines at Swansea, but the protests from Cardiff, Trefforest and presumably Swansea Technical College (which taught mining at an advanced level and out of which the new university college had been formed) were sufficiently vociferous to quash the idea. Sibly had previously argued that the Swansea Technical College should be part of University College, Cardiff, but once he had been appointed principal of University College, Swansea, he tried to undermine it. Sibly may have felt able to attack the qualifications of the teaching staff at Trefforest compared with his own, but Viscount Haldane of Cloan, when later invited to address the enlarged Court of the University of Wales in 1920, which by now included Swansea, felt compelled to warn it against a policy of nepotism whereby unsuitable academic appointments were being made and the best qualified people for the job were not always used. Nepotism was widespread in the public sector in Wales. For example, the historians Chris Williams, in relation to Rhondda politics between 1885 and 1951, and Robert Smith, on elementary schools in Wales between 1870 and 1906, both provide details of corruption: of bribes given to secure teaching and other posts to local councillors, and of councillors providing jobs for their families and friends regardless of their ability to perform them. In contrast to this widespread sleaze in the public sector, the School of Mines at Trefforest only appointed well-qualified people with proven track records to its academic staff.

Further illustrations of the mutual dislike between the two institutions can be gleaned from the hostile comments of many of the expert witnesses giving evidence to the Haldane Commission. As well as the comments above, Sibly had, earlier in his evidence, also pointed out the Trefforest effect on the Cardiff mining department:

> . . . unfortunately, the whole activities of our mining department have been seriously affected by the constitution of the School of Mines at Treforest . . . The establishment . . . has practically killed coal mining at the University College, Cardiff.[8]

Principal George Knox was asked by the Royal Commissioners for his opinion as to what useful purpose the Cardiff B.Sc. qualification served compared with that of the Trefforest diploma. He contemptuously responded: 'I do not think it serves any useful purpose, so far as our coalfield is concerned.'[9] When asked if the label of B.Sc. would be useful elsewhere, he again replied dismissively: 'Yes it certainly would be, even in the coalfield of the future, I think; but for the present it is almost a dead letter as regards the Cardiff Mining Department.'[10] The real rudeness, however, was left to the rumbustious and ebullient Sir Clifford Cory, who was chairman of the Trefforest Board of Management, member of a powerful local family and head of one of the leading coal-owning firms, Cory Brothers & Co. Ltd: 'I am very much responsible I am afraid for rescuing, if I may use that term, the

School of Mines from the Cardiff University College.'[11] He was further asked why he wished the School of Mines to enter the university structure. Heaping further venom upon the perceived inadequacies of Cardiff, he replied sarcastically:

> You rather misunderstood me, I think, in what I said just now. It was not that we should be represented on the governing body of the University, but that they should send representatives to us.[12]

Cory had been one of the earliest supporters of E. H. Griffiths's call for endowment funds for the departments of mining and geology as had Joseph Shaw, chairman of Powell Duffryn. They later both came bitterly to regret their generosity as a complete waste of money. The reason for this resentment was that Cardiff had originally encouraged the employers of their mining students by promising cooperation with courses tailored to suit their needs in return for paying the costs, but subsequently Griffiths had to renege when blocked by the Senate who exhibited personal hostility to the coal owners as a class. They were not prepared to allow the coal owners any say in staff appointments or course structure. As Cory explained to the Haldane Commission:

> the negotiations which took place in 1908/9 with the University College with regard to the foundation of the School of Mines . . . in conjunction with . . . the Principal Companies required as a condition to their subscribing to a Mining School at the College that the Coalowners should have control (a) of the Finances (b) of the appointment of Staff (c) of the Curriculum.
>
> The reason for this was that the Mining Department of the College which had been in operation for several years had entirely failed to provide the class of instruction which the Coalowners required to give for the purposes of their business.
>
> The College purported to pass Resolutions and Statutes which gave effect to the above conditions, but these Resolutions and Statutes, on being submitted to legal advice were held to be *ultra vires* the Charter of the College.[13]

Cory continued by noting that the Trefforest School of Mines, which had been formed on 4 November 1912, had only gone ahead after 'it became patent that the College did not intend to take any steps to alter their Charter to give effect to the conditions to obtain the direct support of the Coalowners to their work'.[14]

Another cause of tension, which was referred to by HM Inspectors in their 1927 report, was that some of the students spending their first year in Cardiff subsequently transferred there to complete their studies, in the belief that there was far greater prestige in obtaining a B.Sc. from a university (which took just three years to complete) as opposed to a mere diploma from a school of mines which took a total of four years of study, including time spent working in collieries. It was possible for the Trefforest student to obtain a B.Sc. (Technological Sciences) as an external student of the University of London. But that meant further study beyond the four years of the diploma course and so was unattractive to many.

Trefforest had opened for business on 8 October 1913 with seventeen students including three from China. Before the Chinese Revolution of 1911 which overthrew the Manchu dynasty, there had been a number of Welsh mine engineers and managers working in China and so there would have been some familiarity with Wales and the Welsh. One of the first tasks of the new school was to form a rugby team and two of the Chinese were constrained to join, in order to make up numbers. It is tempting to speculate as to what they really thought of the alternative Welsh religion. George Knox was appointed director of mining and principal at the then vast salary of £650 (more than double the rate for an Oxford professor), assisted by John Samuel as senior lecturer and assistant director of mining. Also among the six initially recruited staff were R. M. Metcalfe, who was based in Trefforest, and James Dobie, R. Evans and Robert James, based at the branch school in Crumlin, all of whom had come from Wigan. Robert James was deputy principal. He was later appointed principal when George Knox retired. The school was financed by a levy based on the tonnage of coal raised by the participating firms. This was set at one-tenth of a penny. Initially, there were eighteen firms in the scheme. Later, others joined in. In the first year the income was £8,500. By 1922 this had risen to £12,000, with twenty-seven firms in the scheme. The year of opening, 1913, marked the peak of Welsh coal production. Thereafter there was a steady decline, in spite of Britain's involvement with the Great War from the following August. The Royal Navy, which had traditionally burned only the finest Welsh coal from the steam coal pits of the Rhondda in the boilers of her warships, had largely been switched over to oil-burning boilers after the extremely ill-tempered 1911 Cambrian Combine strike. Officially, the reason given was greater efficiency, but it was Winston Churchill who had been home secretary (he had introduced the Mines Act amongst other measures) and involved in the dispute in 1911 which saw considerable militarism – to the extent that troops were placed on standby in the area – and the same Winston Churchill, subsequently First Lord of the Admiralty, who took the decision to turn to imported oil and therefore to end reliance on supplies of Welsh coal which, he realized, were subject to interruption. This turned out to be a hazardous resolution when British merchant shipping, importing the precious oil for the Fleet, as well as foodstuffs and other essential goods, came under sustained attack, for a time, from German U-boats during the First World War.

The newly opened school of mines, in common with most other institutions, suffered considerable disruption during the Great War. After it, a large number of ex-servicemen were enrolled on courses and caused something of a discipline problem. They refused to be treated as callow students in need of *in loco parentis* supervision and live in the hostel provided in Radyr, in the same street as the principal had his house, and from where he could keep a fatherly eye on them. They preferred to live in lodgings in Trefforest and Pontypridd and come and go as they pleased.

An official inspection was carried out by HM Inspectors at Trefforest in 1915. Copies of this report are unavailable at the Public Record Office in Kew, but another report, this time of the sister school at Crumlin in 1916, and a third carried out at both schools in 1927 give a good idea of the high standards of work carried out in both. Crumlin had opened in 1914 at Crumlin Hall, near Newport.[15] Another school to cover the western area of the coalfield where anthracite was mined, at Swansea, was proposed but never opened. The two schools shared George Knox as principal. Several of the six staff taught in both schools, travelling for their lectures and demonstrations between the two. Financially, the two schools were treated as being one. Crumlin took only part-time students, Trefforest both full and part-time. The report noted that research was being undertaken into the application of science to industry and crucially, having in mind the causes of so many mining disasters, an investigation of explosions due to coal dust. This and the accumulation of gas pockets (the horrific explosion at Senghennydd which had killed 439 miners on 14 October 1913, just six days after Trefforest opened its doors for the first time to receive the earliest cohort of students, was caused by an accumulation of gas) were the principal, largely avoidable, reasons for the hazardous nature of the industry and provided at least part of the explanation for the difficulty in recruiting enough students, even in the Depression years of the 1920s and 1930s. Having in mind the deep and widespread anger caused by the Senghennydd explosion, the second such disaster at this pit, it was probably not very tactful of the School's Board of Management to invite the 77-year-old Sir W. T. Lewis, first Baron Merthyr of Senghennydd, to perform the official opening ceremony on 24 January 1914. As the head of Lewis Merthyr Collieries, which owned the Senghennydd pit, although retired to his castle in Pembrokeshire and no longer active on a daily basis with his company, he was possibly the most unpopular person in south Wales at the time. He died in August of that year.

Life as a mine manager or engineer was relatively well paid, but the hours were long, conditions often unattractive and stressful and it was potentially very dangerous. The inspectors commented on the isolation the two schools suffered from linkages with mainstream education apart from the joint diploma scheme with Cardiff, and with the lack of any cooperation from the local education authorities: 'Students attend on their own initiative, not because of co-operation between this "important" school and the local authorities.'[16]

One of the suggestions that George Knox had made to the Haldane Commission was that there should be only one place in south Wales for the teaching of mining at the highest level. The other colleges would feed their students into it. In practical terms, this meant that either Cardiff or Trefforest would have to give way. Knox believed that the logical site for such a school of mines would be Trefforest as it was far better equipped than Cardiff, which was hampered by its city centre location, well away from the coalfield. The University of Wales duly amended its charter in 1922 to permit the establishment of a faculty of technology, having resisted this a decade or so earlier. The School of Mines at Trefforest applied to become the technological outpost of the University where mining was taught at an advanced level.

However, a complication in the form of the Miners' Welfare Fund now entered the equation. The lure of riches clouded the judgement of those parties involved in the merger talks. The money on offer proved to be both a blessing and a curse. The Miners' Welfare Fund had been formed under the Mines Act, 1920, Section 20 of which authorized the levy of one penny per ton of output from Britain's coal mines. Money from the fund poured into the mining areas and was used to pay for improvements to colliers' working conditions, most notably in the provision of pit-head baths, and leisure facilities such as meeting halls, bowling greens and tennis courts. It was also used to pay for a network of mining colleges and for scholarship funds for miners and their families to attend university. The Fund promised substantial funds to whichever institution, Cardiff or Trefforest, was chosen as the site of the new proposed National School of Mines for Wales. The University of Wales, always on the trail of generous benefactors, now decided to attempt to scuttle Trefforest in order to enrich itself from this golden stream. Nevertheless, it was obliged to go through the motions of evaluation and so appointed a team of distinguished visitors to appraise Trefforest's standards to see whether it was capable of teaching mining as part of a university institution. Although the terms of reference are not exactly known, it would appear from its fallacious and negative conclusions that the task of the visitors was to find reasons why Trefforest should *not* be permitted to join the University.

A conference had been held at Trefforest on 16 October 1922 which made reference to the bad working relationship. Cardiff had called for a

> reconsideration of the relations at present existing between the University of South Wales & Monmouthshire and the School of Mines on the one hand, and those between these two centres of Mining Education and the University of Wales on the other, with a view to the progressive development of Mining Education in South Wales on lines more closely related to the University.[17]

It is obvious that Cardiff, with very few students of its own and jealous of the success of Trefforest, felt quite resentful at teaching only the first year of the Trefforest diploma course. Cardiff had already felt the indignity of the School of Medicine's breaking away to form a separate college within the federal University of Wales structure, after losing a long and bitter struggle to retain it, and certainly did not want the humiliation of the loss of another important, if relatively small and unsuccessful, department. There was a lot of prestige at stake should the University College, which was sited in the city which was home to the then largest coal exporting port in the world, fail to make a success of its departments of mining and geology. The report of the visitors was debated by the Council of the University in a meeting dated 23 April 1923. Trefforest had requested that the departments of colliery engineering, chemical engineering and mining engineering be recognized in its application of 16 November 1922. However, the University wanted to appraise them as mining, engineering and applied chemistry as the main subjects, with mathematics, physics and geology as subsidiary subjects.

The visitors were John W. Cobb, Livesey professor of coal, gas and fuel industries at the University of Leeds; G. W. O. Howe, James Watt professor of electrical engineering at the University of Glasgow; F. C. Lea, Beale professor of civil engineering at the University of Birmingham, together with K. Neville Moss, professor of coal and metal mining, also of Birmingham; and G. A. Shott, professor of applied mathematics at the University College of Wales, Aberystwyth. This distinguished line-up was completed by the openly hostile principal of University College, Swansea, T. Franklin Sibly. He attended later than the others due to ill health. The visitors were full of praise for Trefforest, but they were unable to recommend that the School be recognized until substantial changes had occurred. They reported that the School was 'in many respects admirably equipped and managed and is doing excellent work in meeting the demands of the coal industry for technical training'.[18] They noted that the School had, in the main, confined its working to the coal industry. However, they also poured scorn on many of the staff, by suggesting that only a few of them, such as Dr S. Roy Illingworth, were capable of teaching to a high university standard. Illingworth was a prolific researcher and publisher of papers into the chemical composition of coal. He held the South Wales Institute of Engineers Gold Medal in recognition of this each year from 1918 to 1925. His successor in the receipt of this prestigious medal was Professor George Knox who held it until 1928.

The visitors criticized the high teaching load imposed on the staff, as this detracted from the time necessary to do research. They commented that:

> in spite of these defects which in our opinion are fatal to recognition under present conditions . . . It must be clearly understood that this does not mean that the Institution is failing to fulfil its function. On the contrary . . . the work now done is well organised and is suitable for the purpose for which the school was founded.[19]

With breathtaking hypocrisy they also attacked the sandwich system and the fact that full- and part-time students worked side by side: 'Such an arrangement is not conducive to the best results, and would be most unsatisfactory in the case of students pursuing degree courses.'[20] This is just what Cardiff was subsequently to do with its own mining students, to ape the Trefforest model including the sandwich system which had originated in Glasgow more than forty years earlier and from where two of the visitors came. The sandwich system was by now accepted practice and had spread to include most of the English civic universities. The real objection was contained in a single sentence:

> The task of training officials for the mining industry, within the limitations prescribed by Statute is one which is by no means easy to combine with the freedom of teaching and the opportunities for research which are essential to the conduct of a true university course.[21]

What the visitors said, in essence, is that a university course must by its very nature disregard the practical considerations of training and the acquisition of skills for a specific career, but should only pursue the truth or enlightenment, through the discipline studied. Hence the almost obsessive demand that research is all, even though few students were interested in it, only in gaining promotion into a good job at the end of their taught courses, and even though many of their teachers simply wanted to ensure that the students succeeded in this goal. It was this attitude on the part of Cardiff, until it belatedly changed to follow the Trefforest way of doing things, which had caused the coal owners in the first place to establish their own school. In a rider to the report, outside the terms of reference, K. Neville Moss had written:

> Recognition by the University of Wales would necessitate the School having materially to alter its organisation, which even then may benefit only a small percentage of students and would in my opinion tend to spoil the training of the remainder, unless a special staff was employed for each.[22]

This would obviously be impractical. Many of the visitors' comments are ludicrous for vocational courses such as mine management or mine engineering – just as they would be in the case of medical practitioners, dentists or vets, who clearly needed to train at a teaching hospital where they would learn their profession, under supervision, on patients requiring treatment, rather than spend all of their time on abstract theory. Equipped with only this, they would be quite incapable of practising their profession to any degree of competence.

Bloodied but unbowed, Trefforest carried on. It had received a grant from the Board of Education, a fact which caused outrage among certain education officials and which was to lead to a deputation, headed by some Glamorgan county councillors, to the president of the Board of Education to protest against this alleged misuse of public funds which they felt should not be used to assist a much-loathed (by them) privately funded mining college within their area. This was part of a £1 million government grant which had been allocated throughout Britain with the two-pronged purpose of financing research connected with safety in mines and of improving facilities for higher technical education in the mining communities.

In the mean time, Cardiff carried on with its plans to isolate Trefforest. In consultation with all the other parties interested in technical education in south Wales, Glamorgan County Council produced a report, the *Proposed Mining Education Scheme for the South Wales and Monmouthshire Coalfield*, which was published in March 1925. This report, somewhat over-ambitious, called for twenty-five mining centres, fourteen of which were to be located in Glamorgan – and an additional four in the Rhondda area which had gained its educational independence, after a long struggle, from Glamorgan in 1913. One of these was to be an advanced centre. The publication of this report was to lead to a bitter battle by the Rhondda councillors who now felt they had a good reason not to send their students to Trefforest, which they disliked on principle because of its private status.[23] The total cost was estimated at £233,125. The report placed University College, Cardiff, at the apex of the scheme, but it did request that Trefforest should receive a grant of a modest £11,000 for research purposes as a sort of consolation prize. It also established a joint advisory committee with its membership drawn from all of the interested parties including local education authorities, represented by their directors of education and of mining education, and nominated officials of the Coalowners' Association, the South Wales Miners' Federation and the University of Wales and the colleges themselves. Although Trefforest had representation on the joint committee, it was in a minority and unable to influence the direction of future development and was thus placed in a position of potential discrimination.

In the Trefforest archives is a copy of an undated and unsigned memorandum, almost certainly the work of George Knox. This acknowledged the general belief that there was room only for one mining school of 'university' standard in the coalfield of south Wales and it gave a number of cogent reasons why this should be Trefforest, not Cardiff. The report quoted from Professor Louis's *Report on Mining Education in England with special reference to India* which said: 'It is not the duty of a University, nor is it within the scope of a University to teach mining. All that a University can or should teach is the principles upon which mining is based.'[24] When a school of mines was subsequently established at Dhanbad in India by the government in 1926, it was Trefforest which served as the model. The anonymous author of this memorandum produced detailed costings which proved that it was cheaper by far to continue with Trefforest than establish a brand new facility in Cardiff.

Whatever the struggles going on behind the scenes, Trefforest continued to flourish in its main function. Exam results proved Trefforest's standing in the field of training colliery officials. George Knox wrote to Hugh Ingledew on 4 March 1927 to note that 60 per cent of the passes for the Home Office first-class certificates at the Cardiff centre and 16.2 per cent of all passes nationally in November 1926 were gained by Trefforest students. Eighty-two students had completed the full- or part-time diploma, with a further 179 completing the group course certificate. Of this total of 261, some 174 had obtained their first class colliery manager's certificate: equal to two-thirds. The second part of the letter suggested ways in which economies could be made. These were necessary because of the devastating impact of the 1926 General Strike (or lockout), the effects of which brought on the beginning of the end for Trefforest as an independent college. But Knox argued against making any drastic cutbacks in the academic programme:

> I cannot recommend the dropping of any of the courses as the continuity of any educational policy is the first essential towards efficiency and economy. Just as it requires 4 or 5 years to build up a complete course of training to obtain results, it takes the same period to destroy it.[25]

With no willing purchasers for the school available, Knox wrote to Ingledew again to express astonishment that the management board should now be considering giving the school away to the local education authorities who had made life so difficult by their refusal to cooperate with the venture: 'They surely do not expect that our Board is going to make a free gift of the School to them, even if this did carry with it representation of our Board on the Management Committee for the future without further payments.'[26] This is, in fact, exactly what transpired. But in spite of the growing financial storm clouds now buffeting the school, which were not discussed within it, the 1927 HMI report detailed the educational success of Trefforest. The inspectors commented favourably on the accommodation as 'good' and the equipment as 'excellent' although they rued its isolation from the mainstream of Welsh education:

> It is a matter of regret that except for the relationship between the University College of South Wales and Monmouthshire and the School of Mines in regard to the Joint Mining Diploma, there is no other kind of co-ordination with other educational activities in the coalfield. This lack of co-ordination and collaboration is the more to be regretted because all the material necessary to complete

the educational ladder for persons engaged in coal mining in South Wales is ready to hand; it merely awaits correlation.[27]

The inspectors noted that room for thirty students at one time meant a total capacity for 150 full- and part-time students (there were in fact forty-six full-time students in November 1926 and sixty-nine part-timers attending Trefforest). There were forty-one students taking the full-time diploma courses, of whom thirty-eight had attended secondary or higher elementary school. Thirteen of the students had attended evening classes. Most of the students were aged between sixteen and twenty-two; four of them had reached twenty-five. Of the sixty-nine part-time students at Trefforest, thirty-seven had attended secondary schools and fifty-three, evening classes. Ages of the part-time students, as might be expected, were somewhat higher. Eight of the thirty-two taking the five-year mine managers' course were over twenty-five. Fees chargeable on full-time courses were £16 per annum for students employed by the sponsoring collieries and £24 for others. Additionally there was a registration fee of one guinea and a further guinea payable to the Students' Representative Council. Students were apprenticed for between five and six years at the associated collieries who paid the fees of their employees. The fees charged for the first year spent at University College, Cardiff, were higher, but the School of Mines made up the difference. Fees for students on part-time courses were £3 4s for employees of the associated collieries and £4 16s for others. The school provided some eight entrance scholarships, two of them worth £60 per annum and tenable for four years. There was a research scholarship worth £75 per annum, tenable for one year, but capable of being extended for up to five years. There were also internal scholarships worth £10 per annum and gold and silver medals for the students producing the best work.

Shem J. Davies was one such student. He was appointed graduate assistant technical lecturer by Rhondda Urban District Council on 2 October 1922. Here he assisted Tom Harries, the council's mining lecturer (later promoted to director of mining education). Davies had started out as a boy miner at the age of thirteen, and attended evening technical classes at Bridgend County School. He became an official at Wyndham Colliery in

Ogmore Vale and took evening classes at Ogmore Secondary School where he taught mining, mining drawing and mining surveying. In 1917, at the age of twenty-three, Davies went to University College, Cardiff, for two years, where he was first page prizeman in machine design and construction and second page prizeman in applied mechanics and heat engines. After he had obtained a colliery manager's first class certificate, he transferred to Trefforest. Here he carried out post-diploma research work. In 1922 he was awarded the top prize of gold medallist (final).

Trefforest, because of its ownership by the Welsh coal owners who sponsored its employees as students, made a far greater contribution to the professionalization of mine managers and engineers than any of the purely university mining schools in Britain. The Trefforest alumni worked, in the main, in supervisory or managerial capacities in the mines of their sponsors and so were able to influence directly the raising of standards with the latest knowledge of best practice. By contrast, only one of the eighteen graduates of the Royal School of Mines who gained University of London degrees between 1870 and 1914 went into mining. Most of these and the diploma holders took up lucrative posts abroad, went into teaching or used their specialist chemical knowledge in other more congenial industries such as brewing. Few did research. And Armstrong College, Newcastle (an offshoot of the University of Durham), became famous for producing more government inspectors of mines than any other institution. A pattern was set whereby the alumni of the various schools of mines, excluding Trefforest, used their qualifications to avoid employment in the mines.

It was because it was not part of a university that the Trefforest School of Mines evolved to become arguably one of the most important institutions of its kind. This was certainly the description of the HM Inspectors. The mine owners who operated the school were able to conduct the school on the single-minded lines of the pursuit of training excellence: providing a first-class education to students without the complications and compromises necessary to fit into a university structure with its clashing mixture of disciplines, whose adherents constantly jockey for positions of influence or dominance. Within the university or polytechnic structure, influence is generally granted to those departments and their heads who can attract substantial research monies: this can act to the detriment of those smaller departments who concentrate on the excellence of their teaching and do little research. They can, therefore, get squeezed out of existence if they are noted as being unprofitable. Trefforest's principal problem, in the aftermath of the 1926 General Strike, was purely financial. The coal owners could no longer afford to keep it going. They tried to sell, but to no avail. In the end, in desperation, they gave it away, writing off an investment of some £200,000, but even this contained a cost – one of a humiliating loss of face – and it was this loss of face which later was nearly to destroy the school as the ousted coal owners turned and took their savage revenge.

The financial plight of the School of Mines became ever deeper during the course of 1926 and by the following year, in spite of the high praise lavished on it by HM Inspectors, the outlook was desperate. The gross cost of the school for the year ending 31 March 1927 was £10,167. Staff had already been obliged to accept a reduction in salary. George Knox had his reduced by 20 per cent, others by 5 per cent. Salary costs at Trefforest were now down to £6,800, but this was still unaffordable to the coal owners and so contingency plans went ahead to close the School. When confronted with this news, Percy Watkins, secretary of the Welsh Department at the Board of Education, wrote a letter to Hugh Ingledew which outlined the problem:

> The Coalowners are not prepared to continue holding themselves responsible for the maintenance of the schools.
>
> They have offered them as a free gift to the Local Education Authorities, subject to conditions.
>
> The Local Education Authorities, owing to financial stress which is real, are unable to accept responsibility for the cost of maintaining the schools.
>
> The Miners' Welfare Committee are unable to make a grant to the Local Education Authorities towards such cost of maintenance.
>
> Consequently, the Local Education Authorities do not see their way to accept the offer of the Coalowners, and if nothing is done Mining Education in South Wales will lose the Schools.[28]

He suggested two alternative courses of action, first, that the coal owners 'might be induced to maintain the *status quo* for another two or three years in the hope that at the expiration of that period a solution might be found'.[29] The second suggested that the coal owners might gift the school to Cardiff to be used as the mining department, with Glamorgan having the use of it for a peppercorn rent in the evenings. The first suggestion was rejected, but the second, although unpalatable, offered the basis for further negotiations as money was believed to be available through the University Grants Committee. The difficulties in reaching an agreement were discussed in a round-table conference in Cardiff, with Lord Chelmsford in the chair, on 18 April 1928.

The county education authorities were prepared to accept the two schools as a free gift, but this would have to be on the basis that a grant was made available to cover the running costs for the 1928/9 year. The Board of Education would not provide a grant: 'as during this period the School would have been neither privately owned nor supported from the rates'.[30] The Miners' Welfare Fund, when initially approached, had said that it could only pay for capital projects, not subsidize income deficiency – though it did have some discretion in this because ultimately, after months of arguments, cajoling and special-case pleading, A. M. Anderson, on behalf of Lord Chelmsford, was able to write: 'For the year September, 1928 to August, 1929 your Authority is to be relieved of the entire cost of maintaining the School.'[31]

In the mean time contingency plans to close the school had been put into train and letters of termination of employment were prepared to be issued to the staff. It was envisaged that Crumlin would be closed and that two of the staff there transferred to Trefforest to make a core of nine. No new students would be taken on and the staff to be retained in the run-off period would be the oldest and longest serving and thus the most expensive to sack. It would also be easier, according to Knox, for the younger members of staff to obtain new posts. George Knox wrote to Hugh Ingledew:

Should the Board after reducing the staff as suggested still find the financial strain too great I believe (although I have not broached them on the matter) that the remaining members of the staff would be prepared to refund if necessary a portion of their salaries to meet the difficult situation with which the Board is likely to be faced.[32]

This was an impressive sacrifice from ill-paid academics, already suffering from the effects of a pay cut, to their still wealthy industrial employers. Knox wrote again the following week in reply to a letter from Hugh Ingledew to enclose a statement showing the numbers of students who would be left at Crumlin and Trefforest at the end of the present session the following June. There would be thirty full-time students at Trefforest for the next session and twenty-two for the 1929/30 session, with forty-eight part-time for the present session and thirty-five for the 1929/30 session. The figures for Crumlin were forty-eight for the present session and thirty-one for the 1929/30 session – all part-time. Ingledew requested a clarification and Knox duly replied stating that for the 1929/30 session there would be eighty-seven students at both schools; for 1930/1 fifty-eight; and for 1931/2 twenty-four, all of whom were part-time.[33]

Having received notification of the grant from A. M. Anderson at the Miners' Welfare Fund to pay the running costs of the 1928/9 session to the two local education authorities involved, Glamorgan and Monmouthshire, the board of governors of the Mining School was thus enabled to pass the resolution gifting Crumlin to Monmouthshire and Trefforest to Glamorganshire on 13 August 1928. The deed executing the transfer of Trefforest was signed by Sir Clifford Cory as chairman of the board of governors and Hugh Ingledew as secretary to the board; it was dated 11 February 1929 in favour of Glamorgan County Council through county alderman the Revd William Saunders and Henry Rowland, the clerk. Once in possession, Glamorgan used Trefforest as a base for its peripatetic lecturing staff. Additionally, the Fuel Research Board took up residence, and the rent paid by them undoubtedly helped Glamorgan at a time when its income from the rates was plummeting. With the free transfer went a number of scholarships including the Cardiff Chamber of Commerce Viscount Rhondda Memorial Scholarship Fund and the South Wales Colliery Officials Scholarship Fund, together with other scholarship monies. Some of these were attached to Crumlin, such as the Edmund Powell Scholarship Fund and the Monmouthshire Colliery Officials Association First Fund, and were thus transferred to Monmouthshire County Council.

It was Frederick Thesiger, third Baron Chelmsford, the

chairman of the Miners' Welfare Fund Committee, who had been instrumental in saving the Trefforest School of Mines from closure by slicing through the Gordian knots of bureaucracy which threatened to prevent the transfer into local authority control. He was a member of a distinguished, but decidedly accident-prone family. He had been viceroy of India when the Amritsar Massacre occurred on 13 April 1919. His hitherto glowing career in public life was somewhat damaged when he initially supported the actions of General Dyer in the face of the strong odium of Indian public opinion, although he stayed in post until 1921 when he was awarded a viscountcy at the age of fifty-three. Back in London, he was made First Lord of the Admiralty. Chairmanship of the Miners' Welfare Fund Committee, although part-time, was something of a come-down. It was seen as a safe, non-controversial retirement job. His father, Frederick Thesiger, second Baron Chelmsford, an army general, had been blamed for the disaster of Isandhlwana during the 1879 Zulu War by entirely underestimating the fighting prowess of the Zulus, whilst his grandfather, Frederick Thesiger, first Baron Chelmsford, was sacked in a bitter and public row as Lord Chancellor by Benjamin Disraeli as almost his first action when he took over from the ailing earl of Derby as prime minister. Disraeli's career was greatly helped by the wealth generated by Welsh coal miners. He had married Mary Anne, widow of Tony Wyndham Lewis, a coal owner whose large fortune, left in a lifetime trust to his wife, gave Disraeli the private income necessary for him to ascend the greasy pole to the top political job.

Glamorgan had gained control of the School of Mines, and for no capital outlay, which was a sweet political victory, but yet another complication now entered the reckoning. It looked for a time as if they had been lumbered with a white elephant. Glamorgan had written to the neighbouring councils' education committees to assess future demand for their courses and to establish the fairest means of funding them. In reply J. W. Nicholas, clerk to Carmarthenshire's education committee, wrote to state that Trefforest was unpopular with its students because of its remote location. Carmarthenshire students would in future go to Swansea Technical College, which he regarded as adequate for the purpose. Monmouthshire agreed to pay the cost of students nominated by them; Rhondda believed that the only equitable method of payment was that they should pay on the basis of assessable value; Breconshire replied by saying that they would not send their students to Trefforest; Merthyr town council wrote that they would pay towards costs, but only on the basis of the number of miners employed; Swansea noted that it would only send its students to the technical college in the town; Pembrokeshire would pay individually for any students attending Trefforest, but noted that none of them would. So Glamorgan had a problem, the other local LEAs, all, like Glamorgan, financially strapped in the prevailing depressed economic climate, were for the most part reluctant either to use its facilities or to contribute towards its costs. Undaunted by this, Glamorgan conceived ambitious expansion plans. Henry Rowland for Glamorgan education committee contacted Sir Percy Watkins at the Welsh Department of the Board of Education to ask for a grant of £110,000 to turn the School of Mines into a full-scale technical college with the provision of more buildings. The new departments were envisaged as: senior technical department – motor engineering; building trades including carpentry, joinery, plumbing; a commercial course; general education; an art department; and a junior day school. This was regarded as somewhat overambitious and was scaled back to £50,000. Of this sum, it was hoped that the Miners' Welfare Fund would contribute £42,000. The *Western Mail* of 29 January 1930 noted that there was approval for this in the community and that the council had passed the plans with a huge majority.

However, the proposed new Glamorgan Technical College did not get this money. The Miners' Welfare Fund was prepared to contribute only towards mining education and only then once the quarrel with University College, Cardiff, had been settled. And, instead of being settled with the hated coal owners (now pushed from a position of influence), the quarrel re-erupted with much greater virulence. The coal owners staged a volte-face which threatened the very survival of their old institution. They offered a scholarship scheme to University College, Cardiff, if they established a new mining department. Cardiff had in the mean time appointed Dr David Jones as a professor to oversee a newly revitalized department. Initially the intention was that he would work at Trefforest and that the mining department would be based there. It was becoming necessary to take urgent action because the economy had started to recover from the depression of the early 1930s, and it rapidly became apparent that a recruitment crisis was fast looming in the south Wales coal industry. Many managers and engineers were reaching retirement age or leaving for alternative employment, but were not able to be replaced because of a shortage of suitably qualified men. Thus it was crucial to train more, and quickly. Renewed German militarism under their dynamic new Chancellor, Adolf Hitler, indicated to the prescient that a European war was again a distinct possibility.

The records of the Monmouthshire and South Wales Coalowners' Association in the National Library of Wales at Aberystwyth show feverish activity on the education front during 1937–9. Education had not been discussed in their minutes since 1914. Letters were sent to the headmasters of all the leading public schools in Wales and the west of England and of the Welsh grammar schools. On offer was the chance of being given a university education without cost. In fact, students would be paid a generous salary while they studied. In return they had to commit themselves to the sponsoring company for several years where they would enjoy accelerated promotion. The idea was to spend thirty weeks at the University, and twenty with the employer, including three at a summer surveying camp. It was intended to take on twenty to thirty students in each year of study, making for a total under training of between sixty and ninety. Initially twenty-four scholarships were available, ten of them with the Powell Duffryn Company and with no more than two allocated to any other company. A student needed a further three years' experience after graduation prior to sitting the first class certificate examination as a condition of the Coal Mines Act. There was then a 'golden handcuffs' requirement to work for the company for five years after achieving this. Thus the total commitment was for eleven years. Salary scales were generous. The starting salary for a student spending three years at university was £120, rising to £300 as a full-time junior official after graduation. The scheme guaranteed a minimum salary of £400 for the five years after obtaining the first class certificate. It suffered something of a setback because many of the applicants were not of the right calibre. Others were, but were discouraged by their families from entering the coal industry, which had a bad reputation for job instability and poor working conditions, even though the pay could be very good when compared to other occupations.

On 4 January 1939 the Coalowners' Association informed the registrar at University College, Cardiff, that its offer of scholarships valued at £5,000 per annum was conditional on the establishment of a school of mines at Cardiff as part of the University. This offer was to pay the scholarships for a minimum of seven years and was on the basis that the total costs, estimated at £12,000 per annum, would be provided. In an earlier unsigned memo, believed to have been written by the joint secretary of the Coalowners' Association, Iestyn R. Williams, to his counterpart, Finlay A. Gibson, the ground had been prepared for retaliation against the humiliation of the loss of Trefforest. He wrote: 'It will be remembered that the Coal Owners were unaware of the agreement which had been entered into between the University and the Glamorgan County Council for the mining department of the University to be transferred to Treforest.'[34] On the face of it, this comment is quite astonishing since they had representation on the joint committee and could hardly have been unaware of the plans for a new national school of mines for Wales and of the discussions taking place. However, knowledge of how some local councils conduct their business leads this writer to speculate whether the advertised agendas of meetings excluded discussions on this subject which then took place; whether the minutes were doctored and did not represent a true and fair record of the resolutions passed; and whether the times and locations of certain meetings were changed at very short notice with only a quorate of sympathetic committee members advised in time to prevent or frustrate the Coalowners' Association representatives attending meetings at which key decisions were passed. They could then be noted as 'absent'.

Glamorgan County Council reacted badly to the news that the Coalowners' Association planned to cut out Trefforest from the professional training of its employees and sought to halt this by preventing the Miners' Welfare Fund releasing the money to Cardiff instead. The Coalowners' Association had seemingly dangled a large stick and a carrot in front of Professor David Jones, who had been appointed to head Cardiff's mining department in 1935. Without the cooperation of the coal owners and their endowment fund for his department to set up a scheme to train all of their managerial grade mining students, Jones would have few, if any, students and possibly be out of a job. When he went out to Trefforest to check up on the accommodation, he made his first priority that of securing the best room in Trefforest House for his own office. It was inhabited by the principal, Robert James, who had succeeded George Knox on his retirement in 1931. Jones insisted on the principal's office being allocated to him as he was the senior academic. James indignantly refused to vacate it. And, as Basil Isaac has written, 'an acrimonious dispute resulted of such ferocity, that at least one witness was reluctant to discuss the event 40 years later'.[35]

The row was witnessed by several shocked members of staff including H. P. Richards, the head of the mining department, and C. C. Evans, lecturer in physics and mathematics. It is evident that either Jones had no wish to work at Trefforest or, much more likely, that he was under strong pressure not to move from Cardiff, otherwise he would not have gone to the trouble of alienating the Trefforest academic staff over such a trifling matter as the size of his room. He would evidently have to cooperate with them in the future whatever happened. Because of his action, however, Glamorgan County Council was enabled to block the release of the £42,000 promised by the Miners' Welfare Fund to develop the Trefforest site if it was not spent there, but in Cardiff. They were able to effect this due to an earlier agreement signed between Glamorgan, University College, Cardiff, and the Miners' Welfare Fund, which stated that the proposed school of mines would be sited at Trefforest. A stalemate resulted and nothing happened until the war, which put a stop to all such development work.

In the late 1930s, Professor Jones established the Coalowners' Research Association which did valuable work into coal dust suppression, including developing the idea of water sprays fitted to coal-cutting machinery. David Jones, after whom the Cardiff students' mining society, Jones' Heading was named, died in a car accident in 1947. After the war, the Coalowners' Association did not have to redeem its promise of funding Cardiff's mining students. They were coal owners no more. All they had achieved by their petty spite was to put back the development of the Trefforest site for a decade or so. From 1940 the college was known as the

School of Mines and Technology. During the war Trefforest was active in training the 'Bevin Boys', but it was after the war that the real expansion took place as the Polytechnic of Wales and, ultimately, as the University of Glamorgan.

NOTES

1. Cited by Michael Sanderson, *The Universities and British Industry, 1850–1970* (London: Routledge & Kegan Paul, 1972) p. 9.
2. Oldfield-Davies, *Technical Education in Wales: Report of the Central Advisory Council for Education (Wales)* (London: Ministry of Education, HMSO, 1961), p. 2.
3. South Wales Miners' Federation minutes, 18 July 1910.
4. Correspondence: Gee, David & Evans to Ingledew & Sons, 11 November 1909.
5. South Wales Miners' Federation minutes, 28 June, 29 September, 14 November 1913.
6. Haldane, *Royal Commission on University Education in Wales: First Report* (Cmd. 8500; London: HMSO, 1916), T. F. Sibly minutes of evidence 936, p. 60.
7. David Dykes, *The University College of Swansea: An Illustrated History* (Stroud: Alan Sutton, 1992), p. 69.
8. Haldane, *Royal Commission* (1916), T. F. Sibly minutes of evidence 907/8, pp. 58/9.
9. Haldane, *Royal Commission on University Education in Wales: Appendix to Second Report* (Cmd. 8699; London: HMSO, 1917); George Knox minutes of evidence 6162, p. 70.
10. Ibid., 6163, p. 70.
11. Ibid., Sir Clifford Cory minutes of evidence 5931, p. 61.
12. Ibid. 5976, p. 62.
13. Ibid., Sir Clifford Cory statement, para 2, p. 60.
14. Ibid.
15. For further information on Crumlin see Paul Croke and Mike Roach, *From Crumlin to Crosskeys: The History of the First Tertiary College in Wales* (1914–1987) (Cwmbran: Croke and Roach, 1987).
16. PRO, ED114/1200.
17. Copy of Resolutions passed at Trefforest Conference, 16 October 1922.
18. University of Wales Council minutes, 27 April 1923. Appendix A, p. 2.
19. Ibid., p. 3.
20. Ibid.
21. Ibid., pp. 3–4.
22. Ibid. Appendix II, p. 9.

23. For a discussion on this see P. H. G. Harries, 'The Rhondda Revolt', *Welsh Journal of Education* 9/1 (2000), 91–102.
24. 'Outline suggestions of a Scheme for the establishment of a School of Mines in Wales.' Marked Confidential, unsigned and undated. University of Glamorgan archives.
25. Letter from George Knox to H. M. Ingledew, 4 March 1927, p. 1.
26. Letter from George Knox to H. M. Ingledew, 20 May 1927, p. 2/3.
27. PRO, ED114/1211.
28. Letter from Percy E. Watkins to H. M. Ingledew, 15 March 1928.
29. Ibid.
30. CE C5, Accession 382, Correspondence – Monmouthshire Education Committee.
31. Ibid. Correspondence from Miners' Welfare Committee, 2 June 1928.
32. Letter from George Knox to H. M. Ingledew, 16 March 1928, p. 2.
33. Letters from George Knox to H. M. Ingledew, 22 March 1928 and 27 March 1928.
34. MG1071, Memo to the Joint Secretary, 15 January 1938.
35. Basil Isaac, 'The quest for university status', *University of Glamorgan Mineral Surveying Society Magazine*, 7 (1992), 15.

FROM SCHOOL OF MINES TO THE UNIVERSITY OF GLAMORGAN

Basil Isaac

In 1940 the South Wales and Monmouthshire School of Mines was given a new title: the School of Mines and Technology. Despite the new name, the premises remained much the same as they were in 1913, when the school first opened. The nucleus of the institution was still Forest House, added to which was the wing which had been built to accommodate the mining, engineering and chemistry laboratories. Just beyond Forest House were the caretaker's cottage and the old Crawshay stables. There was also a well and pump and, at a distance of a few hundred yards, rough land on which stood the famous stone circles which were demolished in the 1950s.

After the outbreak of war in September 1939, a number of corrugated-iron Nissen huts were built near the stables. Their purpose was to house trainee radio-operators attending classes in the School. Students, both full-time and part-time, were encouraged to join the newly formed Officer Cadet Corps, which was affiliated to the Royal Engineers. The head of the department of fuel technology and chemical engineering was Sidney Watkins, who became the commanding officer of the cadets with the rank of major. His second-in-command was John Benjamin, a lecturer in mathematics, who was now promoted to the rank of lieutenant. There may have been some difficulty when at least one student rose through the ranks to the same eminence.

Students attended classes in drill and weaponry training on their 'free' afternoons, both at the School and at Maindy Barracks in Cardiff. The officers' uniforms worn by the cadets gave them a faintly First World War appearance, particularly as they wore puttees – strips of khaki cloth carefully wound around the leg from ankle to knee – as a kind of gaiter. It sometimes happened that, due to a lack of care, the cloth unwound, with disastrous consequences for the cadet while marching on parade.

When German bombing raids began in south Wales, staff and students volunteered for fire-watching duties. Small teams spent the night in Forest House, taking turns to keep an eye out for incendiary bombs. On one occasion a team suddenly realized it had no experience of dealing with bombs and decided to practise the drill. Their inexpertise with fire hydrants and hosepipes led to the flooding of the ground floor of Forest House.

In 1940, George Knox, the retired first principal of the School, was awarded the highest honour of the South Wales Institute of Engineers when he was made a life member of that august organization. The principal of the School throughout the war was Robert James, affectionately known to all as Bobby. The School's departments at this time were mining and mining surveying, engineering, fuel technology and chemical engineering, and mathematics. The department of mathematics was also responsible for courses in physics. Diploma courses in some of these subjects had been provided since 1913 on 'sandwich' lines: the students spent six months in industry and six at college. It was also possible to take the external B.Sc. examinations of London University in mining, civil engineering, chemistry and mechanical engineering; students who were successful in these examinations might go on to take higher degrees. In addition, there was a great variety of part-time day and evening courses which enabled students to take their ordinary and higher national certificates. Many of these courses were tailored to suit the mining industry and the industrial character of south Wales.

The principal had only one administrative assistant, a secretary named Anne Hart, who was responsible for all the typing and duplication work for the entire academic staff. He gave lectures in engineering and inspired many students to follow successful careers in that field.

A student who entered the school at this time on a part-time basis has given a picture of life there. Royden Greening came to Trefforest as a first-year ordinary national certificate surveyor while working for the Powell Duffryn collieries. His work entailed visiting five different pits each week from a base at Porth in the Rhondda Valley. He set out early in the morning on his bicycle, and in all weathers, to visit pits in the Rhondda, Pontypridd and Pontyclun. Each colliery had a different surveyor and, after a visit underground, he returned to Trefforest. There were no pithead baths or canteen facilities in those days and his weekly wage was 12s 6d. His employers allowed him to spend one day and one evening at the School of Mines and Technology. At this time the School's day lasted from 9.15 a.m. until 4.30 p.m., and from 5 p.m. to 7 p.m. for part-time students. Students who attended only evening classes had classes and practicals from 6.15 p.m. until 9.15 p.m. During the war there was no refectory and students either had to bring their own packed lunches or bought tea and cakes from the caretaker at Forest House. The school was also without library facilities at this time.

As the war went on, other students wearing uniform appeared on campus, in addition to the officer cadets. They were regular army cadets who came to learn practical engineering workshop skills, such as welding and soldering. In April and May 1944 the old railway line above Forest House was filled with wagons and trucks containing the military equipment of American forces awaiting D-Day and the invasion of Europe. Some of the American servicemen would come down from the line to watch the officer cadets at drill and were greatly taken with their weaponry, particularly the Bren light machine-guns. They also gave demonstrations of the finer points of American football. After D-Day it was reported that 75 per cent of all American supplies had passed through south Wales.

Open days were held at the School for sixth-form pupils from local grammar schools, particularly for those studying physics. The pupils were greeted by Principal James and then passed on to C. C. Evans, head of physics, assisted by H. J. Shepherd. The last-named would try to baffle the young visitors with a series of optical illusions, though most were easily solved. His most memorable demonstration was his unique method of blackboard illustration, in which he appeared to hang by his fingertips from the edges of the blackboard, with his back to the class, and addressing them over his right shoulder. C. C. Evans was an expert at Esperanto, the artificial language which some hoped would become a means of international communication. He gave lectures on Esperanto during lunch-breaks and some students became quite proficient in it.

By the end of the war the School of Mines and Technology still consisted of only four departments. There were approximately 150 full-time students and about 800 part-timers. They were taught by seven full-time members of staff and ten part-time day lecturers and nineteen part-time evening lecturers; in addition, there were twenty-three visiting lecturers. One of the students who enrolled in 1944 introduced herself at a reunion almost fifty years later as Lorna Davies, the first female student, who had studied electrical engineering.

The immediate post-war period was marked by a steady expansion and diversification of the School's courses. There was now a great interest in technical education of all kinds. Full-time and sandwich courses were established in mathematics, physics, mining, chemistry, mechanical and electrical engineering, and civil engineering, for the successful completion of which diplomas were awarded. Student numbers remained similar to those during the war years but the number of part-time students increased by about half. The administrative staff also increased – to two female clerks and the principal's secretary.

In the academic year 1945/6 the first refectory was provided for staff and students in a large hut near the lower main gate of the School. Lunches were served in two sittings, there was no choice of menu and the staff sat at two reserved tables; teas and light refreshments were also available. A grave disadvantage was the absence of any kind of shelter for the students waiting to enter the refectory, and they were soaked whenever the weather was unkind, whereas members of staff were allowed to jump the queue.

The School was still without a library. There was a single shelf of books in Forest House and Mr Stone, the caretaker, acted as librarian, entering the names of borrowers in an exercise book. The former officer cadet training hut near the refectory was now converted into an optics laboratory. A number of prefabricated workshops and laboratories were put up and four aluminium classrooms erected behind Forest House. In 1949 the School of Mines acquired a new name: it became the Glamorgan Technical College.

Before this time there had been few communal activities among the students. The rugby and football teams began regularly to play matches on pitches at Rhydyfelin. Table tennis became the most popular indoor sport and a large room was made available for players in Forest House during the lunch-hour. Three scientific societies were organized for students of mining, engineering and chemistry, each of which held weekly meetings. Debating and photography societies were also established. One former student recalls a very noisy debate on the subject of 'Religion versus Science', in which H. P. Richards, a lecturer in mining and surveying, argued in favour of religion and C. C. Evans, a lecturer in physics, took the side of science; the result of this debate was not recorded. The student magazine *Breccia*, founded in 1929, appeared regularly every year. It took its title from the geological term 'breccia' – a sedimentary rock composed of angular bits and pieces; a student with some knowledge of Italian, however, observed that the word may also be translated as 'rubbish'.

In 1952 Dr D. P. Evans, principal of Bridgend Technical College, was invited by the local education authority to fill the post vacated by Robert James. Thomas Powell, head of the department of mining and surveying at Trefforest, went to Bridgend as the new principal. D. P. Evans showed a good deal of energy and initiative in his new post. The number and variety of courses provided at Trefforest, particularly for part-time and evening-class students, rapidly increased. He adopted a rather abrasive style in dealing with staff, perhaps as a consequence of having come from a more junior college. Throughout most of his career at Trefforest he did not have the assistance of a deputy principal and allowed heads of department to represent him only when it was absolutely necessary.

The new head of mining was H. P. Richards. He had been a part-time student at the School of Mines under its first principal, George Knox, before taking a mining degree at the University College, Cardiff. He believed that members of his department should be capable of teaching any subject connected with mining. On one occasion the present writer found himself conducting a practical demonstration of the testing of mine gases. The passing of the examination in this subject was an essential qualification for the class of mine officials and the process had not even been observed before by the lecturer. Fortunately, the actual examination, held later that same day, was carried out by a mine manager, as the regulations required. All the dozen candidates passed, so it was a great triumph for H.P. and his method of using mining 'stand-ins'.

The various 'characters' on the academic staff were known throughout the college by their initials. Apart from H.P., the principal was D.P. and the head of physics was C.C. Some of the senior technicians also had special titles to indicate to which department they belonged. The chief mining technician was known as Jones the Coal, to distinguish him from Jones the Caretaker and several other Joneses on campus.

H. P. Richards was a keen amateur historian and a member of Plaid Cymru who served for many years as a local councillor, albeit as an Independent. One day when he entered the geology laboratory he saw a large wall-map on which the place-names were given in both Welsh and English. Observing, however, that the county of Monmouthshire was shown as part of England, he immediately sent for a technician and ordered him to correct the boundary between Wales and England with a pot of red paint; this was some time before Monmouthshire was officially incorp- orated as part of Wales.

In 1953/4 the link between the mining departments at Trefforest and University College, Cardiff, was severed with the termination of the joint mining diploma. This had been a four-year sandwich course in which the basic sciences were taught at Cardiff and the practical mining subjects at Trefforest. The diploma dated back to 1913, but the relationship between the two institutions had always been a rather uneasy one.

Student numbers at Trefforest in 1953/4 were 149 full-time, 1,282 part-time day and 871 evenings only. Full-time students pur- sued diploma courses in chemical engineering, mining and mine surveying, civil engineering, mechanical engineering and physics. Part-time students followed courses which, in the main, led to ordinary national or higher national qualifications. A preliminary diploma course began in this year in the recently formed com- merce department, which represented a new departure from the array of technological subjects. The fees for these courses seem extremely reasonable by today's standards. The annual cost of a sandwich diploma course, for two terms in college and one in industry, was £16, and the cost of a full-time three-term diploma was £24. The annual fees for part-time ordinary national certificate courses were 10s and £1 for higher national. The Gla- morgan Education Authority provided sixteen scholarships annually for diploma courses. The teaching staff at this time con- sisted of fifty-four full-time and fifty-nine part-time lecturers.

The expansion of a number of courses led to the need for add- itional accommodation. In 1953/4 the Ministry of Education sanctioned the building of a double-storey block near Forest House. Work began in March 1954 and the building was finished in late 1956. The departments of mining, electrical engineering and physics moved into the new block and the rooms vacated in Forest House were taken by the departments of chemistry and mechanical engineering. The numbering of buildings, as each was completed, began at this time: Forest House became A Block, mining became B Block, and so on.

In 1956 a British Transport film unit visited the college to make a short feature entitled *Every Valley,* for which part of the commentary was spoken by the Welsh actor Donald Houston. It showed a scene of a student arriving late for a lecture on the geological structure of the south Wales coalfield given by H. P. Richards in Forest House. Thereafter H.P. always claimed that the film showed him looking far too anxious.

The building programme begun in 1954 was completed, and work began on a new series of buildings for the departments of business studies, civil engineering and building, chemical engineering, and mechanical and production engineering. Work also began on the construction of an assembly hall, a library and a refectory.

In February 1956 the government published a White Paper on technical education. The sector was envisaged as a pyramid structure with a base of local and area technical colleges, leading up through regional colleges to an apex consisting of a small number of colleges of advanced technology. These CATS, as they were soon called, were to provide a type of education comparable with, but distinct from, the courses available in universities. The White Paper also considered the increasing demand for scientific manpower and the supporting role of technicians and craftsmen. At first, there were to have been eight colleges of advanced technology. The two rivals for the coveted title in Wales were the Glamorgan and Cardiff Technical Colleges. In the event, in March 1957, it was the College at Cardiff that was designated as a CAT; it was the only college in Wales to achieve this status.

In 1956 it was decided to wind up the courses at Trefforest which led to the external degrees of London University, thus ending an association which had lasted for more than twenty years. In retrospect, this move seems to have been an unfortunate one. The College had a good success rate and the Council for National Academic Awards would later criticize the staff at Trefforest for lacking experience of teaching to degree level.

A significant initiative during this period was the introduction of the diploma in technology, which was awarded and validated by the National Council for Technological Awards; this body was the predecessor of the Council for National Academic Awards. The diploma in technology was designed to be of honours degree standard but with a technological emphasis. The award was made after a four-year sandwich course and the end-product was intended to be of use in industry.

In 1958 Trefforest became a regional college and, to indicate its enhanced status, its name was changed to the Glamorgan College of Technology. Its role was now to develop advanced full-time, part-time and sandwich courses. The first diploma in technology courses were offered in 1963 by the department of chemistry and chemical engineering and by the newly created department of civil engineering.

In 1960 the Pontypridd College of Further Education at Rhyd-yfelin had opened and rapidly took responsibility for all non-advanced work. The building programme begun on the Trefforest campus in 1954 was now complete and a new phase was put in hand. The completed buildings were opened by the minister of education, Sir Edward Boyle, in May 1963.

In view of the extensive building programmes undertaken, it is surprising that, in the early 1960s, the principal and some members of the senior staff considered the possibility of moving the College to a new site. Among the areas considered were Bridgend, the Vale of Glamorgan and Wenvoe. But such a move could never have been seriously considered at this late stage.

With the opening of the refectory in the basement of B Block, the principal attempted to boost revenue by banning the consumption of food and drink in the College staffrooms. The staff immediately boycotted the refectory and local people were treated to the spectacle of lecturers walking up Forest Grove to eat their picnics on the side of the Barry Mountain, the hill along the bottom of which the railway line to Barry used to run. After several days with an almost empty refectory, the banning order was withdrawn.

The early 1960s were regarded as a fairly relaxed period by academic staff. Students following sandwich courses usually returned to their places of work after Easter, thus greatly reducing teaching hours in the summer term. The term also included the annual golf match, in which all staff participated, and a tennis match; some enthusiasts played a game of cricket. Staff numbers were still suffi-ciently small for all members to know one another. At Christmas there was a carol service and a children's party.

The annual summer school, which took up three weeks of the summer vacation, was an eagerly anticipated event. Selected members of staff, assisted by lecturers from more junior technical colleges, took up residence on the campus of the University Col-lege, Swansea. Students came from various colleges throughout south Wales and lived in the University College hostels. The aim of the summer school was to help students to overcome any diffi-culties they might have in their academic work, usually for the ordinary national certificate. The principal of the College was also head of the summer school. Invitations to attend the school were always prized by lecturing staff because they meant extra remuner-ation. During the week of the National Eisteddfod, H. P. Richards, a Welsh-speaker, would always disappear for a few days. The prin-cipal was well aware of where H. P. Richards was but went through a daily routine of asking about his whereabouts. Each time, loyal members of the mining department would pretend to have seen H.P. on campus earlier that very day.

The last act performed by H.P. before he retired in the early 1960s was to present the collection of miners' lamps which was owned by the mining department, and which he did not want to see dispersed, to the National Museum of Wales, where for many years afterwards they were displayed in glass cases.

In 1963 the Robbins Report on Higher Education led to a massive expansion across the entire field of higher education. The report established a correlation between social class and educa-tional achievement, and argued that all students with the necessary ability could pursue higher educational studies. It also recommended that the existing colleges of advanced technology should be designated technological universities. Regional colleges such as the one at Trefforest might choose to develop along paths that led to university status. The proposals were intended to give a new impetus to vocational education in the United Kingdom.

An important outcome of the Robbins Report was the setting up of the Council for National Academic Awards (CNAA). This body was given power to validate courses and award degrees in non-university institutions, replacing the National Council for

Technological Awards. The teacher-training colleges were now to be called colleges of education and would have the power to award B.Ed. degrees after validation by the CNAA. It was also suggested that the colleges of education could be integrated with universities.

Regional colleges such as the one at Trefforest could now offer CNAA degrees if their courses achieved a sufficiently high standard and if they were validated by the appropriate CNAA subject panel. Higher degrees could also be awarded. Students who had previously obtained diplomas in technology could now have their awards converted to degrees. The implementation of these proposals brought about the 'student explosion' of the 1960s.

In the mid-1960s three small classes of mining diploma students, twenty-two in all, were interviewed with a view to eliciting their opinions of the college and its courses. They were all employed by the National Coal Board and were considerably older than students in other departments. Most were mine officials who received full salary and a lodging allowance while attending the sandwich diploma course at the college. Their previous careers included the occupations of RAF pilot, trawlerman, former member of the Danish Resistance, trained teacher, physics graduate, two international rugby players and champion boxer. Their aim was to gain a post as a mine manager on leaving college. Their diploma course was regarded as being fairly satisfactory but a major complaint was the lack of free time, since lectures and practicals took up thirty hours a week. They also deplored the lack of sports facilities, the absence of a library and the non-existence of student hostels. Because of their maturity and the fact that they were relatively well-off, they did not make much contact with students from other departments.

In the early 1960s the students' union had been given a room in B Block from which to conduct its affairs. Alan Thomas, a student from the mining diploma class, was given the rare honour of life membership of the union. He had won several Welsh international rugby caps, played for the Barbarians, and had been a member of the Newport team which inflicted the only defeat on the All Blacks during their tour of 1963–4.

With the establishment of the CNAA, it became a matter of personal and departmental prestige to have a degree at the college validated. This was certainly the ambition of John Short, a young Yorkshireman who had replaced H. P. Richards as head of mining. He was keenly aware that some of the north of England regional colleges were preparing mining degree courses and decided to attempt to be first with such a course. At this time the mining department had a large, well-qualified staff and had recently had a successful general inspection by HM Inspectors, so there appeared to be a reasonable chance of success. After a good deal of work in the preparation of syllabuses, the proposed scheme was presented to the academic board of the college. It was rejected – for no apparent reason – and was never sent for consideration by the CNAA. The academic board had developed from the original board of studies. The principal was its chairman and the other members were mainly heads of department, with a few specialist senior lecturers in addition.

In April 1965 the Secretary of State for Education, Anthony Crosland, gave a speech to the Association of Teachers in Technical Education, the main union of the academic staff at Trefforest. His speech introduced the concept of the binary system: higher education was considered to consist of a university sector and a public sector comprising the leading technical colleges and the colleges of education. The public-sector colleges would be controlled and financed by local education authorities, while the universities would be autonomous and funded by central government, advised by the University Grants Committee. The university sector would now include the colleges of advanced technology which were promoted to become universities. The two sectors would be regarded as equal in prestige, each making its own distinctive contribution to higher education.

In 1966 the government's White Paper, *A Plan for Polytechnics and Other Colleges,* proposed that higher education outside the existing universities should be concentrated in centres which had staff, buildings and equipment of a high standard. They would be called polytechnics and would be comprehensive in scope. Their main function, unlike that of the existing universities, would be to develop as teaching institutions. Their courses and degrees would be validated by the CNAA. Each would have about 2,000 full-time students as well as a substantial number following part-time courses. The polytechnic courses would include science and technology, business and management studies, the humanities, social sciences, and arts and design, and would range from sub-degree to post-graduate level. The secretary of state would have to be satisfied with the proposed administration of the new institutions. Anthony Crosland came to Trefforest to explain the organization and functions of the polytechnics to the academic staff.

Before further developments in higher education could be confirmed, there was a local mining disaster which became world-famous. On 21 October 1966 the Trefforest campus resounded to the noise of sirens and ambulances and many other vehicles racing down Llantwit Road on their way to Aberfan, near Merthyr Tydfil. The head of the mining department, John Short, spent several days digging in the slurry of the collapsed coal-tip as part of the recovery operation. Senior members of the National Coal Board's surveying and planning departments visited the geology section to examine the large-scale maps of the Aberfan area which had been used by Principal George Knox when writing his paper, 'Landslides in the south Wales valleys', some forty years before.

In April 1967 a parliamentary statement was issued by the secretary of state for education and later incorporated in the administrative memorandum, 'Notes for guidance'. The Glamorgan College of Technology was proposed as one of thirty polytechnics to be created in England and Wales. At this time there were 632 full-time and approximately 1,500 part-time students at the College. In the same year the first hall of residence was opened on the campus, with accommodation for a hundred students. Work was begun on a multi-storey building for the department of civil engineering and building, and then on the students' union, the library and the department of business studies.

There was some discussion at a staff meeting about a suitable name for the proposed polytechnic. Among the suggestions was the South Wales and Monmouthshire Polytechnic but it was pointed out that the acronym SWAMP might give the wrong impression to prospective students and staff. Some thought the word 'Wales' should be included in the title, since the polytechnic was to be the only one in the country, but in the end the title chosen was the Glamorgan Polytechnic.

In 1967 the department of civil engineering and building

received a visit from a CNAA subject panel. The department had a large, well-qualified staff and was confident the panel would have no difficulty in validating the proposed degree course. A diploma in civil engineering had been approved in 1952 but four years later, despite the vigorous opposition of D. P. Evans, HM Inspectors had suggested that the course should be wound up, owing to insufficient student numbers. It came as something of a shock when the department was asked to rewrite and resubmit the degree scheme, and an extensive inquest was carried out. Scapegoats were sought in the departments involved in the scheme but the inquiry petered out when one of the alleged culprits was invited to join a CNAA subject panel. In due course and after some modification, the degree scheme received full approval.

The Academic Board of the Polytechnic was now reorganized. It still consisted of the principal and heads of departments but it was made more democratic. An election was held for the appointment of six members of the lecturing staff from among the 157 who were eligible to vote; some of those elected would retire each year, thus allowing for new members to join the board. Another innovation was the appointment of a student member nominated by the students' union. The Academic Board was intended to assist the principal in the planning, coordination and development of the Polytechnic.

In 1969 the Haslegrave Report, *Technician Courses and Examinations*, recommended the establishment of a technician education council and a business education council which would oversee courses and examinations. The TEC came into existence in 1973 and the BEC in the following year . The TEC was primarily concerned with course validation and rather similar to the CNAA but at a lower academic level. The first chief officer of TEC was Francis Hanrott, who had been registrar of CNAA. Examination awards were validated at certificate, diploma, higher certificate and higher diploma levels. The BEC provided non-degree courses for students who worked in business or public administration. Awards were made at three levels: general awards, national awards and higher national awards. The general similarities between TEC and BEC eventually led to the creation of the Business and Technician Education Council (BTEC).

The Glamorgan Polytechnic was officially designated on

1 April 1970. The document of designation was presented by the parliamentary under-secretary of the Department of Education and Science, William van Straubenzee. At that time the Polytechnic consisted of ten departments: mining and mine surveying; chemical engineering; chemistry; physics; civil engineering and building; electrical engineering; mathematics and computer science; mechanical and production engineering; business studies; and management studies. A department of social studies and arts was added in 1972.

The department of mining and mine surveying had come under serious threat in 1969 when not a single student applied for the first year of the sandwich diploma course. The department's academic staff had been informed that they could be transferred to other departments after the summer term. However, pressure was exerted by the National Coal Board with a view to winning a reprieve and, as a consequence of fluctuating world oil prices, this was achieved. The principal admitted that he had considered having the colliery beam-engine that still stands in front of A Block removed to a museum. Dating from 1844, this machine had stood as a monument to mining in the area since 1920 but it had proved impossible to find an industrial archaeology museum that was interested in acquiring it.

Shortly after the granting of polytechnic status, a scale model showing the future development of the campus appeared in the foyer of the administrative block. Members were intrigued to see a building with a flat roof that was described as a helicopter port. Some were reminded that, in his address to students in 1917, Principal George Knox had prophesied that one day the valleys of south Wales would be served by aircraft competing with fast electric trains.

Before he retired, Principal D. P. Evans was invited to visit a large polytechnic in England to observe its methods of organization and administration. On his return he called a general staff meeting to report his observations. What had most impressed him, it seemed, was that the institution he had visited employed six uniformed porters, a point to which he returned several times. The staff at Trefforest had not realized until now that they suffered from a serious gap in the provision of porters, a lack which was soon corrected.

At the end of 1971/2 the principal retired. In the twenty years he had served at Trefforest many new developments had been initiated and now the Polytechnic had been established. For his work in higher education D. P. Evans was awarded a CBE. His successor was Dr D. W. F. James, who had been deputy principal since 1971, and Dr Frank Hybart was appointed in his place. The title of principal was now replaced by that of director.

The new director had a more relaxed style than his predecessor, particularly in his role as chairman of the Academic Board. The most bitter argument ever to take place at the board's meetings occurred when the question of bilingual signs on campus was discussed. The chairman implored members to conduct discussion of this issue in a calm and rational manner. Unfortunately, he chose a head of department to open the debate who was not known for his sympathy with Welsh matters. This man began by saying the issue before the meeting was 'an extremely simple one: either we advance towards the 21st century or we all return to the trees'. There was, of course, immediate uproar which the chairman had great difficulty in quelling. After protracted argument, it was decided that signs in both Welsh and English should be put up, but that was followed by another discussion about whether the Welsh signs should be placed above or below their English equivalents.

By 1973 a new series of buildings had come into service, including premises for the department of civil engineering and building, the students' union and the department of business studies. The first phase of the library (later called the learning resources centre) and a new refectory were also completed and a new student hall of residence was opened in 1974. At last the students had a proper home for their activities.

One of the enterprising schemes undertaken by students was the raising of funds for charities by organizing a journey by raft down the river Taff all the way to Cardiff. Publicized as the Taff-Tiki expedition, after the famous journey of Thor Heyerdahl across the Pacific, it proved very successful; in the years following, students from other colleges brought their rafts and it became an inter-college race. After several years the event was abruptly ended when a man, though not himself involved in the race and not a student, caught a fatal disease from the polluted waters of the river.

As degrees could now be awarded by the Polytechnic, it

became necessary to devise an awards ceremony. A select panel of senior academic staff under the guidance of John Benjamin, the registrar, held a series of meetings to discuss the matter. A large and imposing metal mace was purchased and a mace-bearer appointed to lead the academic procession and other dignitaries onto the stage. The ceremony was rehearsed several times and eventually deemed satisfactory after elimination of the synchronized but excessive doffing of mortarboards. The first ceremonies were held in the large refectory, with music supplied by a volunteer organist, and they proved a great success, although some members of the audience were put in mind of performances of Gilbert and Sullivan.

In the early 1970s a distinguished academic from Oxford Polytechnic visited Trefforest and addressed the staff. His theme was the future of higher education and the possible role of the polytechnics. Having toured the campus, he had observed the disused railway line that is now used as a car park. He felt the line was symbolic of the Polytechnic: no one could remember where it came from and it went into a dark tunnel which might lead anywhere. The deputy director was then prompted to hold a series of events on campus in which speakers would be invited to visit the Polytechnic and deliver public lectures on topics of general interest. The lectures proved very successful and attracted large audiences. Speakers included Vic Feather, general secretary of the Trades Union Congress, Donald Soper, the Methodist minister, and Emlyn Evans, assistant keeper of geology at the National Museum of Wales. There was also a musical evening, put on by a group of musicians and singers from the Welsh National Opera Company.

In December 1972 the government's White Paper, *Education: A Framework for Expansion,* proposed the development of all types of higher and further education and suggested that some colleges of education should be encouraged to merge with neighbouring polytechnics. The Glamorgan Polytechnic and the Glamorgan College of Education at Barry seemed to be obvious candidates for such a merger.

The Barry college had opened in 1914 with 120 female students. The report of the 1925 Burnham Committee had suggested there should be close liaison between such colleges and local universities; joint examination boards could be set up for the validation of courses. In 1929 the University Board for Training Colleges was formed and by the 1960s a bachelor of education degree had been introduced. The B.Ed. degree at Barry was awarded after a four-year course and a final examination, successful students being able to register for a higher degree.

The James Report of 1973, *Teacher Education and Training,* considered the roles of unversities, colleges of further education and colleges of education. It recommended that a new two-year course should be introduced for a qualification called the diploma in higher education. Students who obtained a Dip. H.E. could continue their studies and gain a degree after completing an additional third year. The James Report was unhappy with university-type education degrees, believing that such courses contained an excess of theory and insufficient practical teaching experience. The suggested remedy was to ask the Council for National Academic Awards to provide new courses to overcome these shortcomings, and the CNAA would validate both the Dip. H.E. and the B.Ed.

One of the main difficulties facing the Glamorgan Polytechnic was that it did not achieve the recognition it deserved in its early years. This may have been because it was a new type of institution and, in Wales, any kind of technological education has traditionally been regarded as inferior to university education. The polytechnics were meant to be practical technological teaching institutions but as time went by they aspired to become more like universities. This problem was developed by the registrar, John Benjamin, in a discussion paper delivered at Coombe Lodge in 1973. The venue was the Further Education Staff College near Bristol where senior staff from the Glamorgan Polytechnic went as part of their development. John Benjamin's discussion paper was entitled 'The organization of the polytechnic: the role of the administration'. The author claimed that the administrative staff were regarded by the local education authority as a colony of county hall. They came under the heading of school clerks, the academic staff were classed as teachers who were expected to perform some clerical duties, and the Polytechnic's director was regarded as a headmaster. When, in 1968, discussions began on drafting the instrument and articles of government of the Polytechnic, these views became evident: thcrc was some reluctance to accept that the Polytechnic would be administered very largely from outside county hall.

In 1975 an article entitled 'A short history of Glamorgan Polytechnic' was produced in pamphlet form by the present writer. Intended for publication in a student society magazine at a later date, it was an attempt to elicit constructive comment, and so ten copies were circulated to senior staff. The author, *inter alia*, deplored the fact that the Polytechnic was listed with schools in the local telephone directory. There was an immediate response from the deputy director, who requested that all copies of the article be promptly withdrawn on the grounds that it contained 'carping criticism'. The author explained that it was not possible to retrieve all copies of the article because Reginald Prentice, secretary of state for education, had asked for something interesting to read on the train back to London after his visit to Trefforest two days previously. The outcome of this brouhaha was that the polytechnic was listed with universities and colleges in all future editions of the telephone directory.

In August 1975 the Department of Education and Science approved the merger of the Glamorgan Polytechnic and the Barry College of Education. The plan envisaged that Barry would include its teacher-training element in the merged institution and degree courses would now be validated by the Council for National Academic Awards. Clement Roberts, principal at Barry, became a second deputy director of the newly designated Polytechnic of Wales.

The Barry College of Education enjoyed an excellent reputation and was highly regarded in certain fields such as women's physical education, special education and the teaching of oral Welsh. It had originally recruited more women than men but was now a fully mixed college. The merger would provide a good opportunity to broaden the base of the Polytechnic by the development of the non-scientific and non-technological academic fields.

Some of the Polytechnic's staff now began to visit Barry for discussion of the possiblity of using modules from Trefforest degree schemes in the proposed Dip. H.E./B.Ed. courses. There was some anxiety regarding the proposed initial visit of the CNAA to Barry because the staff had no experience in facing the full vigour of its subject panels. Unfounded rumours were rife that previous Barry degrees had been validated by university staff over a cup of staffroom coffee. By this time CNAA panels were making frequent visits to Trefforest and the academic staff had become used to the validation process. A few staff members had themselves served as members of CNAA panels on visits to other colleges. There were also murmurs in the academic press to the effect that CNAA inspections had become too severe. One Cardiff professor who had served on a panel stated that he looked forward to the day when university departments would be subjected to the same rigorous scrutiny.

Staff from the Polytechnic visited Barry to discuss the final stages of preparation for the inspection. John Williams, a member of the Barry staff, had a most interesting arrangement for students following the environmental science course. In their final year they had to opt either for 'the urban pathway' or 'the rural pathway'. The latter conjured up a pleasant image of walking through idyllic scenery with an almost hypnotic effect. The corresponding degree at Trefforest had a course called 'Environmental Pollution', which did not sound half so pleasant.

The misgivings with regard to the CNAA visit proved well-founded when the inspection panel found the proposed degree unsatisfactory and recommended that it should not proceed. The staff were asked to reconsider and rewrite certain sections before resubmitting their B.Ed. syllabus.

A constant criticism made of some members of the Trefforest staff, according to the deputy director, was that they were always looking to the past. He wanted to create a new, dynamic, forward-looking image for the Polytechnic, and to this end he asked the staff of the art section at Barry to produce a new cover design for the staff magazine. When the large brown envelope containing the new design was opened at a Barry staff meeting, it was found to be a silhouette of the old colliery beam winding engine which stands in front of Forest House, and this caused much mirth.

The rejected Barry degree was revised and resubmitted, this time with success. By 1977 the Dip. H.E. and B.Ed., together with five other schemes resulting from the merger, received approval. Moreover, the Department of Education and Science and the CNAA hailed the merger as a perfect model for other institutions to emulate. This was the first time a teacher-training course in

Wales had been validated by a body outside the University of Wales.

In January 1977, when everything appeared to be proceeding smoothly, the Polytechnic suffered a severe blow. The Welsh Education Office of the Department of Education and Science informed the Polytechnic that it had decided to remove teacher-training courses from the Barry college. The government's plan also envisaged the removal of such courses from the West Glamorgan Institute of Higher Education at Swansea. The governing body of the Polytechnic immediately tried to persuade the government to allow the college to keep teacher training, an essential part of the integrated degree scheme. The chairman of the Welsh Joint Education Committee at the time was Lord Heycock, a prominent figure in the public affairs of Wales. This body had accepted the plan to merge the Barry College of Education with the Glamorgan Polytechnic and so its support was anticipated. But despite a battery of potent arguments, the Welsh Office pressed on with its plan to remove teacher training from Barry.

The West Glamorgan Institute of Higher Education at Swansea also launched a vigorous campaign to retain teacher training. In this it was stoutly assisted by the University College which would be validating the education degree. The Institute of Higher Education at Swansea, assisted by Lord Heycock and the West Glamorgan Local Education Authority, managed to keep its teaching course, but the Polytechnic of Wales failed to do so. Throughout the process the WJEC and its chairman remained completely silent. This meant that the Polytechnic was the only college in Wales which had terminated validation arrangements with the University of Wales and lost its B.Ed. course. It is tempting to suggest that there was a connection between the two. The director of the Polytechnic, D. W. F. James, believed the loss of teacher training at the college was due to political rather than educational factors. It was suggested that one of these factors was the use of the Welsh language as a medium in the training of teachers. This argument had been successfully used to retain Welsh courses at Bangor Normal College and thus to avoid a proposed merger with the University College of North Wales. The decision by the Secretary of State regarding the Polytechnic meant that the College would no longer train teachers after 1981.

Representatives of the Barry staff started attending meetings of the Polytechnic's Academic Board and some began to consider the possibility of a permanent transfer. Not all were impressed by the Trefforest campus with its modern buildings, which one disenchanted Barry lecturer likened to a factory complex. He failed to be convinced by the suggestion that the stream running through the campus, with its lily-ponds, was reminiscent of Venice.

At the time of the merger the number of full-time students at the Polytechnic had increased to 2,450, while part-time students numbered about 1,500. Among the full-time students there were about 300 who were following the teacher-training course which was now due for closure. At this time the Polytechnic offered thirty-two degree courses in various disciplines, including honours and ordinary degrees.

Research by the academic staff was actively encouraged, with more than a hundred being given timetable allowances in order to carry out this work. In the period 1973–8 a total of twenty-one D.Phil. degrees and fifteen masters' degrees were awarded to staff members. Course development led to the establishment of a new estate management and quantity surveying department; new buildings for the department of management studies, the first phase of the learning resources centre, a new refectory and the students' union had all been completed. A new student hostel opened in 1974 and two more in 1977. The department of mathematics and computer science, new science laboratories and a workshop unit with stores opened in 1976 and an extra 30 acres of playing fields were made available at Tyn-y-wern, some three miles distant. In 1977 the first phase of the new buildings for electrical engineering and mechanical engineering was opened, with a main computer centre and lecture block. Another student hostel opened in 1978 and a groundsman's house completed. A playing field was under construction, as well as an extension to the students' union. The computer centre was also significantly improved with the acquisition of a large multi-access machine.

At the end of 1977/8, D. W. F. James resigned as director of the Polytechnic of Wales and took up a post as chief executive of the British Ceramic Research Association at Stoke-on-Trent. The new director, J. D. Davies, had been principal of the West Glamorgan Institute of Higher Education and had been a student at Trefforest in 1945. He recalled being greeted by Royden Greening and taken on a tour of the laboratories on his arrival as one of three scholarship students.

With the removal of teacher training, the Barry site became scheduled for closure and the transfer of staff to Trefforest now became imminent. Some of the Barry people found the prospect difficult to accept and were encouraged to take early retirement by means of a financial inducement known as the Crombie Award which was calculated on the basis of pensionable years plus a lump sum. The Crombie was offered throughout the United Kingdom to college of education staff who had their career prospects affected, or had been made redundant, by college closures beginning in the 1970s. A limited number of the Trefforest staff affected by the closure at Barry also accepted retirement terms.

The late 1970s were marked by a surge of interest in staff development. Academic staff were encouraged to pursue higher degrees and to visit the Further Education Staff College at Coombe Lodge, where short courses intended to improve the professional and personal expertise of staff were on offer. Typical topics at Coombe Lodge were the planning of college resources, effective communication, the management of meetings and so on. Apart from polytechnic and other college staff, such courses were attended by representatives from local education authorities, government departments and other bodies concerned with education and training.

Some members of the Polytechnic's staff developed an interest in voluntary work. Royden Greening, who had entered the college as a student in 1939, was appointed principal lecturer in engineering design in the department of mechanical engineering. For many years before his retirement in 1980 he worked on the design of aids for disabled people; he was awarded a Churchill Travelling Fellowship which enabled him to visit several European countries, encouraging university students to set up design groups. He was awarded an MBE for his contribution in this field and later visited Russia.

Arthur Lewis, a former colliery manager, joined the mining department as a senior lecturer in 1976 and became interested in the work of the British Executive Overseas. He spent several of his summer vacations in the Philippines and Indonesia, advising governments on modern coal-mining techniques and promoting the sale of British equipment. He was awarded an OBE before retiring in 1987.

By the late 1970s the influence of the Council for National Academic Awards had become extremely evident at all polytechnics. The council now began to turn its attention to the standards of the institutions which its members had visited for validation purposes. Such scrutiny is well illustrated in a report issued by the CNAA on Teesside Polytechnic in 1978. The local education authority was criticized in this report as well as the director of the Polytechnic. Improvement was demanded in most areas of the college's work and the deadline of the 1979/80 session was given for the correction of alleged defects. Failure would mean that the CNAA might invalidate many of the courses, which in turn would lead to the inevitable closure of some departments or even perhaps the entire institution. The report set alarms bells ringing in other polytechnics and probably had the effect of making directors more appreciative of the advantages of corporate status and independence from the CNAA. Some now began to question the powers of the CNAA under its royal charter. Two other polytechnics received adverse reports, but eventually the perceived defects were corrected and it was agreed that the process had benefited the three colleges concerned.

In the face of regular inspections from the CNAA, the staff of the Polytechnic of Wales had become used to dealing with visits. Questions about the aims, focus and objectives of a syllabus were now handled with ease. The only reprimand received in later years was when a CNAA panel was collected from a Cardiff hotel and taken on a circuitous route to the Polytechnic so that its members could view Castell Coch at Tongwynlais and the castle at Caerffili. The theory was that such a picturesque route would put the panel in a relaxed and agreeable mood, but it had the opposite effect and the Polytechnic was reprimanded for wasting its time.

In June 1979 the CNAA published its report, *Partnership in Validation*, which was intended to modify validation for public-sector institutions. The council would now grant approval for 'well established courses', for indefinite periods, instead of examining courses every five years, as had previously been the case. The report was intended to produce greater flexibility and more autonomy in the colleges.

In April 1985 the Lindop Report, *Academic Validation in Public Sector Higher Education*, suggested that some polytechnics and colleges of higher education should be given autonomy by the secretary of state to validate their own courses. The government published two consultative documents two years later which suggested that the polytechnics in England should be granted corporate status in April 1989. They would be funded by a new body called the Polytechnic and College Funding Council. The Polytechnic of Wales would also be granted corporate status but would be retained within the local authority funding sector.

In September 1988 an article by Siân Griffiths appeared in *The Times Higher Education Supplement* under the heading, 'An exhausted seam'. The seam in question was the mining department of the Polytechnic of Wales. The article pointed out that mining had been not only the core subject of the syllabus at Trefforest but the one which had brought the School of Mines into existence. A brief review of the institution's history was given and the suggestion made that the year-long miners' strike of 1984–5 had sounded the department's death-knell. The remaining mining students would complete their courses by 1992 and the staff would be dispersed elsewhere. The article also pointed out, quite accurately, that local people still referred to the bus-stop near the gate of the Polytechnic as the School of Mines.

On 11 November 1988 a seventy-fifth anniversary dinner was given by the Polytechnic at the Angel Hotel in Cardiff to mark the closure of the mining department. The dinner was attended by 190 past and present staff and students of the department and the after-dinner speakers were J. D. Davies, the director, and Ken Rowlands, the international rugby referee and a former student.

By 1988 the Polytechnic was a flourishing single-campus institution with 4,200 full-time and sandwich-course students and 1,300 part-time students. A three-storey sports complex was due for completion in 1989 and enlarged buildings for the learning resources centre were nearly complete. The Welsh Regional Management Centre had been set up with government support in 1977 and was now one of twelve such centres serving England and Wales. It supplied long and short courses in management studies and was active in consultancy and research. Courses for management studies certificates were also developed for other colleges.

The Polytechnic had three academic faculties in 1988. The faculty of environmental studies consisted of the departments of civil engineering and building, estate management and quantity surveying, mining and mine surveying, and science. The faculty of engineering studies contained the departments of chemical engineering, electrical and electronic engineering, mathematics and computer science, and mechanical and production engineering. The faculty of professional studies comprised the departments of arts and languages, behavioural and communication studies, business and administrative studies, and management and legal studies. The campus had three student halls of residence providing accommodation for 500 students, and there were three much smaller off-campus hostels for a further 100 students.

The Polytechnic was now the leading institution for higher education in the maintained sector in Wales and pioneered several innovative courses such as police studies, which entailed study by day-release and evening work, a course which produced its first graduates in 1988. As the only polytechnic in Wales, it faced stiff competition from Welsh colleges and institutes of higher education which enjoyed the support of the Welsh Joint Education Committee.

The government consultation papers on 1987 suggested that the Polytechnic of Wales should be excluded from full corporate status and that its funding should be retained by the local authority of Mid Glamorgan. This would put the Polytechnic at a grave disadvantage vis-à-vis its counterparts in England. The secretary of state for Wales, in anticipation of this problem, arranged to revoke the funding power of the LEA, if the need should arise. He also requested a report by independent auditors as a result of critical comments made by the district auditors in 1988 to the effect that the financial accounts of the Polytechnic's management centre were totally inadequate and completely contrary to current regulations. As a consequence of this adverse report the LEA threatened to defer consideration of the Polytechnic's becoming independent.

J. D. Davies, the Polytechnic's director, had been unhappy with the proposed funding arrangements since they were first mooted. It was estimated that the Polytechnic would suffer a funding deficit of 11 per cent, compared with its counterparts in England. Support for full corporate status was quickly provided by the Committee of Polytechnic Directors and the Council for National Academic Awards. The latter pointed out that a deterioration in funding would bring into question the Polytechnic's ability to maintain the required high standard of courses and degrees. Any financial restrictions imposed by the government or an LEA could therefore not be tolerated.

In the days before polytechnics existed, local education authorities had required colleges to meet the needs of their surrounding area. An LEA usually regarded a polytechnic as having evolved from one of its own institutions, as having been nurtured from a lowlier level, as it were. In the case of the School of Mines it had had links with university colleges in London and Cardiff before it was handed over by the coalowners in 1928; its academic staff had also carried out research of national importance. As the Polytechnic's registrar, John Benjamin, had stated, the staff at county hall had never seemed to appreciate these facts, being more used to dealing with junior technical schools and colleges.

The report presented to the Secretary of State for Wales by his independent auditors made the award of corporate status to the Polytechnic of Wales inevitable. Funding was now removed from the LEA and from now on would be provided by the Welsh Office.

In 1992 the Further and Higher Education Act created two Further Education Councils, one for England and the other for Wales. They replaced the Universities' Funding Council and the Polytechnic Funding Council. These new bodies were required to set up quality control bodies to ensure that high academic standards would be maintained. The Act also allowed polytechnics to assume university titles and full corporate status. By the end of 1992 a total of thirty-six former polytechnics had become universities, doubling the previous number. There was some discussion within the Polytechnic of Wales as to a suitable title for the institution in its new form which would be commensurate with its enhanced status as a university. Among the titles briefly suggested was Crawshay University but this was soon discounted for the reason that the name of the local ironmaster who had lived in

Forest House might revive unhappy memories of times gone by among local people. Eventually, the title University of Glamorgan was chosen and approved.

The Further and Higher Education Act of 1992 marked the end of the binary system which had separated the polytechnics from the universities. The Council for National Academic Awards, which had carried out such excellent work in maintaining standards for so many years, was now dissolved.

The University of Glamorgan did not become part of the federal University of Wales, as might have been anticipated. A separate and independent university was created by the Privy Council in June 1992. The official opening ceremony was performed by David Hunt, Secretary of State for Wales, on 1 September 1992.

Thus ended a chapter in the story which had begun with the foundation of the South Wales and Monmouthshire School of Mines nearly eighty years before.

ACKNOWLEDGEMENTS

The author would like to thank members of staff from a wide range of departments who supplied reports, articles, letters and personal memories over many years. They include J. Benjamin, G. T. Bolan, D. M. Dummer, C. C. Evans, D. P. Evans, R. Greening, L. Jones, L. Morgan, G. Pitt and H. P. Richards.

BIBLIOGRAPHICAL NOTES

A Symposium in Honour of L. H. Thomas, 22 February 1989. Tributes to and memories of the former head of chemistry, member of staff 1940–82.

Breccia, the Student Magazine of Glamorgan Technical College (1951/2). This publication retained the School of Mines cover and contains two articles on the career of Robert James, the retiring principal.

Cantor, Leonard M. and Roberts I. F., *Further Education Today: A Critical Review* (London: Routledge & Kegan Paul, 1986). This work deals with the formation of the CNAA and the BTEC; the merger of Barry College of Education and the Glamorgan Polytechnic; and the loss of teacher training at the Polytechnic of Wales.

Daugherty, R., Phillips, R. and Rees G., *Education Policy-Making in Wales: Exploration in Devolved Governance* (Cardiff: University of Wales

Press, 2000). This work discusses the problems encountered by the Polytechnic of Wales in achieving corporate status and the role of the LEA.

Isaac, Basil, 'A study of the educational, social and personal characteristics of three small groups of students at a regional college of technology', a short thesis on NCB students at Glamorgan College of Technology, part of a University College, Cardiff, MA thesis in education (by examination), 1966.

Lewis, D. Gerwyn, *The University and the Colleges of Education in Wales 1925–1978* (Cardiff: University of Wales Press, 1980). This book deals with the history of teacher training in Wales, including the work of the Barry College of Education; the loss of teacher training at Barry and the merger with the Polytechnic.

Mining Society Magazine of the Polytechnic of Wales, 21 (1978). This number contains a short history of the Polytechnic of Wales and updates Basil Isaac's pamphlet on the history of Glamorgan Polytechnic.

Minerals Surveying Society Magazine, 7 (1992–3). This number includes an article by Basil Isaac on the quest for university status; the same article appeared in the *School of Applied Sciences Magazine* (December, 1994).

'School of Mines reunion day, 10 August 1993', 80th anniversary celebration of the School of Mines mining department; reminiscences of former students. *Glamorgan Alumni Bulletin*, 3 (1993).

Universal (the magazine of the University of Glamorgan Graduate Club), 4 (Spring–Summer 1998). This number contains an article on the award of an MBE to Royden Greening.

CLASSES, COLLEGES AND COMMUNITIES

ASPECTS OF A HUNDRED YEARS OF ADULT EDUCATION
IN THE SOUTH WALES VALLEYS

Keith Davies

The relative innocuousness of the term 'adult education', with its connotations of evening classes offering a 'second chance' at qualification garnering, instruction in practical skills, off-the-job training or the opportunity to acquire the basic linguistic requirements for added holiday enjoyment, can sometimes obscure its deeper significance for political and social empowerment. As a medium for both encouraging and sustaining a sense of collective self-value, adult education, when geared to the self-expressed needs of a society, can provide a mechanism through which that society can declare itself and its intentions to continue and prosper.

No more so was this the case than in the Valleys of the south Wales coalfield during the last century, where traditions of adult learning for communal advancement, or sometimes for simple survival, proved strong and vibrant. In communities throughout the area, responses to perceived political insensitivity, economic exploitation or social inequality have often been expressed through demands for purposeful and self-targeted adult learning to comprehend and cope with their consequences. Through this means, it was often confidently believed, meaningful change in the collective experience could be effected. Though easy to deride as naive and utopian, this trust invested in adult education bore much fruit in creating a particular consciousness of society and their place within in for those who took advantage of the educational opportunities which comprise the history of adult learning in south Wales.

This collective, class-based analysis of the role of adult or, as it is sometimes tellingly labelled, 'workers' education' has, however, sometimes predominated to the relative denigration of its role as a means of personal self-betterment. A more rounded and inclusive interpretation would see the latter as equally valid and its denial as tantamount to a crude politicization of adult education that contravenes its liberating essence. Indeed, adult education has often formed the battleground between opposed 'visions' of the nature of south Wales society and its various forms – liberal, vocational, political, ideological, conservative, Marxist – trumpeted in turn as the most appropriate for the area and its needs. One thing lacking in all these generalizations has often been the personal motive of the individual adult student, overlooked in the quest to harness adult education to politics.

This chapter will attempt to strike a balance by examining the achievements of adult education for both society and the individual in south Wales during the period covered. To concentrate on the one to the exclusion of the other would be to impose a subjective and judgemental framework upon a phenomenon that warrants more subtle examination – an examination that is not merely rooted in history but which has a contemporary relevance for the south Wales of today where, in a post-coal era, the need for 'education', in its broadest sense, is obvious if an understanding of current predicaments and possible future solutions is to be acquired.

The chapter will, by presenting a survey of some of the manifestations of adult education and the confrontations it provoked, show how it played such a key role in south Wales during the last century. Inevitably, given the constraints of space, such a survey can only be partial and focus on a sample of the methods utilized by adult educators of differing political, cultural, philosophical, intellectual and motivational persuasions to reach their intended audiences and how those audiences responded. More comprehensive treatments are already available.[1] For this reason, the chapter will focus on a limited number of instances when disagreements over the precise nature and purposes of adult education emerged particularly strongly and often obscured, through a tendency towards sectarianism, its more general *raison d'être*.

In the light of this historical survey, I intend to offer some thoughts on the present nature and possible future direction of adult education and its relevance to current debates on the optimum method of achieving social transformation and community regeneration in the Valleys through the fostering of individual and community self-assurance, self-confidence and self-reliance. The argument is made that the past informs the present as much in adult education as in any other context.

Taking a broad approach, the chapter deals with the early debates on the meaning of adult education – the so-called battle of the 'two traditions' where, depending upon one's standpoint, it was seen as either a method of encouraging social harmony, fostering social revolt or imposing social control. I examine the work of the Workers' Educational Association (WEA) and that of its ideological arch-rival, the Independent Working-Class Education (IWCE) movement, exemplified by the Plebs League and the

National Council of Labour Colleges. The often controversial role of the universities, through the extension movement and the extra-mural tradition, will be covered. This was particularly evident during the Depression years of the 1930s, notably concerning the establishment of educational settlements throughout the area at that time. The part played by that most powerful of local institutions, the South Wales Miners' Federation (SWMF) in the provision of adult education, particularly in the years following the nationalization of the coal industry in 1947, will be outlined. Finally, the re-emergence of an arguably more progressive university role in the provision of education in the community during the last decades of the twentieth century will be examined. It is with the latter that the chapter emerges from history to concern itself with important contemporary issues.

This admittedly selective overview, whilst largely ignoring the valuable contributions of agencies such as the Sunday schools, the co-operative societies, the political parties, local education authorities, Coleg Harlech and others, as well as informal workplace-based learning – notably at the coalface – will, at least, provide a flavour of the variety of aims and objectives of adult education in some of its more prominent guises.

THE ROLE OF THE WORKERS' EDUCATIONAL ASSOCIATION (WEA) [2]

The WEA was established at an Oxford conference of adult educationalists in 1903 with the express intention of delivering impartial education on political, social, historical and economic issues through classes organized by university-calibre tutors for groups of workers who wished to study. Choice of tutor and topic was to be made by the students themselves to avoid charges of outside control, although the initial impetus for the establishment of classes might be made by local authorities, trade union branches or other interested groups. Eventually, the university tutorial method of learning was to be adopted.

The first Welsh branch was formed at Barry in 1906 and, the following year, an autonomous south Wales region of the WEA came into existence. By the outbreak of the First World War, just over 500 students, a relatively small number and almost exclusively male, were attending WEA classes at its four branches in industrialized south Wales – Cardiff, Barry, Caerau near Maesteg and Llanelli. Figures were, however, to improve significantly in the post-war decades.

Undoubtedly, the WEA possessed a genuine concern to assist working-class students to develop a capacity for study and an ability to apply the knowledge thus gained to the political, economic and social problems of the day. Those involved in its establishment and development, though usually middle class, generally identified with the aspirations of Labour and believed in the need for equality of opportunity through open access to education (of a university standard) for those who, in earlier years of life, had been denied such a chance.

The education offered by WEA classes was to be impartial and non-partisan, aiming at explaining, if critically, the current political and social order, rather than seeking to change it radically, at least in the short term. Essentially, it believed in the concept of education for citizenship, equipping the individual with the knowledge required to play a full and active part in society and, eventually, thus bringing about its transformation. Inevitably, this gradualist outlook would bring it into conflict with those who took a more militant attitude towards the possibilities of education, seeing it, rather, as the means to revolutionary enlightenment and an inspiration to a more immediate overthrow of the existing social order. Denigrating the efforts of the WEA as 'collaborationist', overly dominated by the universities and intended to bring the workers to an acceptance of the current capitalist system, such critics also pointed to its willingness to accept grants from the Board of Education and local government authorities as evidence of its role as an arm of state control.

Furthermore, those who advocated what was termed 'Independent Working-Class Education' (IWCE) – though, as we shall see, the reality of any independence was somewhat dubious – accused the WEA of being more interested in encouraging individual self-improvement, antiquarian scholarship or pursuit of knowledge for its own sake rather than aiming to educate, and hence raise, the working class as a whole. This conflict between the 'two traditions' – liberal versus radical – was to be particularly keen in south Wales in the opening decades of the twentieth century. This was a period that, of course, coincided with immense upheavals in the mining industry and its dependent communities, not the least of which were the foundation of the first area-wide trade union and its emerging militancy; the Tonypandy Riots; the dabbling in ideas of syndicalism, industrial unionism and workers' control; and the emergence of the Labour Party. IWCE was a natural concomitant of this vibrant radicalism.

INDEPENDENT WORKING-CLASS EDUCATION

A class analysis of society and a revolutionary view of social change argued that the working class itself should strive for its own emancipation and not rely on what was seen as the paternalism of the WEA. Thus, as the need for economic self-organization had led to the growth of trade unionism and the absence of political representation had led to the formation of working-class and socialist parties, so there was a similar requirement for self-organized working-class adult education.

In south Wales, support for this concept developed out of a new and more militant attitude that began generally to permeate the area in the years between 1905 and 1910. These were the peak years of the industry, with coal production approaching its 1913 zenith of 56 million tons, more than a quarter of a million men directly employed in the collieries, and the height of population influx to the Valleys – 129,000 had arrived in the coal-producing counties of Glamorgan, Carmarthenshire and Monmouthshire in the decade 1901–11. Presiding over that scene of apparent limitless expansion was the South Wales Miners' Federation (SWMF), the 'Fed', set up in 1898 as the first effective area-wide union in the coal industry, and presiding over the union was its first president, William Abraham (Mabon). A key figure in both politics and industrial relations in the coalfield, Mabon, and 'Mabonism', epitomized the essential moderation that guided the SWMF in its relations with the coalowners during the first years of its existence. Compromise and conciliation were deemed the most appropriate tactics in seeking concessions from a group of employers not generally known for their benevolence or philanthropy.

Towards the end of the first decade of the new century, however, Mabonism came under increasing criticism from a younger group of leaders who had come into contact with the revolutionary ideas of Marxism, of extreme socialism and of syndicalism.[3] As they attempted to seize control of the SWMF and turn it in a more confrontational direction, they sought to use the medium of education to influence the rank-and-file miners of south Wales in the ideas they themselves had come to embrace. The movement developed in two related ways – attendance of individual miners from south Wales at Ruskin College, Oxford, and later the Central Labour College in London, and the evening-class network which began to take root throughout the coalfield after 1909.

Ruskin had been founded in 1899 as a specifically 'Labour College' with a view to establishing an institution where working men received an education which, it was hoped, they would be able to pass on to their colleagues on returning to their communities. The crucial point was to educate men and women to raise rather than rise out of their class.[4] Initially, the college offered residential places to about twenty-five students on fees of £52 per annum and its curriculum concentrated on those subjects considered to be of interest to the working-class activist – political economy, sociology, industrial history, history of social movements, etc.

In its early years a number of south Wales miners attended Ruskin, paying their own fees. By 1906, however, a successful campaign had been waged to get the SWMF to sponsor students at the college. Gradually, a number of districts in the coalfield began to send one or two men to Oxford each year. Great care was always taken to ensure that these men would pass on the education they received, through the medium of evening classes on their return to south Wales, for the benefit of the union and the labour movement in general rather than for any personal advancement.

The result of careful selection procedures ensured that only the most active and committed union members went to Ruskin. They were usually men who were politically aware, with some definite, if not dogmatic, views on the relationship of labour to capital that had been developed through their own reading. Often this reading would have taken place in one of the miners' halls or institutes which became such a feature of practically every town and village in industrial south Wales. True cradles of adult education, the libraries of these buildings often provided the only access, certainly before the advent of public library provision in the 1920s, to literature, learning and ideas.[5]

In 1909, a famous strike took place at Ruskin which was to have enormous consequences for adult education and which confirmed the firmly established dichotomy of the 'two traditions'. The emergence of the Labour Party at the general election of 1906 had convinced many of the need to educate a working class which was now seen to be reaching out for political power. One way in which this could be achieved was to take firmer control of adult education and the nature of that education itself. In 1908, an important report on *Oxford and Working-class Education* was published which, amongst other things, called for closer contact to be established between the university and Ruskin to achieve just such a supervisory relationship.

Tension had already been building within Ruskin itself amongst students who felt that the education they were receiving was not radical enough or commensurate with their growing industrial militancy. In particular, they criticized the lack of classes on Marxism, socialism and class issues. Consequently, in March 1909, these students, including men from south Wales, refused to attend lectures and effectively went on strike, forming themselves into a group known as the Plebs League which was to become the instigator of a nationwide evening-class network promoting the merits of IWCE.[6] A further result of the strike was the foundation of an alternative institution, the Central Labour College (CLC), sited originally in Oxford and later in London, which lasted until 1929 and sought to offer the kind of education seen as lacking at Ruskin.[7]

The aim of the CLC was to build up an adult education movement with solely working-class support and addressed to working-class needs and demands. It was recognized, however, that no single college could hope to create such a movement overnight. Therefore, from the beginning it encouraged the growth of local, non-residential colleges throughout the country, complementing those classes organized by the Plebs League. To supplement these, the CLC established a correspondence-course department with a lectures-by-post scheme. During the period 1909–15, the number of non-residential courses grew slowly, and more dramatically after 1918. Eventually, a nationally coordinated network of such classes was formed under a body known as the National Council of Labour Colleges (NCLC).[8]

Out of the Ruskin College, Plebs League, CLC and NCLC mix
were to emerge many of the leading figures in industrial and political life in south Wales during the middle decades of the twentieth
century. Men such as Noah Ablett, A. J. Cook, James Griffiths and
Aneurin Bevan received a formative education as well as politicization through attendance at one of the colleges or at evening classes.

How unbridgeable was the alleged divide between the concep-
tions of adult education advocated by the WEA or by the
proponents of IWCE and how much did it matter to the general
student unmoved by such sectarianism? Whilst the former was
accused of peddling conservative 'dope' with the intention of
diverting or defusing the class struggle, the latter were charged
with the spread of a propaganda designed to indoctrinate with
dogma. In reality, the distinction was not always so stark. Both
began from the worthy premises of seeking improvement in the
lives and lot of the working class and both placed as much emphasis on a general raising of standards as on facilitating
individual advancement. True, their political visions differed
greatly, but their ultimate ends were not so fundamentally dissim-
ilar. In their ways, each was to make a significant contribution to
the development of adult education in south Wales.

A distinction between a liberal education for citizenship and a
'political' one for social transformation need not rule one or the
other out. Certainly, for many of those who benefited from
evening-class education it often hardly mattered who was its
organizer; many would move from WEA to Plebs League to
NCLC and back, taking from each what they wished and using it
as they saw fit. Furthermore, if this sometimes led to individual
advancement then, it can be argued, this could serve as equally
inspirational, in a role-model sense, to the community and,
indeed, was a good deal more achievable than the rather utopian
notion of raising an entire class. Not everyone could be an
Aneurin Bevan but many could aspire to a bettering of their lives
through adult education which could also prove inspirational to
others even if it 'only' led to a better job, more money and that
sought-after respectability which so ordered life in the Valley communities. This is often overlooked by those who view the history
of adult education in south Wales in a politicized, 'what-should-
have-been rather than what-was', way.

AN EARLY ROLE FOR THE UNIVERSITIES

The suspicions that greeted the emergence of the WEA simply mirrored those which had already accompanied the entry of the universities into the field of adult education. Although the university extension movement, whereby colleges sought to offer adult education provision to their surrounding communities, began at Oxford and Cambridge in the 1860s and can be seen operating in south Wales in the following two decades, its real beginnings here date from around the turn of the century. At that time, the University College of Cardiff, through the efforts of three enlightened academics, Ronald Burrows, Sydney Chapman and J. S. Mackenzie, rekindled a waning interest in extension work and also urged the establishment of an educational 'settlement' outside the walls (extra-mural) of the college itself to provide a university presence in the community. This was opened at Splott in 1901. The university was also to be closely concerned with the setting up and early history of the WEA in Wales. Again, of course, this linkage was to spark more criticism from those who argued the necessity of independence in working-class education, albeit a circumscribed independence that should, in their eyes, revolve around an unquestioning acceptance of Marx, Engels, Dietzgen and other socialist luminaries.

The main emphasis of the university extension movement was to aid in the task of diverting the working class away from these writers, with their emphasis on class conflict, towards more moderate, incorporative ideas of community and citizenship. Again, in south Wales, the period before the First World War is crucial when, in an attempt to defuse rising industrial unrest, the *South Wales Daily News* sought to encourage the universities to 'show the workers the duties and privileges of citizenship and to gently lead them on to a nobler conception of life based on the enlightened and practical interest of the masses in the government of the community'.

This view was reiterated during the war itself when, in the aftermath of the much-criticized strike by the south Wales miners against existing wage levels in July 1915, the periodical *Welsh Outlook* argued that 'what is needed is a university with a missionary spirit that will spread its teaching to the Valleys of the coalfield and will equip minds, now immature, to deal with the great problems that vitally affect the social life of the nation'.[9]

Education for citizenship was also to be a constant theme in adult education in south Wales in the inter-war years and was given added impetus by the entry of the Labour Party into government. The *South Wales Daily News* was again prominent in urging that 'We must educate our masters of the new democracy if we would strengthen the bulwarks against revolution, and ensure the ordered progress of our national life.'

The charge of social control was one that could easily be levelled against the notion of education for citizenship as provided by the universities by advocates of IWCE. Yet, again, if the parameters of adult education are extended beyond partisan political posturing, this work, together with the complementary efforts of Coleg Harlech from 1927 onwards, can be seen to have had a beneficial effect on south Wales in the areas of social service and trade unionism, as well as in politics.[10]

Furthermore, although the university extension movement, just like the WEA or the promoters of IWCE, nominally subscribed to the ideal of 'raising the class not the individual', in practice all these approaches fostered social mobility and personal advancement. Just as products of the Labour College and Plebs League network progressed to high-ranking positions with the trade union movement or politics, even up to and including the office of Cabinet minister, so many members of WEA or university extra-mural classes went on to full-time higher education and a wide range of subsequent careers. The role of adult education as a 'second chance' became increasingly stressed. Once more, it might be argued that the example such 'success stories' of adult education had on their communities might be of equal, or even greater, value to its more elusive supposed collective purposes.[11]

THE INTER-WAR CONTEXT

In south Wales, the 1930s were truly the nightmare years, the 'Devil's Decade'. Whilst the mining industry had been in comparative decline since 1918, the extent of its problems during the Depression seemed likely to threaten the very life of the mining valleys. The industry which, at the beginning of the 1920s, employed 270,000 men was severely affected by mass unemployment, with an area average of 36.5 per cent but with particular pockets suffering much more drastically than this. Merthyr Tydfil, for example, had 61.9 per cent unemployment, with nearby Dowlais peaking at 73.4 per cent. Many sought a solution in flight, with over a quarter of a million people leaving south Wales between 1929 and 1935, and those that remained faced a grim and relentless battle for survival.

If protest, demonstration, escapism and apathy represented some of the varied responses to this predicament, adult education was also seen as a way of dealing with the complexities of a shattered world and investing in a more promising future. Once more, however, the old fractures re-emerged, enhanced by the supposition that a new generation of adult educators were more intent on imposing a patronizing form of 'missionary work' on south Wales, designed to ameliorate and disperse an inevitable sense of grievance at the trauma of unemployment, poverty and social decay.

This voluntary 'social service' response, beginning with the involvement of the Society of Friends, operating through a Coalfield Distress Committee, in the aftermath of the General Strike of 1926, came to form a strong element of adult education in inter-war south Wales and one best evaluated through an examination of two particular facets of its work, the educational settlement phenomenon and the work of the Carnegie Trust.[12]

The former began to develop from the late 1920s and displayed many of the aspirations of the original university settlements of the late nineteenth century, such as that at Splott in Cardiff. Notably, this included a belief in the mutual benefits that might accrue from an association of university graduates and ordinary working people within the community. Between 1903 and 1918, ten such settlements were established, throughout south Wales. The foundation of the Educational Settlements Association (ESA) in 1920, emanating from recommendations incorporated in the *Final Report of the Committee on Adult Education to the Ministry of Reconstruction* in 1919, galvanized a new wave of settlement provision. Between 1920 and the coming of the Second World War, twenty-seven new settlements were established throughout the United Kingdom, nine of them based in south Wales. In the latter, due to the particular extremities of economic and social distress engendered by the Depression, educational provision was combined with social relief work.

The first of the nine new settlements, with their complement of academic and administrative resident staff, was that at Maes-yr-Haf at Trealaw in the Rhondda Valley, opened in 1927. Whilst this and a number of others were inspired and financed by Quaker involvement, this was not always the case at subsequent settlements opened in Merthyr, Risca, Bargoed, Pontypool, Brynmawr, Dowlais, Aberdare and Pontypridd.[13] They were collectively overseen by the Education Committee of the South Wales and Monmouthshire Council of Social Service as 'self-managing and self-governing' units.[14] Their tasks, over and above the provision of educational classes at the settlements themselves and at outreach centres in their vicinity, included giving aid and guidance to existing local clubs and associations – especially the many unemployed men's clubs set up since the onset of the Depression – or the creation of new clubs for women, boys and girls; practical training in handiwork and crafts; the setting up of work projects such as allotment schemes; physical training; and dispensation of legal advice. In sum, this was a complete range of educational and social relief measures.

The rationale behind the concept of a settlement was that it should provide the opportunity for self-help initiatives to the local community and attempt to make itself 'an organic part of the life of the district'.[15] This was, of course, designed as a defence against those who criticized the settlement movement as 'missionary work' and who distrusted its moderate – in their view, socially mollifying – ethos. These charges had been levelled against both the WEA and the universities in earlier times and, whilst there was some truth in them, and the aim of reducing the likelihood of a more militant response to their situation by a people angered at the apparent impotence of the state to provide effective remedies was part of the settlement philosophy, to dismiss them as simply instruments of social control would be unfair.

Competitive strategies, both political and industrial, might decry the efforts of the settlements as palliative rather than curative and urge the adoption of more radical tactics of protest. The practical achievements of the settlements were, admittedly, limited, the life of some relatively short. However, there is no doubt that, in their way, they did provide one channel of survival and assistance during their existence to a population seemingly bereft of most other forms of external help, whether or not the self-stated aim of ensuring that 'men and women can achieve for themselves inner joys and material advantages thorough the power of community life . . . at a time of stress and challenge' was actually attained.[16]

The settlement at Aberdare, for example, known as the People's College or Coleg Gwerin Cymru, provides a good model by which the whole movement might be evaluated. Opened in 1936, its governing body consisted of some of the leading lights in both adult education and social service in south Wales at the time. These included Principal J. F. Rees of University College, Cardiff; Ben Bowen Thomas, first warden of Coleg Harlech; Thomas Jones ('T.J.'), former Cabinet secretary and secretary of the Pilgrim Trust; and Percy Watkins, former secretary of the Welsh Department of the Board of Education and now secretary of the Welsh branch of the National Council of Social Service. Working with both employed and unemployed in the area, the settlement aimed to become 'a true university of a true democracy'.[17]

Not everyone was convinced. The local *Aberdare Leader*, in an editorial, acknowledged that there were those of 'rebellious spirit' who claimed that settlements would not solve unemployment or remove the 'inequalities' of the economic system. To this, the writer replied that the Aberdare settlement would not, indeed, 'preach a political creed', but would aspire to become the basis of a 'new and better society' by encouraging 'knowledge, fellowship, tolerance, sympathy and kindness'.[18]

A further dispute arose over whether the work of the settlement impinged on that of the education committee of the Glamorgan County Council which was also active in the provision of adult education throughout south Wales in the form of both regular evening classes and summer schools.[19]

To the people of Aberdare and the Cynon Valley in general, this sectarian wrangling proved somewhat irrelevant. In its first years of existence, the *Annual Reports* of the settlement show both growth and popularity, with weekly attendance figures at classes rising from an initial 200 to over 800 in late 1938.[20] As well as classes in academic subjects such as political science, international relations, psychology, law, economic theory and public administration, others covered woodwork, weaving and cobbling. Work also went on with local unemployed men's clubs, women's clubs, boys' and girls' clubs, either at the settlement itself based in Fairfield House, Aberdare, or at its numerous outreach centres in the surrounding locality.

Criticism could, no doubt, be levelled at the limited scope, and indeed vision, of the settlement's work in a time of economic and social catastrophe. However, for many ordinary people whose views appear in the letters columns of the local newspaper, the *Aberdare Leader*, or are contained within the *Annual Reports* of the settlement, it appears to have been welcomed as, at least, an attempt to provide some form of relief and sense of purpose in a time of confusion and despair.

A similar judgement could be passed on another venture in adult education which developed in south Wales during the Depression years, namely, the work of the Carnegie United Kingdom Trust. This had been established in 1913 as part of the international philanthropy of the Scottish-born, American steel magnate, Andrew Carnegie, with a brief to engage in educational, health, social welfare and pacifist initiatives. In 1929, the trust decided to grant a total of £5,000, to be shared between the coalfields of Durham and south Wales, to be spent on adult education provision. South Wales was seen as an ideal area for this work as 'there is a more intense intellectual activity here than is to be found among any working class in the United Kingdom'.[21]

To administer that proportion of money allocated to south Wales, £3,000, a Joint Committee for the Promotion of Educational Facilities in the South Wales and Monmouthshire Coalfields was established. This Joint Committee, under the chairmanship of the indefatigable Percy Watkins, continued in operation through the life of the trust's involvement with south Wales, lasting from 1929 until 1933, and was later subsumed within the South Wales and Monmouth Council of Social Service (SW&MCSS). In essence, a collective and community-wide network of adult education providers was established in an attempt to counter the usual charges of missionary work and sectarianism. This resulted in the cooperation of the University Extension Board, the WEA, the YMCA, the Welsh National Council of Music, the Welsh Drama League, regional directors of education, as well as representatives of the management of the miners' institutes and halls. Undoubtedly, however, a political dimension crept in with a self-declared intention to counter the work of the 'advanced leaders' and 'propagandists' of the SWMF who, allegedly, used these institutes as bases for the spread of that 'economic determinism' seen as so destructively prevalent in south Wales and its workforce.[22] This old charge had also been made against the Plebs Leaguers and others in the years before the First World War, albeit in more colourful language as 'vipers of a viperous brood'.[23]

By 1933, over 4,000 students were attending a variety of one-year, terminal and short courses organized by the Joint Committee at numerous venues throughout the coalfield. In addition, more than 3,000 students attended day schools that year. Much of this provision was culturally based, with lectures, concerts and dramatic presentations featuring strongly. Whilst the various participating organizations were responsible for most of this provision, it was also argued that

> not only have the people taken advantage of the facilities which the scheme provided, but they have in many cases made this the basis of a vigorous organisation, and also have themselves developed a sense of responsibility to the work of adult education in general.[24]

With the cessation of direct financial involvement by the Carnegie Trust in 1933, funding was maintained by the local education authorities, the National Council of Social Service, and by private donation. Ultimately, the Joint Committee transformed itself into the education committee of the SW&MCSS in 1934 and was responsible for the continuation of the work begun by the trust as well as its linkage with the various educational settlements.

Given the current advocacy of technology as a means of addressing contemporary problems of access to education in south Wales, due to geography, transportation or other difficulties, one particular initiative funded by trust money might be noted. This was the provision of radio sets to miners' institutes and welfare halls throughout the area in order that local community listening groups could be afforded the opportunity of receiving the growing adult education output broadcast by the BBC. The intention was to stimulate interest in subjects that might subsequently be more fully covered by establishment of a tutorial class. Of particular note were those programmes that sought, constructively, to link the past history and heritage of industrial south Wales with its future prospects for revival and regeneration.[25]

The overall effects of the radio scheme were positive and served as a complementary aid to more traditional adult education classes. It represented an early attempt to overcome problems of geographical remoteness and the lack of local opportunities for study that continue to pose difficulties for adult education provision in south Wales to the present day. As an embryonic experiment in 'distance learning', it bears some comparison with ongoing attempts to use modern technology to reach otherwise disadvantaged communities.

The rationale behind the Carnegie Trust initiative was certainly apolitical. In reality, it represented a partial response to a socio-economic crisis that defied a general solution. However, if limited in scope, it still saw the merits of community-centred learning, whilst noting the essential need to engage the participation in its provision by those to whom it was directed. In sponsoring a partnership between the various adult education providers in the area it sought to eliminate duplication in favour of the optimum use of limited manpower and resources. In seeking to take advantage of available technology it anticipated some of the benefits of diversity in modes of supply advocated by adult educationalists today.[26]

Both the educational settlement movement and the Carnegie Trust initiative, despite their contextual relevance to the 1920s and 1930s, can be seen to have something to contribute to the current debate on the regeneration of south Wales through, amongst a wider armoury, the provision of adult education opportunities. Whilst the nature of that provision may have changed, not least through the advancement of technology, many of the reasons for its necessity remain.

THE SOUTH WALES MINERS' FEDERATION
AND ADULT EDUCATION POST-1945 [27]

It has already been shown how close the relationship was between the South Wales Miners' Federation and adult education, in its independent working-class form, before the Second World War and how the Fed maintained a committed support of the ideals fostered by the Plebs League, CLC and NCLC. This policy had borne remarkable fruit with the emergence of a generation of miners' leaders of outstanding abilities, of whom A. J. Cook and Arthur Horner were only two of the most prominent. Intellectually, this linkage also supplied a working philosophy which, pre-1926, could promise major social change and, during the Depression years, could then offer a mode of comprehension and survival.

The 1950s was a period of challenge for the south Wales area of the National Union of Mineworkers, as the Fed became known after the nationalization of the coal industry in 1947. Responding to the changed relationships now evident under the new management of the National Coal Board, the union sought to rekindle rank-and-file interest in union affairs to cope with the different demands of industrial relations. Again, it saw adult education as the vital component in the achievement of this objective.

From the point of view of many within the union, the existing links with Coleg Harlech and the NCLC were flawed, with the former seen as more interested in offering its students a way out of the industry and the latter weakened by dwindling attendance at its classes. Consequently, a move was initiated to persuade the executive council (EC) of the union to consider the establishment of an independent education scheme with 'clearer Trade Union and socialist principles'.

The scheme, which began operating in 1956, provided initially for ninety-six students receiving tuition in political economy, social history, history of the miners' union and union organization in one-day classes spread over fifteen weeks. Its aim was to attract lodge activists from all over the coalfield with a view to providing them with a systematic Marxist analysis of society – in effect, the objective of the Plebs League, CLC and NCLC. During their study, the students, aged between twenty and forty-five, would have their wages made up by the union. However, this amounted only to basic shift payment, less any bonuses, and students were required to pay their own travel costs. Anyone who indicated that his motive in studying was to 'get on' was excluded from the course.

Take-up of the education programme proved very good, with over 400 students attending classes between 1957 and 1960. Many of these were new to adult education, having been previously unmoved by the varied offerings of the NCLC, WEA or university extra-mural departments. This may have been a consequence of the strong relationship forged between the union and its members and the latters' trust in an adult education scheme organized especially for them. Certainly, some of the students regarded the scheme in this way, comparing it favourably with others:

> The unfortunate part of any centrally sponsored educational scheme is that a distinct danger of too much control over the subject matter . . . usually exists . . . Immediately the true purpose of education is departed from in the interest of any political or industrial group, it becomes propaganda . . . [28]

In its early years, the education scheme largely succeeded on its own terms of preparing students for an active union life, with the intention of raising the general level of ability rather than encouraging individual ambition. It served to provide a continuity of outlook with the past as the society of south Wales changed, with the ongoing programme of pit closures that was to have such a devastating and long-term effect on the area. The course succeeded in stimulating an educational interest amongst those who had previously shown little or limited interest. Much anecdotal evidence from students of the 1957–60 period, collated in annual reports prepared by the programme's first educational officer, Ronald Frankenberg, testifies to its impact on participants' attitudes and outlook. The aim to strengthen commitment to and understanding of a Marxist analysis of society and unionism, rather than facilitate a route out of the industry for the individual student, was achieved. Many of those attending went on to prominence in local and national union activity or in politics.

In the end, of course, this proved no more than a temporary holding action. By 1971, when the scheme was wound up, the number of miners in south Wales was little more than a third of what it had been at its inception in 1956. Within a few years, however, the banner of an alternative educational perspective was picked up with the establishment of a new programme organized by the union in conjunction with the extra-mural department of University College Swansea. In many ways, this link was also to prove the starting-point for a renewed and modernized role for the universities in the provision of adult education throughout south Wales, one that continues to the present day.

The role of education in informing a particular view of society and its possible transformation was one which continued throughout the history of unionism in the south Wales coalfield in the twentieth century. The education programme of the 1950s and 1960s was founded upon those of earlier generations. Many of its basic tenets and larger purposes, not the least of which was the advocacy of a communal self-help strategy, remained the same as its predecessors. A similar need exists today.

ADULT EDUCATION IN SOUTH WALES
TODAY AND TOMORROW

Earlier in this chapter, the role of the university extension move-ment and the extra-mural tradition was discussed. It would be fitting to conclude with a brief analysis of some aspects of the adult education work of the universities in south Wales in more recent years and with some comments on their future role in the economic, social and cultural regeneration of the area.

It would be fair to say that, prior to the beginning of the 1990s, much of the work of extra-mural departments at the Uni-versity Colleges of Cardiff and Swansea, at that time the two longest-established higher education institutions serving the south Wales area, was in the liberal adult education tradition. At Swansea, for example, much of the provision was centred on the humanities, with the majority of students coming from a middle-class background and already possessing a relatively high standard of education. This group was not concerned with gaining qualifications or in progression but in attending classes largely as a hobby or leisure interest. Provision was mainly organized on the main campus at Singleton Park, although a number of community outreach centres throughout the western valleys were also util-ized. Provision for those who had largely missed out on the first opportunities for higher education and who now wished to take up degree-level study was mainly confined to a small access pro-gramme designed to prepare them for full-time attendance at the university.

At that time, however, a conscious decision was taken to change the nature and direction of the extra-mural department towards widening the participation of under-represented social groups in higher education. This was accompanied by a name change, to the department of adult continuing education (DACE). Henceforward, more emphasis was placed on access and foundation work aimed at part-time courses for non-traditional students from a variety of backgrounds including the unemployed, low-waged, those with disabilities, women returners, etc. To cater for the particular needs of these groups, additional mechanisms in the shape of educational guidance, counselling, study skills support, help with fees, crèche provision, etc. were put in place.

The response from targeted groups began to change the profile of the department's work. Whilst liberal adult education remained, rightly so, as part of its output, other courses had a more vocational dimension, especially in the areas of information technology, social studies and counselling. The idea of progression through a structured framework incorporating non-award- bearing and award-bearing courses with multiple exit points became implemented.

One particular development was the extension of outreach work up to and including the provision of degree-level courses. This was in direct response to the geographical remoteness of many Valley communities, and the difficulty of their transport links with the city of Swansea. Here the university presence had been, at best, patchy; its reputation was still that of an elitist, city-based institution. The siting of degree courses in these areas served to break through this barrier and establish, albeit on a small scale, a closer link and less of the sense of an inferiority complex as far as higher education was concerned.

The oldest and, thus far, most successful of such ventures was the establishment of the Community University of the Valleys (CUV) in 1993. This followed on from the development of a BA humanities (part-time) degree programme on the Swansea campus in 1991 and represented the first outreach-based degree programme in Wales. Working in collaboration with local community groups – notably the locally based training organization Dulais Opportunities for Voluntary Enterprise (DOVE)[29] and Onllwyn Community Council – DACE organized a daytime, part-time programme, leading to a full degree qualification, at the offices of DOVE in Banwen at the head of the Dulais Valley. Eventually, the scheme was to attract the partnership of the University of Glamorgan and the Open University in Wales.

The scheme aimed at attracting adult students who, for many reasons, would be unable to take up places at the main Swansea campus. It targeted the unemployed, those with caring commitments, lone parents, those on low income and women returners. A full range of support mechanisms, including fee bursaries, library provision – with the opening of a branch of the South Wales Miners' Library – guidance, crèche facilities and IT training were put in place. The opportunity to study at Banwen for a full degree by part-time study proved successful with, at its height, more than fifty students taking modules on the programme. For those not yet ready for degree study, a plurality of provision – non-accredited, accredited, access, return to learn – was provided to enable progression to that level.

Though innovative, the CUV programme was essentially following in the long tradition of community-based adult education initiatives as detailed in other examples cited in this chapter. Its historical dimension, however, was more than balanced by its contemporary relevance as one way, albeit limited, of contributing to the desperately needed regeneration of areas of south Wales, in a post-coal-mining era. Its most lasting effect was to point up the merits, indeed the necessity, of working not only in but also with local communities in response to their own self-perceived needs and dreams.[30]

The essential ingredient that fuelled the success of the Community University of the Valleys scheme was the part-time mode of delivery. This is the method of study often most appropriate to those students from non-traditional and disadvantaged backgrounds. It enables those with employment, family, health or other personal commitments to undertake entry to higher education that would, otherwise, be impossible. Whilst the very essence of adult education in the past has, of course, been its part-time nature, the possibility of obtaining a degree by that method has been of relatively recent origin. Interestingly, the first opportunity for part-time degree study was not presented by either of the universities whose area of responsibility includes the numerous Valley communities of south-east and south-west Wales, Cardiff and Swansea. Rather, it came from the erstwhile Polytechnic of Wales, now the University of Glamorgan, whose BA humanities (part-time) degree programme began operating over twenty years ago.

Today, there is a greater than ever emphasis on the importance of adult education, or, as it is now fashionably termed, lifelong learning. Progress has been made in both further and higher education in attracting more mature students, with a majority of adults, predominantly part-timers, attending FE institutions and 40 per cent of all enrolments in HE institutions also coming from this group. Moreover, Welsh HE institutions have a higher proportion of mature entrants from under-represented groups than the United Kingdom as a whole.[31]

Much more remains to be achieved, particularly in the Valleys of the South Wales Coalfield where, regrettably, HE presence has, in the past, been sparse. This was partly due to issues of political territoriality, whereby the HE institutions whose hinterlands incorporated the Valleys, fought shy of 'infringing' upon one another's areas of responsibility, but with a more enlightened and less precious approach this situation is changing, if slowly. Mirroring this trend is a new appreciation of the merits and capabilities of adult students which, if not yet common amongst academics, is, thankfully, increasing.

The recently published *Policy Review of Higher Education in Wales* pays close attention to these issues.[32] Whilst primarily concerned with the 18–24 age group, the review also acknowledges the need to foster a culture of lifelong learning which recognizes that students may need to move in and out of higher education as their personal needs and circumstances alter; that many may wish to study part-time; that they may not necessarily want to undertake campus-based learning; and that community initiatives have a vital role to play in initiating interest in higher education whether at pre-degree or degree level.[33]

The University of Glamorgan is now at the leading edge of these developments in its involvement with the proposed economic, social and cultural regeneration of the Valleys. In particular, its close association with the Communities First initiative of the National Assembly for Wales demonstrates this. That project seeks to stimulate regeneration in the Valleys through a joint-partnership approach incorporating the university, the business sector, local authorities and, crucially, the community itself.

The vision of regeneration presented here is a broad-based, holistic one that includes, not only urban, economic and social renewal, but also cultural revitalization. It is in the latter area that strong continuities with adult education provision, of whatever political or ideological persuasion, in the past can be identified. It is worth quoting in some length here from a document published by the Housing and Community Renewal Division of the National Assembly of Wales which reviews best practice in community regeneration schemes in the UK and elsewhere:

> The existence of past organisational structures, cultures of self-help and mutuality, ideologies that empower and political values which foster resistance to external pressure will all provide support for contemporary community development initiatives. This is evident to a considerable degree in many parts of Wales where an attachment to the notion of community is a significant feature of the local culture. The high level of social organisation evident in mining communities has been a critical influence on the development of the community and development trusts that have emerged. The current pattern of self-organisation evident in many communities in Wales demonstrates a continuity with past political and cultural practices.[34]

Lessons from the past can, therefore, inform the future. These include the need to generate a sense of ownership by the community itself in what is being provided for it; a willingness to listen to the self-expressed needs of that community rather than impose 'top-down' solutions; the need to recognize that both individual and collective motivations are of equal relevance; the need to create a belief in the permanence of adult education initiatives rather than a cynicism towards what might be seen as a 'parachuting' in and out as new policies emerge on the higher education agenda.

For a university to contribute to the economic and social health of its surrounding region it must invest both financial and human resources for the long term and be aware of the present and changing needs of the community. In delivering educational opportunities in disadvantaged areas, or to relatively disadvantaged groups such as ethnic minorities in more affluent areas, it also requires patience and the willingness to engage in partnership with the community rather than a prescriptive approach.

More than the socio-economic dimension, however, lifelong

learning can, and should, have the additional goals of personal development, cultural renaissance and democratic renewal in the belief that 'education and democratic involvement in social change are political, and that education should resource the struggle of people to challenge democracy's limitations and extend its possibilities'.[35] Similarly, there is a role for the universities, and all higher education institutions, in stimulating the imagination and encouraging an interest in the humanities, science and the arts if, as the recent review by the National Assembly of arts and culture in Wales argues, 'Culture is at the heart of our national enterprise'.

Here we can, once more, turn to history. It is easy to romanticize this history and over-emphasize both the participation in and achievements of adult education in south Wales. Of course, not everyone either could or wanted to spend their time in evening classes or deep reading at the local institute library. Other interests and attractions might hold sway. Sport and leisure activities, for example, are equally valid expressions of the local culture. Nevertheless, the ongoing place of adult education in the life of south Wales throughout the twentieth century and its contribution to resisting, if not solving, the many problems that have beset the area would seem to show that it has been consistently valued. The problems remain, have indeed multiplied, but a role for lifelong learning (formerly known as adult education) must surely still exist if ever they are to be tackled systematically and resolved.

NOTES

1. See, in particular, Richard Lewis, *Leaders and Teachers: Adult Education and the Challenge of Labour in South Wales 1906–1940* (Cardiff: University of Wales Press, 1993).
2. Much of the following is taken from Brian Simon (ed.), *The Search for Enlightenment: The Working Class and Adult Education in the Twentieth Century* (London: Lawrence & Wishart, 1990), part 1.
3. See D. K. Davies, 'The influence of syndicalism and industrial unionism in the South Wales Coalfield, 1898–1921: a study in ideology and practice' (unpublished Ph.D. thesis, University of Wales, Cardiff, 1991).
4. See P. Yorke, *Ruskin College 1899–1909* (Oxford: Ruskin College, 1977).

5. See Hywel Francis, 'The origins of the South Wales Miners Library', *History Workshop*, 2 (1976).

6. See Richard Lewis, 'South Wales miners and the Ruskin College strike of 1909', *Llafur, Journal of Welsh Labour History*, 2, 1 (1976).

7. See John Atkins, *Neither Crumbs Nor Condescension: The Central Labour College 1909–1915* (Aberdeen: People's Press, 1981).

8. See J. P. M. Millar, *The Labour College Movement* (London: National Council of Labour, 1980).

9. *Welsh Outlook* (August 1916).

10. Consideration of the work of Coleg Harlech is beyond the scope of this chapter. For a full treatment, see Peter Stead, *Coleg Harlech: The First Fifty Years* (Cardiff: University of Wales Press, 1977).

11. Much of this section has been based on Richard Lewis, 'The inheritance: adult education in the Valleys between the wars', *Adult Education in the Valleys: The Last Fifty Years* (Llafur Conference Report, 1986), pp. 7–14.

12. For an analysis of Quaker involvement in adult education in south Wales, and its reception here, see Alun Burge, Hywel Francis and Colin Trotman, *In a Class of their Own: Adult Learning and the South Wales Mining Community 1900–1939* (London: Economic and Social Research Council Report, July 1998), pp. 39–45.

13. For information on the Aberdare Settlement, see D. K. Davies, ' "An oasis of culture": the Aberdare Valley Educational Settlement 1936–67', *Transactions of the Honourable Society of Cymmrodorion*, 6 (2000), 135–48.

14. Percy E. Watkins, *Educational Settlements in South Wales and Monmouthshire* (Cardiff: Western Mail & Echo, 1940), p. 5.

15. *Men without Work: A Report Made to the Pilgrim Trust* (Cambridge: Cambridge University Press, 1938), p. 382.

16. *Aberdare Valley Educational Settlement: Warden's First Annual Report 1936–37*.

17. 'John Victor Evans, first warden of the Aberdare Settlement', *Aberdare Leader* (12 September 1936).

18. *Aberdare Leader* (3 October 1936).

19. For a colourful account of the adult education work of Glamorgan County Council, see Harold M. Watkins, *Unusual Students* (Liverpool: Brython Press, 1947).

20. *Aberdare Valley Educational Settlement October Bulletin* (1938): Salisbury Library, Cardiff University.

21. *Report of the Joint Committee for the Promotion of Educational Facilities in the South Wales and Monmouthshire Coalfields* (27 May 1929). South Wales Workers' Educational Association [WEA] Records, Cardiff.

22. Unattributed report, attached to the minutes of its fourteenth meeting, 29 January 1930: WEA Records, Cardiff.

23. *Western Mail* (27 February 1912).

24. Unattributed report, minutes of the fourteenth meeting.

25. *Report on the Wireless Sets installed under the auspices of the Joint Committee* [no date]: WEA Records, Cardiff.

26. For more on the Carnegie Trust scheme, see: D. K. Davies, ' "A healthier and more profitable choice": the Carnegie Trust initiative and adult education in the South Wales Coalfield in the early 1930s', *History of Education Society Bulletin,* 63 (May 1999), 25–34.

27. Much of this section is taken from Alun Burge and D. K. Davies, ' "Enlightenment of the highest order": the education programme of the south Wales miners 1956–1971', *Llafur, Journal of Welsh Labour History,* 7, 1 (1996), 111–121.

28. Letter from Howard Evans, a participating student, *The Miner,* 6, 1 (January/February 1958), 12–13.

29. DOVE was set up by local women's support groups after the 1984–5 mining strike to enable them to continue to play a role in the future of the Dulais Valley.

30. Hywel Francis and Rob Humphreys, 'Communities, valleys, universities', in Jane Elliot et al. (eds), *Communities and their Universities: The Challenge of Lifelong Learning* (London: Lawrence & Wishart, 1996), 230–49.

31. *The Learning Country: A Comprehensive Education and Lifelong Learning Programme for Wales to 2010* (Cardiff: National Assembly of Wales Paving Document, 2001), 59.

32. See *Policy Review of Higher Education* (Cardiff: Education and Lifelong Learning Committee, National Assembly for Wales, 2002).

33. In 1999–2000, some 30,000 studied part-time in Wales, with 6,000 attending HE courses franchised to FE institutions, and 5,000 studying with the Open University.

34. David Adamson, Helen Dearden and Barbara Castle, *Community Regeneration: Review of Best Practice* (Cardiff: Housing and Community Renewal Division, National Assembly of Wales, 2001), pp. 29–30.

35. Jane Thompson, *Rerooting Lifelong Learning: Resourcing Neighbourhood Renewal* (Leicester: National Organisation for Adult Learning Policy Discussion Paper, 2001), p. 37.

The UNIVERSITY of GLAMORGAN, SOCIAL EXCLUSION and the SOUTH WALES VALLEYS

David Adamson

Throughout its history as a learning institution the University of Glamorgan has had a significant relationship with the Valleys region in which it physically exists. Its origin as a School of Mines in 1913 points to a vocational link to the industry and economy of the region which continues to influence the direction of the University and the programmes it provides. In addition to its developing role as a 'new university' and its presence in United Kingdom higher education provision the University maintains a special relationship with the population of the south Wales Valleys. This relationship is embedded in the University's mission statement: 'to serve and contribute to our communities in terms of education, training, health, wealth creation and cultural development'. Importantly, this intent is fulfilled in a range of programmes and provision which engages local populations in learning relationships with the University. This is initially evident in the University's mainstream campus higher education provision. Currently, almost 2,500 full-time students from the surrounding Valleys communities of Torfaen, Blaenau Gwent, Caerphilly, Merthyr Tydfil and Rhondda Cynon Taff attend on-campus provision at the University.

The University has supplemented this on-campus provision through the actions of its Centre for Life Long Learning which has created relationships with eighty-four community learning centres throughout the region (Saunders and Powell, 1998; Humphreys and Saunders, 2000). This area of the University's operation currently provides 40,000 hours of non-accredited learning per academic year. Over 1,250 community-based students per year take up non-accredited learning opportunities and a further 650 follow accredited courses. Subjects range from the sciences to the creative arts and include astronomy, art and design, information technology, community regeneration and music technology, responding directly to the learning interests and needs of the community. This community relationship extends to compacts with schools in the region (Smalley and Saunders, 2000), in which student-based mentoring of pupils plays a significant role in raising educational aspiration in the region (Saunders and Kingdon, 1998). Additionally the University of Glamorgan plays a major role in the Community University of the Valleys.

In these actions the University is responding to national

objectives as well as its own sense of mission in the region. Key policy changes have been prompted by United Kingdom reports such as the Dearing Report and, in Wales, by Welsh Assembly Government documents such as *Better Wales* and *Learning is for Everyone*. The 'widening access' agenda has become an important backdrop to the work of universities and colleges of further education. The creation and proliferation of learning opportunities are seen as critical components of the wider social inclusion agenda and one of the means to achieve government objectives of increased prosperity and poverty eradication.

However, in operating its own widening access strategies the University is acutely aware of the limitations of its current achievements. At primary, secondary and post-16 levels, the University's hinterland demonstrates a failure of significant proportions of the population to engage with the educational process. Currently 13 per cent of 16- to 18-year-olds have no qualifications, 18 per cent of working-age adults lack basic literacy skills and 42 per cent lack basic numeracy (ELWa, 2001). The culmination of this pattern is found in the University's own difficulties of recruitment from lower socio-economic categories despite the development of strategies and initiatives intended to redress this situation.

The scale and quality of this low level of educational engagement and attainment in the region has been the subject of research in recent years and some insights into the causes and patterns of educational disengagement are emerging. Early concerns were expressed about the existence of a significant proportion of young people who were totally disengaged from the educational, training and employment markets. These 'status zero' young people appeared to be living outside all the support services intended to ease the transition from work to school and were not registered as being in school, higher education (HE), further education (FE), training or employment. Additionally, they were not recorded as seeking work or training (Istance and Williamson, 1996). More recent research has found that attitudes to education and training in the region are determined by a complex combination of age, gender, place and family factors linked to broad-scale economic changes (Gorard et al., 1998a, b, c). This major study of post-compulsory education and training in the region found that non-participation stems from cultural values in which education and training are not seen as appropriate or relevant activities by a third of the population. Consequently, policies that simply attempt to increase access to education founder on a simple perception that education is not relevant to the lives of those they target. The authors conclude that access policies which only address issues of costs, time and lack of childcare have a limited impact (Gorard et al., 1999).

Research in the wider UK context supports this latter view. Similar conclusions emerge from a Rowntree study of a socially excluded council estate in the north of England (Bowman et al., 2000). A mix of economic, cultural and experiential issues conditioned attitudes to adult education. Negative school experience, family pressures, confidence levels and social networks all played critical roles in shaping attitudes. The living conditions imposed by social exclusion also raised major issues for the basic motivation and capacity to engage with education against a backdrop of difficult family life, the pull of the informal economy and the barriers of the benefit system. Financial factors have also played a prominent role in shaping attitudes to higher education in recent years. With the demise of student grants and introduction of tuition fees the well-publicized debt which students can acquire provides a strong disincentive for students from working-class communities. In a recent DfEE study financial concerns were established as one of the key factors influencing decisions not to enter HE.

> Affording the cost of studying and being in debt were also key reasons for not going to university . . . Concerns about costs were wider and more complex than simply about paying fees. They were linked in to other financial concerns about borrowing and future debt, working to earn income during term-time, and not knowing enough about likely costs and income sources . . . (Connor et al., 2001)

This study found such concerns in potential entrants studying in schools and colleges, current students and qualified non-entrants to HE. No research was undertaken with early school-leavers, the non-qualified or excluded where such concerns would be likely to be more exaggerated and perhaps reinforced by the perception identified by Gorard et al. (1998a) that education simply had no relevance to their lives.

These studies indicate a complex pattern of socio-cultural and economic factors which determine patterns of educational disengagement. The University of Glamorgan's experience in this area suggests that the issue is one of equity and social justice and not simply reducible to issues of educational performance. This chapter will explore such a view by examining the patterns of class relations, poverty and social exclusion in the locality in an attempt to understand in cultural terms why education is so undervalued by a significant proportion of the population. It will be suggested that the pattern of disengagement is a visible outcropping of class inequalities which have become established as fixed patterns of social exclusion in the Valleys region and which require major interventions to resolve.

CLASS IN THE SOUTH WALES VALLEYS

During the 1980s and 1990s it was not possible to make the claim that class still existed without meeting major challenge. Politicians such as John Major were able to state with conviction that Britain was a classless society. During the economic boom of the early 1990s, the superficial image of British society was one of increasing affluence. But beneath the surface a section of that society was characterized by growing levels of poverty. Ironically, Major and his predecessor Margaret Thatcher had presided over a welfare regime and an economic policy that had widened the gap between rich and poor to a level greater than at any time since the end of the Second World War (JRF, 1995).

It is fairly easy to understand the claims for the disappearance of class and inequality coming from politicians driven by an ideology which emphasized personal wealth and individualism. Less easy to understand is the same claim emanating from academics during the early 1990s. Peter Saunders, in an echo of the Conservative rhetoric, argued that Britain is a true meritocracy where talent and ability determine your achievements in life (Saunders 1995, 1996, 1997), a claim which has prompted a whole industry of denial by other sociologists and ripostes by the author.

Another leading academic was able to proclaim that 'classes are not social forces at all, and that they never have been' (Hindess, 1987: 8). In the 'end of class' debate of the late 1980s (Meiksins-Wood, 1986) to which this remark contributed, structuralists and

Marxists converted to the attractions of postmodernism. Pushed by the collapse of Marxist regimes and the failure of socialist politics in Europe, sociologists sought new ways of explaining the world. Feminists had rightly pointed to the unreasonable domination of sociology by class analysis and the inequality issues affecting ethnic minorities were correctly being recognized as deserving of study and analysis. But, as the focus of sociology moved to these deserving areas of study, there emerged a mistaken belief that social class and its consequences had disappeared. Anyone researching the economic and cultural changes of the south Wales region would have found such propositions difficult to defend in the face of increasing social and economic polarization (Adamson and Jones, 1996).

Where sociological debate was reasserting a class analysis it was in terms of occupational class and the analysis of changing workforce composition and its implications for class structuration. In the tradition of Glass (1954) and Goldethorpe (1980) writers such as Marshall et al. (1988) were analysing the social class significance of occupational change. Much of this debate was esoteric and understood only by the few, and the conclusions drawn by the writers often derived from the statistical methods they employed rather than the nature of that which they observed. Consequently, it was possible for completely contradictory conclusions to be drawn from analysis of the National Child Development Study Data as evidenced in the heated debate between Saunders (1995) and Savage and Egerton (1997).

However, in all such studies there was a core agreement that society in the post-war period is more mobile, with greater fluidity and movement between occupational categories. Even after controlling for the structural changes in patterns of occupation, all the studies demonstrate a degree of social mobility that has improved over the post-war period. However, they also all point to a stubborn resistance of the life chances of individuals to equalize regardless of class. It is still largely agreed that a child born of professional parents is four times as likely to become a professional person than is an individual born into the family of a manual worker, a claim first put in the 'ratio' argument presented by Goldethorpe in the 1980s. Consequently, class background remains a significant determinant of occupational life chances.

A more qualitative argument for the continued existence of the social class structure can also be advanced. Class is made up of much more than the occupational categories which have concerned the studies mentioned above. Perhaps the most significant outward manifestations of class barriers to equality are the cultural differences between the classes (Hamnett et al., 1989). Sociologists have long been concerned with the class-consciousness which arises from specific locations in the class structure. One of the more sophisticated approaches to this issue can be found in the work of French sociologist Pierre Bourdieu and his development of the concept of the 'habitus'. For Bourdieu, we are born into social class positions which shape our tastes and preferences for everything from food to sport. In his famous work *Distinction: A Social Critique of the Judgement of Taste* (1984), he outlines the mechanisms by which we acquire the social and cultural tastes of our class of origin. Through socialization in the family, through the education system, in advertising and marketing and in the way we consume as social groups, we acquire a pattern of tastes and preferences for everything we consume.

In particular, we consume certain goods and services in society to distinguish ourselves from other social groups. We mark our position in the class hierarchy by specific patterns of consumption linked to our possession of cultural capital. Thus opera and classical music are conventionally the preserve of the middle classes, football and bingo predominantly are seen as working-class activities. A prime example cited by Bourdieu is the working-class appraisal of a restaurant meal by the quantity of food on the plate, in contrast to a middle-class assessment of presentation, colour balance, variety of tastes and a lack of concern about quantity. In this way the habitus creates in us a predisposition to certain behaviours, political choices, career paths, food consumption and leisure activities which accumulate to create class lifestyles. Now clearly, this is rather deterministic and suggests that we are all prisoners of a class background from which we cannot break free. Bourdieu separates himself from a deterministic view and recognizes the individual choices made to consume and exercise tastes outside of our obvious class position. Whilst he offers a theory which does not adequately explain individual behaviour he does draw the boundaries around collective patterns of consumption in a way which usefully delineates the class boundaries. Yes, there is fluidity along the boundaries but significant numbers of people and indeed whole communities conform closely to the predicted behaviours of their class location. The end result is a form of social apartheid that maintains clear social distance between the classes and conditions their behaviour towards each other when they are forced into proximity.

The middle and working classes each in turn recognize social boundaries: restaurants we do not visit, food we do not eat, music we do not listen to, people we do not talk to in public places. The working class avoids places which will expose lack of cultural capital, reveal unfamiliarity with high culture and demonstrate lack of confidence. The middle classes avoid 'unsafe' places where behaviours are challenging, where the food is poor quality, the entertainment unsophisticated. To parody the outcome, one class takes its leisure in working-men's clubs and bingo halls, the other in theatres and restaurants. The rules of engagement are unspoken but widely known. The ultimate marker in this social hierarchy is our place of residence and the tenure of housing to which we subscribe. We are divided into communities of class determined by complex connections between income and taste.

This social apartheid of class is what maintains the class system in the face of increasing occupational mobility. This self-regulating social structure survives despite greater educational equality and higher incomes for working-class people. It is the informal barrier of a social capital of knowledge and of aspiration which significantly prevents class mobility. The majority of people born in working-class locations never see horizons outside a compressed range of possibilities. To summarize, the social rules of engagement hold us in our class places. The working-class habitus fosters passivity, acceptance of the inevitable and a lack of personal capacity and agency. One consequence is that, even an institution such as the University of Glamorgan, which has done much to remove the barriers to university entry, does not reach a section of the population which does not have the word university in its vocabulary of possibility. In the terms identified by Gorard et al. (1998a, b) education has no relevance to the 'habitus' of a significant proportion of working-class people living in the south Wales Valleys. Understanding the relationship between social class, class experience and corresponding cultural outcomes is critical to breaking this pattern of educational disengagement. To reach this understanding requires a detailed knowledge of the local class structure and of the more recent impact of poverty and social exclusion. Past work by the present author (1988, 1991; Jones and Adamson, 2001) has sought to contribute to that detailed picture and is only briefly summarized here to delineate the class boundaries which have become evident in the south Wales Valleys.

It is first necessary to clarify that the working class was never a homogeneous whole and was always characterized by internal division and differentiation. However, there was a compressed range of social experience which created a relatively uniform cultural response. Now the diversity of employment experience, increased social fragmentation, changes in consumption patterns and the break-up of political allegiances are all illustrations of a much more varied working-class experience. Linked closely to changes in the structure of the Welsh economy and the associated patterns of occupational change, I have identified three separate divisions or fractions in the Welsh working class. The model identifies Weberian style ideal-types based on analysis of work and consumption patterns. Perhaps never found in their true form, they represent analytical categories which can shed light on the changing class configurations of south Wales society and corresponding social and political effects.

THE TRADITIONAL WORKING CLASS

The first category is of those who remain employed in the traditional industries in Wales or who were politically and occupationally socialized in them. Possessing conventional manufacturing skills and the skills of the heavy extractive industries, such workers are ill-equipped to survive the restructuring of the industrial base that has occurred. Many are now unemployed and unlikely to re-enter the labour market. They contribute significantly to the high rates of incapacity and invalidity that characterize the working-age population in Wales. Their values are those of a traditional working-class social and cultural practice and are perhaps best demonstrated by the residents of the terraced housing communities of the south Wales Valleys. In survey work conducted by the University of Glamorgan in 1995 (Adamson and

Jones, 1996) and 2001 (Jones and Adamson, 2001) a strong sense of collectivism, a high level of community links and a continued attachment to traditional working-class organizations such as sports clubs and working-men's clubs are evident. This class fraction has traditionally been associated with a high evaluation of education and a commitment to self-education and community-based learning in institutions such as the miners' institutes and the Workers' Education Association. However, it is evident that the decline of this cultural attachment to education predated the acute industrial decline of the 1980s which saw the marginalization of what was once the dominant class character of the region.

THE NEW WORKING CLASS

This class fraction is characterized by those who have taken advantage of increased educational opportunities and have successfully made the transition to the new light manufacturing, electronics and service sectors of the Welsh economy. In higher waged and higher status employment they are able to sustain high-consumption lifestyles by easier access to credit. This class develops new consumption practices, especially in relation to housing, motoring, holidays and eating out. The economic status of this class is dependent on an attachment to education and successful performance at all levels of the educational and training system.

THE MARGINALIZED WORKING CLASS

This class fraction consists significantly of those who have failed to enter the new labour markets or who are caught in the fragile and precarious employment of the lower levels of the casualized new industries. Largely unqualified and unprepared for the contemporary labour market, this section of the population is relegated to the low-pay sectors or almost permanent unemployment. Faced with minimal incomes this fraction consumes housing in the social housing sector, a tenure which has become synonymous with poverty in Britain. Often located in hilltop estates this fraction of the working class suffers multiple disadvantage and is the principal location of contemporary poverty. It is also this class fraction which is the most likely to manifest youth disaffection, educational disengagement, high levels of truancy, school exclusion and the multiple disadvantages of social exclusion. In the

attempt to widen access to education it is this section of the working class which is the key target for improved rates of participation. It is also the class fraction least likely to be reached by
current initiatives and most likely to perceive education as having
no relevance. This class fraction and its experience of poverty and
social exclusion will be the focus of the remainder of this chapter.

POVERTY AND SOCIAL EXCLUSION
IN THE VALLEYS

Writing in 1996 (Adamson) it was possible to identify a hidden
crisis of poverty in that the issue was not on any political agenda
and not the focus of public concern. In 1996 I wrote of the invisi-
bility of the problem, largely isolated in remote housing estates
which the mainstream society had no cause to visit or know of
their existence.

In the UK context a Joseph Rowntree Foundation report had
enormous impact on this situation. The *Income and Wealth:
Report of the JRF Inquiry Group* (1995) provided inarguable evidence of the descent into poverty of whole sections of the British
population. A significant public debate was triggered in which
Conservative government protestations that there was no evidence of poverty sounded increasingly unconvincing and callous.
Poverty was once again on the political agenda.

However, the analysis of poverty was beginning to employ a
new terminology and to recognize additional effects beyond the
simple material deprivation of a traditional view of poverty. Conventionally, poverty has been analysed in terms of a lack of
material well-being and its impact on the physical conditions of
life. Increasingly, during the 1970s and 1980s this was seen to have
multiple effects beyond the financial sphere. Poverty was increasingly seen to have a negative impact on every aspect of life,
including educational achievement, quality of housing, labour-
market participation and health. The multidimensional nature of
contemporary poverty was easily demonstrated as a significant
body of evidence began to emerge for the compound effect of
poverty in all spheres of individual, family and community life.
Additionally, social geographers were providing increased evidence from the early 1990s onwards of major concentrations of
poverty both regionally (the North-South divide) and locally in

local authority housing estates on the periphery of the British cities and in areas like the south Wales Valleys. Where these concentrations of poverty existed, additional social effects were being noted as whole neighbourhoods were being stigmatized by the wider society.

At this time European debates about poverty were beginning to influence British academics and the term 'social exclusion' began to be used to describe the multidimensional pattern of poverty and the resulting social practices of isolation and stigmatization of the poor. Largely influenced by a French analysis of poverty which came to dominate European Union policy, this represented a totally different way of describing and understanding the causes of poverty (Silver, 1994). With its origins in both Catholic and socialist perspectives in France, this view saw poverty and social disintegration as a failure of the state to ensure the full participation of all citizens as equal members of society. This was contrasted with the 'Anglo-Saxon' pattern of policy in Britain which was seen as blaming the poor for their own poverty and seeking to punish them for the personal failings, low morality and fecklessness which were seen as the root causes of poverty in this perspective (Byrne, 1999). French sociologists stressed the impact of globalization, economic restructuring and mass unemployment on the urban poor and shifted the blame for poverty onto the state and mainstream society for failing to protect the vulnerable and precarious in society.

> The notion of poverty is primarily focused on *distribution* issues: the lack of resources at the disposal of the individual or household. In contrast, notions such as social exclusion focus primarily on *relational* issues: in other words inadequate social participation, lack of social integration and lack of power. (Room, 1995; 105, my emphasis)

In Britain a weakened form of this approach was taken up by the Labour Party on its election in 1997. The emerging view from the Cabinet Office Social Exclusion Unit saw labour-market exclusion as the primary route to poverty (Levitas, 1996). The French and European model was intermixed with American notions of an underclass which perceives some sections of society as adopting deliberate choices to remain on welfare and avoid work and associated patterns of family life (Murray, 1989). The government adopted a 'welfare to work' approach as the primary means of social inclusion by providing a mixed regime of incentives and sanctions to promote return to work by the benefit-dependent sections of the population. New Labour stressed the existence of welfare rights coupled with obligations to work when possible. The clearest policy manifestation of this is the New Deal policies which have targeted young people, lone parents, the over-50s and partners of unemployed people. At the same time the Social Exclusion Unit (SEU) launched a series of policy action team reports which have analysed almost every aspect of social exclusion and provided detailed policy recommendations, many of which have found their way into current policy.

So, is poverty in the Valleys characterized by this new phenomenon of social exclusion? The answer must be a resounding yes. Whole communities throughout the area have become marked by high levels of unemployment and patterns of low pay, high rates of lone parenthood and family breakdown, casual employment and long-term benefit dependency. This has created communities where few people experience long-term employment or stable income and social expectations are low. Such communities possess difficult-to-let housing and experience a high rate of tenant turnover. Crime rates are high and physical degradation is abundantly evident. Most fundamentally, such communities are reviled by the wider society and a clear pattern of 'postcode prejudice' emerges to stigmatize and exclude the people who live in these branded communities (Adamson and Jones, 1996). The Regional Research Programme based at the university mapped these communities in 1993 and found a distinctive pattern of coincidence of high male unemployment/economic inactivity, high rates of lone parenthood, poor housing, physical and environmental degradation. At enumeration district level of census data (1991) it was possible to identify communities where nearly 25 per cent of households were those of lone parents, where economic inactivity reached over 50 per cent of the working-age population and up to 90 per cent of households were dependent on housing benefit.

It was communities like these which bore the major features of the poverty which was measured in major reports such as the Joseph Rowntree *Poverty and Social Exclusion in Britain* (2000).

This report argues that 26 per cent of adults live in poverty, defined as an inability to afford a basket of items recognized by the rest of society as essential. In Wales this figure rises to 35 per cent, the highest of all UK regions (JRF, 2000). If we consider the most deprived electoral wards in the UK based on income data we find that seven of the top ten are in the Rhondda Cynon Taff area (National Office of Statistics). The newly established National Assembly Index of Multiple Deprivation also paints a depressing picture of disadvantage. The greatest concentration of Communities First wards selected from the index is in the county borough of Rhondda Cynon Taff in which the University of Glamorgan is situated. There, seventeen communities have been identified as belonging to the one hundred most deprived communities in Wales.

The reality of the south Wales Valleys is that the social class system and poverty come together in a complex mix of cultural and economic deprivation. For the residents of many communities in the region, the level of opportunity is almost non-existent. In the Valleys we have a complex mix of poverty and social class which currently ensures that up to 25 per cent of the population is not participating fully in the economic, social and cultural life of the nation. This pattern of social exclusion contributes significantly to the appalling health statistics that Wales demonstrates, to its low rates of educational achievement, to the low GDP rate which has earned us Objective One status and ultimately to the premature deaths of our citizens from a wide range of illnesses which are directly related to poverty. Class and poverty are close allies in Welsh society and demean the lives of a significant proportion of our population.

EDUCATIONAL PROVISION AND
SOCIAL INCLUSION

Since 1997 we have had a Labour Party administration which has put the eradication of poverty at the core of both its principles and its policies. The prime minister demonstrates a personal moral commitment to the elimination of poverty and a raft of policies have been proposed and enacted to tackle many different aspects of poverty. We have witnessed the most concerted effort by government to marshal expertise and opinion on the causes of poverty and the eighteen policy action team reports commissioned by the Social Exclusion Unit (see SEU, 2001, for a summary) have made dozens of recommendations which are finding their way into a wide range of social policies. Key reports have identified the potential role of education and training in contributing towards social inclusion and there is now a widespread policy platform in which widening educational access plays a key role. The implications for the future relationship between the University of Glamorgan and the south Wales Valleys are considerable.

Central to New Labour's analysis is a return to the belief that the state has a major role to play in the alleviation of poverty. This is not a return to the welfare rights model of Beveridge and the post-war settlement. As well as rights, this new 'Third Way' has stressed individual obligation and is reflected in the domination of policy by strategies to promote labour-market inclusion. In the 'Third Way' the vehicle to a cohesive and integrated society is the labour market. The key policy initiatives to tackle poverty to date have been the creation of the minimum wage, the family tax credit system and labour-market insertion strategies in the form of the many variants of New Deal programmes. The individual is seen as having a responsibility to participate in the labour market in order to benefit from the full advantages of citizenship.

The many outputs of the Social Exclusion Unit have also forced attention on to the most marginalized sections of the population and their lack of ability to perform and compete in the labour market without advanced preparatory work. In the class analysis I discussed earlier, the Welsh 'marginalized working class' are ill-equipped for a return to work even when a more vibrant economy has created opportunity. Lack of skills, skills mismatch, distance from the new industries and the absence of transport all create real physical barriers to work. We can also add to these a range of cultural barriers where collapsed personal and communal confidence, loss of self-esteem and aspiration and an absence of experience of the culture of the workplace prevent sections of the population from even seeing themselves as employable. A clear relationship exists between economic opportunity and local aspiration. In communities where there is little experience of work the aspiration of young people collapses. Payne and Payne (1994) found that young people's employment aspirations fell dramatically in the face of unemployment, following a plant closure in 'Steeltown' in Scotland. More optimistically, they also found that aspiration quickly returned with renewed economic opportunity in the area. Regrettably, for the majority of Valleys communities, there has been no return of economic opportunity to boost aspiration.

In this context community regeneration approaches have proved invaluable in working with communities where confidence and personal capacity is low (Jones and Adamson, 2001). A significant body of evidence was emerging by the mid-1990s that best practice in a wide range of health, housing, training and regeneration initiatives involved direct community participation (Hughes and Carmichael, 1998). It challenges the effects of social exclusion and raises confidence levels as a first stage in promoting social inclusion. Additionally, evidence in Wales suggested that there was a wide range of 'grass-roots' community action taking place which was having major impact on social problems in marginalized communities (Adamson 1997; Jones and Adamson, 2001). Government has sought to harness the advantages of a participative approach by creating a policy framework in which community-based development can flourish. Taking different forms in the devolved administrations, all are implementing major community regeneration initiatives. In England the Strategy for Neighbourhood Renewal is implementing a complex programme of community regeneration delivered through the local authorities in the most deprived communities. In Wales Communities First has created a long-term funded programme of community regeneration across Wales, recognizing the most deprived communities and communities of interest. The emphasis in this 'new social policy' (Finer, 1997) is on inclusion. If the analysis of social exclusion informs the understanding of contemporary poverty, then the anti-exclusion policy of necessity has to be participative.

The concept of multi-agency partnership working has also become orthodoxy, despite the many difficulties associated with building good partnerships (Taylor, 1995). Changes to the single regeneration budget in England following the 1997 election quickly demonstrated the New Labour administration commitment to this practice (Miller, 1999) and it is a central feature of the new policies for community regeneration. In promoting social inclusion the role of higher education in such partnerships has to date been minimal. Whilst the majority of universities have developed 'widening access' initiatives in response to pressures such as the Dearing Report, few have become engaged at community level in direct partnership working. The University of Glamorgan through its Programme for Community Regeneration and University College Newport through its relationship with Community Agents of Change have pointed to ways in which effective partnership can be conducted at community level. However, the conventional role of the university militates against such involvement. Outside the traditional 'extra-mural' activities, universities are largely charged with providing degree and higher degree education. Intervention in the culture of aspiration in local communities is not part of the conventional brief of the HE sector. However, the University of Glamorgan, in its current mission statement and in its community-based actions, identified at the beginning of this chapter, is developing a role which is far more community- and partnership-based. The university has developed a view that truly to widen access and promote social inclusion it has to move beyond its conventional role.

For education to make a full contribution to the struggle for social inclusion it has to challenge directly the cultural and social outcomes of the structure of poverty and social exclusion. The responses which emerge at the individual level are usually encountered in reactions of depressed ambition, low confidence, disengagement, disaffection and disconnection from the mainstream economy and society. These can also be seen as a communal process in which long-term change to local cultures can become consolidated and difficult to challenge. Disengagement from education and training can become an automatic response of those who grow up in such communities. In reality a reactive cultural response emerges in which young people reject academic achievement, belittle those who seek it and establish alternative subcultural markers of social status. These may be linked to anti-social behaviours including use of drugs, car crime or general neighbourhood nuisance.

However, more optimistically, successful regeneration projects in the region have demonstrated amply how young people can be diverted into creative activities in music, drama, dance, theatre and multimedia. The successes of organizations such as Valleys Kids, The Arts Factory, The Pop Factory, the People and Work Unit and a plethora of similar organizations point the way to actions which can both confront and reverse the negative outcroppings of class and social exclusion in the region. Community regeneration provides experiences that take communities and individuals outside their conventionally limited range of experience. It sets them challenges and gives them the skills to meet those challenges. It physically takes children to new places, different cultural contexts, and shows them the external world. It gives people skills and capacity to recognize and make choices as active social agents. It confronts power and enables communities to challenge the structures which govern their lives. Fundamentally, it creates active citizens who do not passively accept the limits placed on their lives by living in a marginalized, impoverished community. In all these ways it challenges the habitus outlined earlier. In doing so it challenges the social and cultural class barriers which help maintain poverty. Community regeneration, implemented holistically, can and is changing the working-class experience in Wales. In this it represents a significant advantage over the past, more passive, welfare relationship which did nothing to alter the social experience of the poor. It has the additional advantage of being virtually immune to changes of government. As a process it is irreversible. Communities once equipped to be active cannot be simply turned off, even by withdrawal of funding. Significant community regeneration organizations have developed without funding and outside of the local and national state. They are local social movements which draw on past radical traditions and collectivist culture (Jones and Adamson, 2001).

The key to widening access and increasing participation in education in the region is in promoting community renewal and developing cultural practices which challenge the culture of low aspiration and negative ambition which has marked local cultures. The University of Glamorgan is now recognizing its place in this equation of change and developing partnerships and programmes in which informal learning (Coffield, 2000) will play a key role. Already the actions of the Centre for Life Long Learning discussed earlier are having an impact in local learning centres and in schools in the Valleys area. More ambitiously, the University is creating its Gates programme to develop centres of intervention in key locations. In each Gate, informal education will be celebrated and promoted in cultural and artistic practice. The intention is to interest, captivate and involve local people in activities which they shape and determine. It is not intended to deliver the formal campus courses but instead to provide an experience of learning which will act as a 'gate' to further learning opportunities. The Gate thus becomes both a physical and cultural entry point to promoting a more aspirational culture.

This development points to the way in which the University will maintain its special relationship with the south Wales Valleys. Through the vehicle of Gates and its other community-based actions as well as maintaining a strong local intake to its more conventional campus-based provision, the university can contribute significantly to the regeneration of the region and thus fulfil its stated mission.

REFERENCES

Adamson, D. (1988). 'The new working class in Welsh politics', *Contemporary Wales*, 2, 7–28.

Adamson, D. (1991). 'Lived experience, social consumption and political change in Wales', in G. Day and G. Rees (eds), *Nations and European Integration: Remaking the Celtic Periphery* (Cardiff: University of Wales Press).

Adamson, D. and Jones, S. (1996). *The South Wales Valleys: Continuity and Change* (Trefforest: University of Glamorgan, Regional Research Programme, Occasional Papers, Series 1).

Adamson, D. (1996). *Living on the Edge: Poverty and Deprivation in Wales* (Llandysul: Gomer Press).

Adamson, D. (1997). *Social and Economic Regeneration in Wales* (Community Enterprise Wales, Eryr Discussion Papers, 1).

Bourdieu, P. (1984). *Distinction: A Social Critique of the Judgement of Taste* (London: Routledge Kegan & Paul).

Bowman, H., Burden, T. et al. (2000). *Successful Futures? Community Views on Adult Education and Training* (York: Joseph Rowntree Foundation).

Byrne, D. (1999). *Social Exclusion* (Buckingham and Philadelphia: Open University Press).

Coffield, F. (2000). *The Necessity of Informal Learning* (Bristol: Policy Press).

Connor H., Dewson, S., Tyers, C., Eccles, J., Regan, J., and Aston, J. (2001). *Social Class and Higher Education: Issues Affecting Decisions on Participation by Lower Social Class Groups*, Research Report RR267, (London: DfEE).

ELWa (2001). *Draft Corporate Strategy* (Cardiff: National Council ELWa).

Finer, C. (1997). 'The new social policy in Britain', *Social Policy and Administration*, 31, 5, 154–70

Glass, D. (1954). *Social Mobility in Britain* (London: Routledge & Kegan Paul).

Goldethorpe, J. (1980). *Social Mobility and Class Structure in Modern Britain* (Oxford: Clarendon Press).

Gorard, S., Fevre, R., et al. (1999). 'The apparent decline of informal learning', *Oxford Review of Education* 25, 4, 437–54.

Gorard, S., Rees, G., et al. (1998a). 'Learning trajectories: travelling towards a learning society?', *International Journal of Lifelong Education*, 17, 6, 400–10.

Gorard, S., Rees, G., et al. (1998b). 'Progress towards a learning society? Patterns of lifelong learning', *Innovations in Education and Training International*, 35, 4, 275–281.

Gorard, S., Rees, G., et al. (1998c). 'The two components of a new learning society', *Journal of Vocational Education and Training*, 50, 1, 5–19.

Gorard, S., Rees, G., et al. (1999). 'Patterns of participation in lifelong learning: do families make a difference?', *British Educational Research Journal*, 25, 4, 517–31.

Hamnett, C., McDowell, L. and Sarre, P. (1989). *The Changing Social Structure* (London: Sage).

Hindess, B. (1987). *Politics and Class Analysis* (Oxford: Blackwell).

Hughes, J. and Carmichael, P. (1998). 'Building partnerships in urban regeneration: a case study from Belfast', *Community Development Journal*, 33, 3, 205–25.

Humphreys, R. and Saunders, D. (2000). 'Beyond rhetoric in lifelong learning', in R. Daugherty, R. Philips and G. Rees (eds), *Education Policy in Wales: Explorations in Devolved Governance* (Cardiff: University of Wales Press).

Istance, D. and Williamson, H. (1996). *16 and 17 year olds in Mid Glamorgan Not in Education, Training or Employment (Status O)* (Swansea: University of Swansea, Department of Continuing Education).

Jones, S. and Adamson, D. (2001). *The South Wales Valleys: Continuity and Change 2001* (Pontypridd: University of Glamorgan).

Joseph Rowntree Foundation (JRF) (1995). *Income and Wealth: Report of the JRF Inquiry Group* (York: JRF).

Joseph Rowntree Foundation (2000). *Poverty and Social Exclusion in Britain* (York: JRF).

Levitas, R. (1996). 'The concept of social exclusion and the new Durkheimian hegemony', *Critical Social Policy*, 16, 5–20.

Marshall, G., Newby, H., Rose, D. and Vogler, C. (1988). *Social Class in Modern Britain* (London: Hutchinson).

Meiksins-Wood, E. (1986). *The Retreat from Class: A New 'True' Socialism* (London: Verso).

Miller, C. (1999). 'Partners in regeneration: constructing a local regime for urban management', *Policy and Politics*, 27, 3, 343–58.

Murray, C. (1989). 'The emerging British underclass', *Sunday Times Magazine* (November 1989). For a collected edition of essays by Murray and other commentators see *Charles Murray and the Underclass: The Developing Debate* (London: Institute of Economic Affairs, 1996).

National Assembly for Wales (2000). *Welsh Index of Multiple Deprivation* (Cardiff: NAfW).

Payne, J. and Payne, C. (1994). 'Recession, restructuring, and the fate of the unemployed: evidence in the underclass debate', *Sociology*, 28, 1, 1–19.

Room, G. (1995), 'Poverty in Europe: competing paradigms of analysis', *Policy and Politics*, 23, 103–13.

Saunders, P. (1995). 'Might Britain be a meritocracy?', *Sociology* 29, 23–41.

Saunders, P. (1996). *Unequal But Fair? A Study of Class Barriers in Britain* (London: Institute of Economic Affairs).

Saunders, P. (1997). 'Social mobility in Britain: an empirical evaluation of two competing explanations', *Sociology* 31, 261–88.

Saunders, D. and Kingdon, R. (1998). 'Establishing student tutoring within a higher education curriculum through the theme of personal and professional development', in S. Goodlad (ed.), *Mentoring and Tutoring by Students* (London: Kogan Page).

Saunders, D. and Powell, T. (1998). 'Developing a European media simulation through new information technologies', in J. Rolfe et al., *The International Simulation and Gaming Research Yearbook, 6, Simulations and Games for Emergency and Crisis Management* (London: Kogan Page).

Savage, M. and Egerton, M. (1997). 'Social mobility, individual ability and the inheritance of class inequality', *Sociology* 31, 645–72.

Silver, H. (1994). 'Social exclusion and social solidarity: three paradigms', *International Labour Review*, 133, 531–78.

Social Exclusion Unit (SEU) (2001). *National Strategy for Neighbourhood Renewal: Policy Action Team Audit* (London: SEU, January).

Smalley, N. and Saunders, D. (eds) (2000). *The International Simulation and Gaming Research Yearbook 8, Simulations and Games for Transition and Change* (London: Kogan Page).

Taylor, M. (1995). *Unleashing the Potential: Bringing Residents to the Centre of Regeneration* (York: Joseph Rowntree Foundation).

CIVIL SOCIETY – CIVIL UNIVERSITY

VOLUNTARY ASSOCIATION IN THE SOUTH WALES VALLEYS

Lesley Hodgson & David Dunkerley

'Civil society' – this is a term rarely heard or used only a decade ago. Yet today civil society is referred to reverentially by politicians, opinion-formers and academics alike. It is held up as a kind of panacea that will change the nature of policy-making and decision-taking, that will signal a fundamental change in the way societies are structured and that will involve citizens in their communities. Wales presents an excellent example of a civil society achieving greater prominence in all these respects and does so from both bottom–up and top–down perspectives.

Devolution in Wales – albeit in its limited format compared with Scotland – has done much to encourage and develop civil society in Wales in recent years. John Osmond of the Institute of Welsh Affairs, for example, suggests that devolution in Wales presents new political and social opportunities and that 'the new Welsh politics is about creating a new democracy and a new civil society to make the democracy work' (Osmond, 1998a: 15). This 'new' civil society is seen by other commentators as the bearer of exciting aspirations and actually follows rather than precedes political devolution. Thus, Assembly First Minister Rhodri Morgan suggests that civil society was 'actually the predecessor of devolution in Scotland' but that it 'may be the successor to devolution in Wales' (Morgan, 2000: 19). In this sense, he is suggesting that civil society in Wales is different from that in Scotland and was possibly less strong before the process of devolution took place.

The National Assembly for Wales (NAW) has done much to foster the development of civil society in Wales. Its rhetoric frequently uses the term itself alongside notions of 'partnership' and 'inclusion'; in practical terms it cannot be denied that new forms of participation and engagement with civil society organizations have been encouraged and promoted. This is very much in line with Osmond's argument that a 'new and interactive network of policy communication will be a building block of a new dynamic civil society' (1998a: 3). Whether a new civil society can be deliberately and spontaneously constructed rather than being allowed to emerge and evolve of its own accord over some period of time is an empirical question which, in the case of Wales, it is probably too soon to answer.

But what is civil society and is the term used univocally by politicians, journalists and academics? Is it as tangible a thing as

Osmond suggests, just waiting to be cultivated and embraced by new political structures? Indeed, is there anything new in the term or are we looking at a twenty-first-century version of the emperor's clothes? The term is a rather slippery one for, as Seligman (1997: 5) suggests, 'Right, Left and Center; North, South, East and West civil society is identified with everything from multi-party systems and the rights of citizenship to individual voluntarism and the spirit of community.' Forms of voluntary association seem to be at the heart of civil society so that individuals engage with one another independently of the state or the market, free from ideology or political pressure. Such association invariably takes place in formal or informal organizational settings such as churches, voluntary associations, the media, educational establishments and clubs. It is through such association that 'social capital' can be developed and inculcated. Thus, Salamon and Anheir (1997) talk of a 'global associational revolution' taking place. They base this dramatic claim on a comparative study of thirteen countries from which they identify a massive growth in the 'not-for-profit' sector where voluntary organizations are stepping in to fill the gaps left unaddressed by the state and/or the market. Deakin (2001) suggests that this 'revolution' is not taking place in or as a self-contained sector but that voluntary associations interact, more or less, with state organizations at local, national and international levels. Similarly there is a certain fuzziness around the borders of civil society and the market.

The 'Third Way' arguments presented by Giddens (1998, 2000) take this position further in that civil society is perceived as a way of fostering social cohesion through the development of a partnership with the state. Thus, state and civil society 'should act in partnership, each to facilitate, but also to act as a control upon, the other' (Giddens, 1998: 79). Such an approach also links to the market since civil society can make an impact on economic development, especially at the level of economic decision-making. According to the advocates of the 'Third Way', civil society's sphere of influence can also extend to participation in and reform of education, health and welfare.

The model being pursued by the NAW reflects this position rather well. There appears to be a genuine desire on the part of the Assembly to work with people and associations throughout

Wales, to take notice of their differing interests and hopes and to draw on previously untapped local expertise regardless of social position. This is almost a defining hallmark of the experience of devolution in Wales to date and certainly one that is giving a legitimacy to the NAW's work.

The stereotypical view of civil society in Wales is probably half a century out of date. Wales is presented as a country knit tightly by Protestant Nonconformism, with the chapels instilling the moral, social and political mores, or by the integrating influence in industrial south Wales of the miners' institute, the welfare hall and the miners' federation (Francis and Smith, 1998). The fact is that the days of radical Nonconformism have long gone, the miners' institute is more likely now to be a bingo hall or to have been demolished altogether. Indeed, Jones (1999: 18) suggests that the welfare halls, where they still exist, are now 'little more than drinking clubs', whereas they were 'previously famous for their level of cultural and political activity'. Is it then the case that 'community' has been replaced by 'individualism'? Alternatively, is it the case that Wales is small enough for notions of nationality, good communications and close social and personal integration to have generated a 'community of communities'? Or, again, is Wales so fragmented and divided and with such an underdeveloped civil society, that the hopes and aspirations released through devolution are likely to flounder and generate disappointment and despair?

Of course, Wales may be far from unique. It is certainly the case that modernity (and even postmodernity) has brought with it a disengagement of citizens with their society. The notion of there being three Waleses certainly has some appeal: *Y Fro Gymraeg* (the Welsh-speaking areas of west and north Wales); 'Welsh Wales' (the post-industrial areas identifying themselves as Welsh such as the erstwhile coalfield area of south Wales); and 'British Wales' (the border and coastal plain areas). Each area is likely to have different notions of identity and engagement. At the same time, each is likely to display declining levels of trust in government and party politics (one such example is represented by the low turnout and actual voting figures both in the devolution referendum in Wales and in the first elections for the NAW). Yet this is symptomatic of a wider malaise affecting not simply Wales or the three Waleses. It is a national and international phenomenon. Tony Blair, for example, has spoken of a 'second age of democracy' where 'people want the freedom to do things differently at local level' (Lambert et al., 1999) and key social commentators such as Fukuyama (1995, 1999) and Giddens (1998) have highlighted the growing disaffection with party politics.

But all is not necessarily doom and gloom. On the contrary, the lacunae left by the demise in the influence of the chapel or the miners' institute may have been replaced by a new form of civil society. Community groups, voluntary organizations, cultural organizations, youth groups and, importantly, educational institutions, among many others, all function in a different way from fifty years ago. Many operate as lobbying organizations and claim to influence the policy process. Several have quickly become adept at monitoring the activities of the NAW on behalf of their members. Organizationally, what is different is that, although large numbers of individuals are involved in one way or another with civil society associations, it is these associations, qua organizations, that make the running in terms of lobbying or influencing decision-making, rather than the active participants.

Recent work undertaken by Dicks et al. (2001) explores this issue in some detail. They are impressed by figures quoted by the Wales Council for Voluntary Action (WCVA) suggesting 'a burgeoning and vital sector' that 'helps make the case for the voluntary sector in Wales as a substantial resource that a devolved Wales would do well to call on (and a substantial constituency it should not ignore)' (Dicks et al., 2001: 105). At first glance the figures produced by the WCVA are indeed impressive: the identification of over 25,000 voluntary groups in Wales where over 80 per cent of the adult population are themselves volunteers, of whom '1.1 million are formal volunteers and 1.7 million are informal volunteers assisting neighbours and their communities outside of organizations' (WCVA, 1999: 1). The Dicks et al. study was conducted with seventy voluntary organizations, largely using telephone interviewing. Of interest is that 80 per cent of the sample organizations were based in south Wales. They conclude that

> those agencies responding to this survey were able, in different
> ways, to orientate themselves to an anticipated new environment
> promised by the Assembly . . . and this bodes well for the

ambitions of the Assembly. Whether these ambitions come to fruition is yet unknown. (Dicks et al., 2001: 111).

WCVA take great pains to establish that the value of volunteering in Wales (including in their definition both formal and informal groups) is worth some £3.4 billion for Wales with an annual turnover of £675 million. These figures appear continually in any literature that discusses voluntary activity in Wales. However, these figures may be little more than conjecture since they are extrapolated from the 1997 UK Survey into Volunteering where a mere seventy-eight individuals in Wales were surveyed!

The extent to which volunteering is actually undertaken in Wales is still unknown and, indeed, raises the question of the extent to which groups and organizations are voluntary. Most informal groups (usually self-interest and cultural groups such as choirs, social clubs and cycling clubs) are all completely voluntary in nature. Formal groups, however, present a different picture from one of voluntary unpaid associational activity. The WCVA has around 800 voluntary organizations as members,with membership fees ranging from £25 for associate membership to £50 full membership and £90 for private associate membership. It would appear, in reality, that the only individuals who are volunteers are the management/executive committee or board. Here again we can question the extent to which these individuals are truly volunteers since the Annual report for 1999–2000 indicates that, of the forty executive committee members, thirty-one are paid members of various groups. The other nine members served in their individual capacity as volunteers, although many of these can be viewed as the local 'great and the good'.

Clearly, there are problems with definition, both of what civil society actually comprises and of the individual elements that make up the whole. So much of the discussion about civil society is based upon 'armchair theorizing' using conjecture rather than fact. In an attempt to address this major problem, we now move to a description of an original empirical study conducted within the 'footprint' of the University of Glamorgan.

METHODOLOGY

Taped semi-structured interviews were conducted with individuals involved in some forty civil society groups located in the

Merthyr, Cynon and Rhondda Valleys. Within five groups, members other than the 'key person' were interviewed in order to gain the views of those involved at grass-roots level. In two cases members of the national (Wales) body of groups were interviewed to examine the difference between groups involved at various hierarchical levels. The monthly meetings of two community-based groups were attended (access being denied in the third) in an effort to determine whether the experience of belonging to a civil society group was the same for everyone. Added to this the study was rounded out by an examination of the literature of groups, where there was such literature, to provide necessary background information.

A list of voluntary organizations was obtained using the *Wales Yearbook* (2000). The *Yearbook* contains a listing of all groups who

TRAINING BY THE UNIVERSITY

There are a number of community revival or regeneration groups in the Valleys. One such is based approximately 10 miles from the university in an area of high social deprivation. Recently formed to produce a coordinated approach to regenerating the community, the strategy group comprises a number of smaller groups such as neighbourhood watch, the local community hall management team and various residents' associations. One of the first functions of the group was to develop a 'regeneration document that was completely flexible, so that depending on which project is achieved first, will mean that all of the other projects can interchange accordingly.' That document was based on a feasibility study undertaken on behalf of the group. The study indicated what the individuals living in the community felt was needed, as the project manager explains, 'the public told us what they needed. The main concern at the time was that . . . there was no

Medical Centre . . . And there is no Police Station and that upsets people. There are no facilities for the kids, no play areas. And these are the things that we are aiming for . . .'

The project manager freely admits that, at the beginning, group members had little idea how to develop a coordinated approach. The first few years were a learning period, which they used well. 'There was an interim period when we were just forming ourselves together and we received training from the University of Glamorgan on a constitution and the way forward and how to form ourselves.' In a recent interview, the project manager bemoaned the lack of speed with which the project has moved forward. With a heavy reliance on volunteers, however (the project manager being the only paid employee), the group has already had some marginal success. Having just secured a large proportion of Communities First monies, however, the group's future looks very bright.

were full members of the WCVA. A second list was made, based on locality. The intention was to interview individuals from groups of varying sizes and who were engaged in a wide range of activities. This information was not available from the *Yearbook* and therefore necessitated a more hands-on approach. A list of twenty groups was drawn up using the data gathered from a brief telephone survey. However, this was far from inclusive since the spread of organizations was not wide enough: all the groups on the list were members of the WCVA and also involved in what may be termed the voluntary 'sector' rather than civil society more broadly, that is, civil society as voluntary association.

It was apparent that the number of voluntary groups within the area of study was far greater than the numbers provided within the *Yearbook*. Using a snowballing technique, groups were asked to recommend other groups, possibly groups that they had links with that were involved in a similar yet different area. Using this information, the interview list grew rapidly. Community and grass-roots initiatives were most helpful in providing the opportunity of reaching those more informal groups. These groups proved to be the most difficult to gain access to, very often because they themselves do not recognize themselves as a 'group' or 'club'. Discussions with friends and neighbours yielded some results. Eventually five such groups were interviewed: a cycling club, a crochet club, a choir and two social clubs.

The semi-structured interviews generated material on a number of core topics in relation to assumptions about civil society and voluntary association. What is civil society actually like? How does it operate and what happens when the state (in all its various forms) attempts to partner civil society groups? More specifically, data were gathered on the reasons behind individuals' coming together in voluntary association; the extent to which belonging to civil society is actually voluntary; how groups operate; how and why they network; whom they partner and why; and the experience of involvement with the local authorities and the National Assembly for Wales.

The interviews generated a large amount of high-quality, qualitative data focusing on the experience of group membership and belonging within civil society. Groups were involved in the following activities:

Accommodation/Housing	Health
Advice and Information	Protest
Art	Social Welfare
Campaigning and Advocacy	Sport
Community	Support
Community financing	Recreation/Leisure
Counselling	Recruitment of Volunteers
Culture	Recycling
Development	Regeneration
Environment	Therapy
Families	Transport
Facilities and Equipment	Youth
Fund-raising	

CIVIL SOCIETY IN THE VALLEYS

This section focuses on the types of civil society groups that are to be found in the Merthyr, Cynon and Rhondda Valleys and investigates the types of activities in which these groups are involved. It is not the intention here to compile a list of groups outlining the quantitative nature of civil society; the dimensions of activities that take place within this sphere preclude that. Rather, the aim is to give a 'flavour' or 'snapshot' of civil society within the hinterland of the University of Glamorgan.

There are innumerable small informal groupings of various sizes, networks of families and friends who come together ostensibly as part of an interest group. These 'clubs' are often not part of any register or directory and are formed through word of mouth. They often comprise what Finnegan (1989) refers to as 'the invisible organization'. These groups are not part of the formal voluntary sector; they do not exist to fulfil a need, nor are they part of the 'grant chasing' system. They often have no formal basis, no written constitution and no coded rules of membership. Rather their membership is based around friendship and shared interests, enthusiasm and enjoyment. In some instances group members deliberately shy away from the 'legal process' of formal group membership often because they have been members of a formal grouping before and do not want to 'go down that road again'. One member of a club that meets weekly as part of a crochet group put it this way:

we decided that we didn't want to do that. It was just purely a little gathering. We did that in [a] club years ago, but it wasn't very good. We had a secretary and a chairman and all that but there was always disputes, and minutes had to be taken, and we had to have organized meetings, we didn't want to do all that again. This way there is no responsibility. There are very few arguments, it's just a case of putting your 50p in the ashtray and having a good evening.

These groups are funded through subscriptions (usually a token amount of 50p or £1 a week or upon attendance) and their only resource, outside of their shared knowledge, is the room or hall they use. The money may be used for hire of the room and social events such as the Christmas party. Although primarily meeting to develop a shared enthusiasm, there is a heavy element of socializing in such groups.

> We just meet up to help each other, have a chat, enjoy ourselves . . . We have general discussions so that if there is anything special going on in the village we all know about it . . . Another thing that's good is that we go out for meals. If it's someone's birthday we say 'right it's time for a meal then' and sometimes we get together and go on a shopping trip at Christmas time. It's a very social club.

At times such groups are insular and do not link with other groups, 'I don't even know of any other group like ours' being a typical comment. They are, however, often linked with others in the sense that members of the group attend other interest clubs, such as slimming clubs or swimming classes, but interviews highlighted that individuals almost always stay within their own circle of friends.

Other groups of this kind are more outgoing and link with other groups with a similar or shared interest or common enthusiasm. For example, a member of a choir stated: 'We love to go and join with other choirs, put on performances together or just practice together. We often sing at charity events and if we combine forces we have a great time and share a few drinks later.'

At times these smaller groups can grow and develop into something larger, taking on the mantle of 'formality' yet still keeping the focus of activities on socializing. One such group that now has upward of eighty members (mainly retired men and women) began as a small informal group of friends who met weekly for a 'drink and a chat about old times'. Gradually, however, this grouping grew until it was felt that it was becoming unmanageable and the 'club' should branch out, find themselves a bigger room (in fact they now meet in the community centre), think of a name, have some form of written 'rules of membership', a chair, a secretary and meet at regular times (Wednesdays between 2 and 4 pm). They are funded through subscriptions of £1 a week, 50p of which goes to a compulsory raffle. The group is now focused entirely on organized social activities. Each week there is either a musician, a dance or a game of bingo, and occasionally there is a trip away or a speaker (a local dignitary or information-provider such as CAB). The core function of these types of clubs is to bring people together in a social atmosphere:

> the interesting thing about it is that 60% of them [the members] are lonely, living on their own, widows, widowers, you know, and the reason they want to come out of their home is that of course to meet each other, have some company . . . so it's basically about getting people out of the house . . . they are happy to just talk to each other.

These sorts of groups sometimes have links with other similar social groups in the area and often share social outings:

> Yes, we have links with a group in [a nearby village], now they've got wonderful facilities which we haven't got, and on three occasions now they've invited us up for the evening, when we've played bingo and listened to their musical evenings, they were very kind to do that you see.

Even where groups begin as social entities in the narrow sense there is evidence to suggest that they often 'branch out' into other areas when a need is perceived. Take, for example, a group of heart patients who met regularly 'once a month, to catch up . . . and socialize. We put various things on, various speakers, various entertainers according to people's moods and what they want.' Over time, however, the realization that there was little provision and aftercare service for rehabilitating heart patients and their families moved this group to become involved in fund-raising activities. After fund-raising the group began 'a help-line for patients, a taxi service for rehabilitating patients and are heavily involved in fund-raising for hospital equipment'. The idea behind many groups of this nature is in 'giving something back'. Having secured funding from various sources, the group now provides exercise classes and first aid training as well as advising the community health council.

At the community level, grass-roots organizations are abundant in the Valleys. These groups are often concerned with addressing specific societal 'problems' and fulfil an array of essential community functions, whether in the form of addressing youth problems, illiteracy, drugs, the provision of after-school clubs and/or playgroups, providing a travel service for elderly or ill people, addressing housing needs or charity work. This is the area where individuals are 'doing it for themselves' – where a need is perceived and filled, as one member of such a group stated:

> there was just nothing here so we, well, decided to do something about the community, we thought that we would do something to benefit our children, because there was masses of alcohol and drugs and do we really want our children to go down this road? We decided that this is what we were going to do, if we weren't going to do something then [the area] would be neglected forever. So it was a case of just getting stuck in there. Nobody else was going to do it for us.

Such groups are often funded initially through fund-raising activities within the local community, such as bring-and-buy sales, car boot sales, raffles and carnival events. Over time they often take on charitable status which allows them to access funding from various sources.

Added to this grouping of grass-roots initiatives are those groups that spontaneously form to address some 'issue'. During the course of this research a number of such groups formed to protest against a range of issues, such as the development of opencast mining, the placement of landfill sites and the perceived threat to sixth-form schooling by the development of a sixth-form college. These groups develop to bring pressure to bear on those in authority and if they are successful they often disband as quickly as they appear. Rarely do they involve funding, but where it is needed, perhaps to produce sloganed badges or T-shirts, it is often provided through the members of the group itself.

The vast majority of the large formal groups both of a philanthropic and mutual character found in the area (and variously defined as falling into the 'voluntary sector', 'third sector' or 'not-for-profit' sector) fall into three main categories – groups that have an international, national, or regional dimension. Of course, a categorization of this kind is open to criticism because of the overlapping nature of groups, yet, for the purpose of investigating the activities in which groups are involved, this categorization proves useful. International and national groups tend to have a historical dimension, are well known to people in general (by name if not in fact) and may have more secure avenues of funding than other groups. Groups such as the Young Men's Christian Association (YMCA), Scouts' Association, Salvation Army, Citizens' Advice Bureau (CAB), Barnardos, Age Concern, credit unions and the like, all have a presence in the Valleys, each providing within their specific 'area' some form of service or fulfilling some form of need at a community level under the banner of their parent organization. Many of these groups are involved in producing 'better citizens' and involve themselves in the development of citizenship skills, through engaging in activities that will encourage people to behave in certain ways. Examples of this are provided through the responses from members of two groups, both with an international dimension. One spoke in terms of encouraging 'local people [in] learning thrift and managing their own savings as a means of eventually controlling their own economic destiny' and the other stated their aim as 'producing the type of kids you'd like to live next door to . . . through engaging in activities . . . and teamwork'. Other groups are concerned with addressing poverty and/or other social problems within specific sections of the community, although many groups widen out from their focus of activity at a community level. These groups are often linked in a hierarchical structure to parent groups, so, for example, the local Citizens' Advice Bureau is linked at a regional and a national level, as well as having 'sister' groups. The local Scouts' Association is linked by district, regional, national and international levels as well as at grass-roots level to other scouts' groups.

Many groups with a national affiliation have reaffirmed their regional status, distinct from the national, by adding the word 'Cymru' to their title. This has especially been the case since the setting up of the National Assembly for Wales. There appear to be two reasons for this. First, the perception is that funding will be forthcoming to groups with a particularly 'Welsh' focus and, second, as an attempt to focus the mind of the public, and perhaps those involved in the group too, on the fact that the group is working for the people of Wales. One member of a well-established national body suggested:

> Well I suppose, when you are looking for funding from the National Assembly it looks good to see Wales or Cymru after the name . . . it does underscore that we do have a focus on Wales and not England. The work I do, I do here, for the people here, in this community, for the people here in Wales and I think people need to realize that.

Within the national category of groups are some 'manufactured' groups. These have come about through government intervention, are often funded, at least initially, by government and are answerable to the state, feeding back information and addressing certain criteria set by the state. These groups are often concerned with community regeneration and/or welfare issues and many have a highly moralistic agenda, concerned with producing 'rounded' individuals, usually through education. Groups such as Sure Start and People in Communities are part of this grouping. The driving force behind these initiatives is to impart skills to enable individuals to develop as citizens and/or to encourage them to take an active interest in their community.

Also to be found in the Valleys are a number of umbrella organizations that safeguard the interests of their members. One such which has been set up in more recent times (1997) is the Valleys Race Equality Council, which seeks to safeguard the rights of various ethnic minority groups in the Valleys, combating discrimination and promoting improved race relations. Other groups, such as the Welsh Council for Voluntary Action (WCVA) and local county voluntary councils, have a long history in the area (in one guise or another, throughout various local authority boundary changes) and are specifically focused on supporting

> the voluntary and community sector in . . . a number of different ways either by working to help their capacity, or supplying information, help and support . . . facilitates networks and forums . . . there's the intermediary role where we work with statutory agencies to ensure that the voluntary sector is being heard.

Clearly, then, the Valleys have an impressive array of civil society groupings, with individuals being involved in innumerable activities, from choirs and crochet circles, self-help and community-based initiatives, to the more formal groups concerned with anti-poverty strategies and citizen development, with a host of others in between. But what makes civil society different from other aspects of society? It has been suggested that civil society is the locus where individuals learn to be citizens – where civic virtue, where social capital and trust and reciprocity develop and where individuals become civilized and moral beings (see, for example, Almond and Verba, 1965; Cohen and Arato, 1992; Hirst, 1994; Etzioni, 1998; Keane, 1998; Putnam, 2001).

CIVIL SOCIETY AS AGENTS OF SOCIALIZATION

All institutions within society socialize their members to learn the rules of group membership. Arguably, when it comes to civil society, this aspect is even 'more important than the practical functions of civil society' (Eberly, 2000: 3). Theorists of civil society suggest a range of roles/habits or 'ways of being' that group membership confers, from the development of political skills to the development of a shared way of looking at the world. Some may be deliberately formed as the group sets out to develop a way of 'being', while others, it is suggested (Eberly, 2000; Putnam, 2001), come about as a by-product of group activity in the sense that group membership develops certain transferable skills. What are those roles and skills that are learned and how does civil society socialize its members into those roles?

There is little doubt that group membership does engender certain basic habits. At a basic level, small informal groups with few members rely on members 'turning up'. Although membership of such groups is fluid, with some members not turning up for weeks, there appears to be a core of members that can be relied upon to attend and 'keep the group alive'. One respondent put it this way,

> No one feels coerced to attend . . . well I suppose I feel obligated today but in a different way . . . if I didn't go I'd be letting the others down, they kind of expect me to be there, and I expect them. I know even when I don't feel like going I do, because I know they'll be waiting for me. If I go down, I know that I won't be sat there on my own but that other people will turn up. So

> although I'm not coerced, I feel a sense of obligation, mind you
> not everyone feels the same way, some people don't turn up for
> weeks but it's still nice to see them when they do.

A number of things become noticeable through this account.
First, joining a group does engender an element of trust – at the
most basic level, trust that other people will turn up. Although
there is no formal rule regarding attendance and members are free
to join or leave as they wish, there is, for some at least, a clearly
understood convention that non-attendance would lead to the disintegration of the group and therefore an element of reciprocity
develops. To safeguard the group, feelings of obligation are generated and implicitly stated. It becomes apparent, however, that the
level of obligation generated through group membership varies
among members. In this instance, some members do not turn up
for weeks while others feel obligated to turn up as often as they
can. It is apparent that in almost all smaller interest groups there is
a core of individuals who feel obligated to attend, and a significant
number of others for whom membership is more fluid; for these,
feelings of obligation or implicit coercion are not an issue.

At this level when disputes arise they are often handled in a
light-hearted way. One respondent described the relationship
within the group in these terms:

> Barbara counts the money and does a headcount and if it doesn't
> tally up she takes the 'mick' but in a spirit of fun . . . sometimes
> there's a conflict of characters but it's sorted out in a spirit of light-
> heartedness and it's pooh-poohed.

Here is evidence that group members put in place strategies,
sometimes unconsciously, to control the behaviour of members.
Unresolved disputes lead to individuals leaving the group but this
usually only happens to newcomers. Other groups suggested that
they face problems and disputes 'head on' by talking through the
issues raised. Discourse is seen as the best way to settle disputes –
'we talk about it' being a common solution.

As groups develop and grow in size it becomes more difficult
to 'control' group membership. Turning up and supporting
appears not to be so important but controlling behaviour in other
ways does and this is often effected by a set of written rules:

> We do have a drawn-up statement of intent to say that . . .

> members will respect each other and each other's differences . . .
> any offensive behaviour including any racist, sexist, ageist or
> defamatory or bad language may not be permitted and will consti-
> tute a breach of reasonable behaviour and any breach of behaviour
> will result in two verbal warnings and if it still occurs then mem-
> bership to the club will cease immediately. If a member is absent
> for 3 months then membership will be terminated, that sort of
> thing, you know.

In this instance there is an element of coercion, with membership
being terminated for a variety of reasons and behaviour being
controlled through sanctions and warnings rather than informally.

It is also evident that people involved in community-based
groups learn over time how to handle disputes:

> we discuss things and we just talk things through because at the
> end of the day we have to talk things through. You just have to air
> your views and at the end of the day, it is not personal. It's very
> open and very informal down here if anyone has anything to say,
> just say it. Whatever happens in here, is in here, it does not leave. I
> think because we started small and did it one step at a time we've
> learnt that's the best way to do things, not let issues get out of
> control. So now we control them [disputes] rather than they con-
> trol us. We keep everybody informed by letter of what's going on,
> I think that helps as well. Local knowledge helps because we all
> live here, we know the different disagreements between families.
> Somebody from outside wouldn't have known . . . and it would
> have just escalated.

In this instance, group membership has enabled group members
to decide on a course of action that would settle disputes. Talking
things through, being open, leaving issues behind 'at the end of
the day', using 'insider' information about neighbourhood disputes are all skills that have been learned through the trial and
error of group membership. It is at this level, too, that a mention
of other skill development arises:

> It's made me go back to college, and get more qualifications. I've
> had a lot of, um, I meet a lot of people, got a lot of contacts, I've
> learnt a lot. I have developed new skills, met new friends and
> gained confidence. It made us believe in something and made us
> believe that we could get it. Before we used to rely on [a develop-
> ment worker] to write reports and bids, they'd just fill them in for

us, but we said, 'excuse me who said that that was what we wanted to do'? and now they don't do anything unless they check with us first.

This person felt that involvement with the group had helped them to acquire the skills necessary to equip the whole group to evolve into a more formal structure and allowed her to take managerial responsibility. This skill development is something that is an integral part of group formation at this level. Whether through trial and error, as in this case, or through more formal avenues of learning, members of groups develop certain skills. This is supported by the following comments from members of various groups. The secretary of a group with environmental concerns stated:

> it's given me the confidence to approach people I wouldn't normally. I've always been confident but I would never approach people from university or anything like that. And I've learnt how to use the computer. I can produce documents, I can write up bids.

One member of a tenants' association noted:

> the group has grown, our minds are much more broader. We are doing a course in sociology and community development at the university, we've done a counselling course and we have done presentations to the Social Exclusion Unit, I did one recently to David Blunkett on volunteering in the community. I would never of done that before.

Skill development has become a clear marketing strategy of those groups involved in the formal voluntary sector. An investigation into the pamphlets and leaflets used by groups to encourage volunteering highlighted that one of the primary reasons given for involvement in voluntary activity is skill development. This features alongside making new friends and helping the community. Here we have a reciprocal arrangement: 'You volunteer for us and we will provide you with friends, engender feelings of goodwill and community service and equip you with skills.' These skills can then be utilized by large groups to help in furthering their goals, especially when they are involved in philanthropic activities within the community. An example of this is provided by a member of a large organization when discussing volunteers: 'I work a lot with the tenants' groups, I can see how they [some members] have changed, you have these people who started off saying I can't do that, I can't chair meetings and all of a sudden they are doing it.'

The respondent went on to relate how the organization then uses these individuals to liaise between the organization, other tenant groups, tenants themselves and the community at large, utilizing their newly developed skills. Skill development in this way may also serve as a basis for the development of mutual aid or new community-based projects (such as when individuals leave a large formal voluntary sector organization and start up or move on to work with a smaller community-based initiative). For some individuals, skill development can be viewed as a means of gaining secure employment.

Other groups deliberately set out to moralize/remoralize. Members of such groups talk in terms of passing on values, encouraging certain forms of behaviour while discouraging others, and promoting good citizenship. One chair of a community-based group voiced it in these terms:

> So at the end of the day it is a responsibility, it is a personal responsibility of everybody, to try and build a better community. If you are going to live in it then let's work to make it a decent

THE VOLUNTEER

Jenny is now entering her second year of a humanities degree at the University of Glamorgan and attributes the confidence she has today to her time spent as a volunteer.

Jenny described herself as a 'bored housewife and mother of three' until she joined her local playgroup as a volunteer. 'I had no formal qualifications but I did know how to look after children', she says.

The playgroup is attached to the local primary school. The school provides a room and some basic resources and the playgroup leader is funded from an outside body. The playgroup itself however is heavily reliant on volunteers. Volunteers not only engage in fund-raising activities, raising money for toys, trips

and basic resources, but are also involved in the day-to-day running of the group.

Jenny became involved in the playgroup when her youngest child was about 2 years of age. She explains how she went to enrol her child in the playgroup near her home and found herself becoming part of the team of volunteers.

'I went to put my child's name down and the woman running the playgroup asked me could I come and help out from time to time when they were short staffed. I started helping out a couple of mornings a week and then the girl who was there most of the time got a full-time job and so I took over her shift. I went in everyday 9–11.30 a.m. I learnt as I went along.'

community . . . If you do that and try and breed into them a sense of responsibility in the community.

A committee member of a not-for-profit business suggested:

> So that would hopefully help them get into the practice of con-serving. Because you notice this is what Mr Blair is trying to do with these young children, is to get people into the practice of having a little bit of money on their side, something we don't do any more. We try and get people into that habit and encourage good money management.

And, finally, a leader of a scouts' group stated: 'All we hope we can do is guide them into society so that they are accepted rather than them being an outcast.'

From the above there can be little doubt that civil society groups are agents of socialization. Through both formal and informal mechanisms they socialize individuals into ways of being, of accepting the norms and values of the group. Smaller groups and community organizations use informal mechanisms of censure to ensure behaviour or attendance, whereas larger groups tend to have written codes of behaviour. For the most

---

The running of the playgroup had changed hands since Jenny's older children had attended. The person running the group was an old friend of hers and so she saw helping out as not only a means of getting 'out of the house but also helping a friend'. When asked why she had never been involved before Jenny quite simply states, 'I had never been asked.'

Jenny felt that a lack of childcare provision coupled with her lack of experience in the job market hindered her from finding employment. She describes her volunteering activity as a means of meeting people, making new friends and having an interest. There is an acknowledgement that volunteering is not always easy. 'Sometimes you feel that you have no time of your own. You seem to be on call all the time. Even when I went to the school to pick up the children, people would come up and say things about the playgroup.' The benefits to the community however outweigh any negative personal aspects. Jenny realizes that without the work of volunteers there would be no playgroup.

With hindsight, Jenny realizes that volunteering imparted something of even greater benefit, 'Volunteering gave me the confidence to go on a short course in computers at my local college. Then I signed up for the Access course and then an 'A' level in sociology and then I came to university. I wouldn't be here now if I hadn't volunteered in the first place.'

THE VOLUNTEER

part, however, if you do not agree with the particular set of values or norms you can leave the group. There is evidence that trust is engendered at least among certain members of groups. Reciprocity is in evidence at all levels of civil society, at least between groups and individual members. Skill development figures highly, either through the 'learn as we grow' model of grass-roots initiatives or through the deliberate policy of engendering certain skills that form the basis of involvement of large formal groups. These are some of the component parts of what Putnam (2001) refers to as 'social capital' and it becomes evident that social capital is developed through voluntary activity. Social capital is developed in a number of ways and used by various actors within civil society for different purposes. For small groups it is a matter of securing, keeping and controlling members' behaviour; for larger formal organizations it enables them to secure their aims and fulfil needs; for others it becomes a means by which to produce individuals who have the necessary skills to function successfully as citizens and individuals use it to develop friendships and secure employment. In this regard, it appears that Putnam is right to speak about social capital having simultaneously a public and private 'good': group membership benefits individual members, the group as an organization and can also benefit the wider community. But social capital is not the prerogative of civil society alone. Social networks, reciprocity and trust can be engendered in any setting where people come together, including the state and the market. So what makes civil society different?

THE CIVIL SOCIETY ETHOS

Implicit in ideas of civil society as distinct from the state and the market has been the idea that this sphere is marked by a specific 'ethos' that is in contrast to the authoritarian manner of the state and the market logic of the economic realm. An ethos can be explained in terms of a distinctive character, spirit or attitude. What can be termed the civil society 'ethos' has come to be viewed as a mechanism for righting societal 'ills', whether in terms of a moralizing agenda or welfare provision. Tony Blair's ill-fated speech to the Women's Institute, for example, implied that civil society groups, like the WI, represent the 'community' and are necessary in building a 'decent' society built on traditional British values.

The public face of voluntary organizations is generally presented through the various mission statements and constitutions of individual groups (where they have them). A good place to begin, therefore, is with an examination of some of the 'legitimized' values or aims of civil society groups. These often tend to be stated in general terms, yet can give an insight into what is deemed to be the ethos of civil society.

> To promote the benefit of the inhabitants of [the area], to empower individuals and advance social education and to provide facilities in the interests of social welfare, training, employment skills and for recreation and leisure time activities with the object of improving the conditions of life for the said inhabitants. (community-based project)

> …giving disadvantaged children the help they need to build a better future (Barnardos Cymru)

> …to help and support families in creating happy, stimulating environments, in which all family members can flourish (Sure Start)

> The dream is of a place where people can come to meet, to find out what is happening in the community, to get involved. (church-based group)

There is an element of commonality here in that all these mission statements speak in terms of the 'other', referring to benefiting or enabling 'others', whether as individuals, families or communities. Rather than profit or power being the motivating force, there is an element of the wider 'social' aspects of life being taken into consideration. However, mission statements and constitutions are often the 'public' or 'legal' face of a group or organization. Groups need to develop constitutions out of legal necessity, especially when applying for charitable or not-for-profit status, and often need to address and fulfil certain criteria. For example, one respondent from a community-based group, which does not have a mission statement but does have a constitution, admitted, 'It's very – it suggests we will do this and that by these means. It's the new model from the Charity Commission.' This was underscored by the comments from a member of a self-help group for women:

> We had a meeting quite early on, and someone from the WCVA, I think it was, some umbrella body anyway, they came along with a model mission statement . . . we just used that and inserted our own words in here and there, where they seemed applicable. To be honest, no one ever uses them, they appear on our literature to give an idea of what we are all about and we use it when we apply for funding. I bet most people don't remember them.

A closer examination of mission statements also highlights the general nature of their content. Generic terms, such as enabling, empowering, benefiting, supporting, promoting, developing and improving, alongside words like capacity, synergy, community and partnership, are often used interchangeably to describe involvement in the lives of others. It became apparent through the interviews that it is advantageous to have a wide-ranging mission statement because this enables groups to apply for funding from an ever-wider variety of sources. There is evidence that, in recent years, groups have reinvented their image – and their mission statements accordingly – in an effort to widen their remit and apply for funding to bodies other than those they traditionally would have. This very telling comment came from the manager of a boys' and girls' club: 'The constitution needed to be widened for funding, you need to widen up the clauses and move away from particulars and speak in the general all the time. It's meaningless really because you could be talking about anything . . .' This is not meant as a criticism nor to undermine the work of such groups but is used to demonstrate that mission statements and constitutions alone are not enough to develop a view regarding the ethos of civil society.

Nevertheless, people involved in civil society groups are concerned with the wider social aspects of life rather than simply the political and economic. One respondent involved in a housing association put it this way:

> It's about people, not money, but people. I could probably use my skills elsewhere and make a lot of money, in fact, I have done so in the past . . . but there's no satisfaction. Here you feel that you make a difference – it's all about people.

Another respondent who had gone into voluntary work some seven years before highlighted the job satisfaction that came from

'seeing kids develop and grow' and described his previous experience of work as being involved in 'a rat race . . . now it's total job
satisfaction'. Rather than describing their work or involvement in
purely altruistic terms, in fact, very few respondents did so; the
vast majority of those interviewed spoke in terms of their own job
satisfaction that grew from seeing others grow and develop,
whether as individuals or as communities.

The idea that groups within civil society are 'people-focused'
and concerned with 'the social' is upheld in groups that do not
have mission statements or constitutions. It is still possible to
detect an underlying theme. One respondent involved in the
crochet 'club' mentioned earlier made this insightful comment:

> It's a social thing. I rarely go into the village any more because of
> work and so this is my way of keeping in touch with all the news
> and gossip in the community. Years ago I'd meet up with everyone
> at the school gate but that's lost now. The club is my equivalent of
> the school gate. It's important to meet up with people in a place
> like this, it's village life isn't it . . . it's important not to lose that –
> the quality of life is important, in a small way it's a way of keeping
> the community together . . . Perhaps there are not always benefits
> but I think it keeps the village together well, perhaps not our
> group alone but lots of these groups, I mean, like the others meet
> up about three times a week in little groups like this and then
> down the pub one night. It's what life is about, and then of course
> at times there is a need to do something to raise money for some-
> one in the village. It's the congregating of people together that's
> important not what they do. I've always done it, always been a
> member of a group when I can.

Again the reference for a desire to be closer to the community and
to quality of life is pronounced.

Similarly, protest or pressure groups, some of which spring up
and fade away as soon as the focus of the dispute is settled, whilst
being insular in their outlook and often being guilty of the 'Not
In My Back Yard' (NIMBY) syndrome, are often primarily concerned with the social aspects of life rather than political or
economic. Although their objectives might be their own, they are
concerned with what are inherently social issues. Their agenda is
often one that puts them at odds with the state, sometimes to the
point of civil disobedience. One individual in a group that

recently formed to protest against changes in schooling for their children argued: 'We want the best for our children and we don't think that the LEA knows what's best . . . they have their own reasons for changing things . . . well it's up to us to tell them.' Another respondent in a protest group admitted,

> I know no one wants opencast mining near them, and yes I'm being selfish because I don't want it near me and my children and my family and my village. And yes, it will bring jobs to the area, but at what cost, there are more important things than money at the end of the day. Health is important, quality of life is important and children are important. That's what I'm fighting for.

Again, underlying the lack of altruistic reasons for joining this group does not take away from the fact that the group is involved in what is an inherently social cause or debate.

If, then, when discussing the ethos of groups, the goals and

FROM VOLUNTEER TO FULL-TIME WORKER

Diane has recently completed a combined studies degree at the University of Glamorgan.

Diane (not her real name) became involved in a nationwide charitable organization concerned with the rights and needs of older people. Despite having a longer historical background, the organization developed in the Valleys area in the mid-1970s and now has offices throughout the various valleys surrounding the University of Glamorgan.

'We started off in Llantrisant as a very, very small organization and it's grown and grown. Within the last four years or three years we have seen our biggest change, when we've taken on various projects and now we have some forty members of full-time staff plus twenty part-time. From being a very, very small organization we've grown to quite a large organization for the Valleys in general.'

Despite this growth the group still relies on volunteers to fulfil most of its day-to-day functions. Diane explains: 'In the office where I was based there were two members of paid staff and the rest were volunteers – over 40 of them. The volunteers are involved in all aspects of the group and are involved in all the various projects that we run.'

Diane had started a degree course at the University of Glamorgan and when she volunteered 'I wasn't being at all altruistic, I just thought it would look good on my CV. I joined purely because of what I might get out of it. Employers look at your CV and I thought they might see someone who was willing to give of themselves.' She soon became 'hooked', however. 'The people you worked for were so friendly and caring and I got on well with the clients, as we call them.' As a single parent, Diane's volunteering was also a means of meeting new people. She volunteered as part of a aspirations are taken as the criteria, it would seem that there is a specific ethos or set of values that drives civil society. There does appear to be an interest or desire to improve the social and cultural aspects of life, whether it be through addressing specific criteria or through improving the quality of life.

Even where groups come together for the fulfilment of private needs, as in the case of interest groups, for example, they serve an important social function, sometimes unconsciously. The building of social ties, at times weaving together isolated individuals into a larger grouping, serves to bind individuals for purposes beyond private interests and develops a sense of mutual obligation, on the smallest scale by turning up and engaging in activities of social cooperation, on a larger scale by moving away from the group's initial activities and widening out to help others. This is fundamentally different from the compulsive aspect of the state and the profit-driven competitive aspect of the markets. Individuals

---

'good neighbour' scheme the organization was running, whereby they match older people with volunteers who can provide a friendly face and care as needed. Despite a heavy workload at university and battling with arthritis, Diane still managed to devote some of her time each week to her voluntary activities. She felt volunteering was important: 'The longer I was involved with [the organization] the more I felt I wanted to be involved and help out in some way. It was hard juggling university and volunteering, but volunteering gave me such a feeling of self-worth. Also volunteering was a means of gaining valuable experience, I developed new skills, went on various training courses and liked being with the older people I visited.'

After successfully completing her combined studies degree Diane continued her work with the organization, and eventually applied to become a member of the adminini-strative team on a part-time basis. She later took over the role of part-time coordinator. Recently Diane has become a full-time member of staff and is the coordinator and outreach support worker for the organization in a nearby valley. When asked to reflect on her experience to date Diane made this observation:

'The combination of obtaining a degree and the experience gained in voluntary work combined to give me the confidence to push myself forward. I definitely lacked confidence before I went to university. I felt I wasn't qualified, that my opinion didn't amount to much. I know now that wasn't necessarily true but now I have the educational qualifications and the experience to be able to talk to people on different levels. I didn't have that advantage before, but I needed them both. Now I feel I can hold my own in any situation. I can fight my corner.'

FROM VOLUNTEER TO FULL-TIME WORKER

within this sphere come together beyond the obligations of law or the self-interest of profit and engage in activities that consciously or unconsciously benefit and nurture the social and cultural aspects of life.

There is, however, another body of literature that suggests that, rather than investigating the aims or practical functions of civil society to determine what makes civil society different and gives it a particular ethos, distinct from the market or the state, there is a need to examine the way civil society operates. We shall look at this idea in the next section.

A DIFFERENT WAY OF WORKING?

Morgan (1990) refers to the values based on 'free association, consensus and cooperation' that are characteristic of civil society groups. Dahrendorf (1998: 81) suggests that it is the 'creative chaos' that makes up 'the reality of civil society'. Deakin (2001: 145) describes the values that drive many civil society groups as

THE DEVELOPMENT OF A COMMUNITY-BASED GROUP

A community-based group involved in recycling developed when a number of individuals involved in another charitable organization (what we might term practitioners) saw a need within the community and a means of fulfilling that need. The project manager explains: 'I was working for [a large charitable organization] ... and we were offered items of furniture that people didn't want any more ... we had no means of transporting the furniture so a lot of the offers were refused. At the same time I was aware that we were working with people who were desperately in need of furniture, who had children who couldn't use a knife and fork because they never sat at a table, and you have people wearing badly creased clothes because they had nowhere to hang them up. So it was frustrating really, that we couldn't put the two together ... We organized a public open evening,

which was attended by over forty people, and from that open meeting five people put their hand up to be a steering committee to develop a new group, and I was one of them. It took us two years to get a constitution, to get charitable status, to get our first lot of funding ...'

Through the determination of this group of individuals the organization has developed into a vibrant concern that offers the community a valuable service. It has not always been easy, however: 'We didn't have any capital money, initially I would use my own home computer to bring in here, we would borrow a van from social services or the probation services in order to get things delivered. We then had our first van donated to us by Whitbread and the Royal Mail. So that meant that we were then independent. That was six years ago. We now employ eight people, seven full-time including 'the importance attached to non-monetary goods and services provided to meet need, altruism as the animating motive . . . and satisfaction measured not by monetary reward but in reciprocal affection'. The suggestion is that civil society operates in a fundamentally different way from both the state and the market and it is this distinction that demarcates civil society.

This seems to be borne out by many of the respondents interviewed. Some had joined voluntary groups after being involved in businesses or the local authority and suggest that the free and easy way in which groups operate internally is fundamentally different. The following five quotes are gathered from people at different hierarchical levels, involved in different groups and concerned with a wide range of activities. One respondent who had worked in social services and now works as an administrator within a large community-based group suggested:

> But it doesn't even compare when you talk about ways of working. I would never go back to local authority, I worked in different areas

and one part-time and we run out of two different sites.'

Despite the number of paid staff the group relies heavily on volunteers; they currently have around twenty individuals who are responsible for all aspects of the operation, from transporting furniture to providing office cover and customer care. This is very much a community-based group: 'we wouldn't survive without the backing of the community, the community donates the furniture, the community volunteers and sits on the board of directors and the community are employed here and the community benefits from it.'

The respondent also feels that it is important not to be insular but to develop links with other community-based groups and indeed the wider community. This is an important means of sharing resources, knowledge and expertise; as the respondent suggests, 'we can share our resources and help each other out and we are stronger as a larger group than we are individually. We are currently trying to develop our own network with the University of Glamorgan, the Wales Council for Voluntary Action and other community groups in the area. We are writing to each community group offering to send them leaflets, to give a talk or a community display. We are actively making one-to-one contact with other groups . . . I think that working in partnership will make us all much stronger, and I actively support that.'

The group has recently employed a graduate from the University of Glamorgan through the 'Cymru Prosper' scheme. This benefits both the student, who gains valuable work experience, and the group, which is able to reap the benefits of employing a graduate student at a subsidized rate.

THE DEVELOPMENT OF A COMMUNITY-BASED GROUP

and you get a feel for it but the council are constantly changing their infrastructure, if something doesn't work let's bin it and do something else. Just too many chiefs, and not enough Indians. That's how I felt anyway, we never seemed to get anything done. People here listen. Although there is a hierarchical structure to the group it feels more informal . . . The council is physically hierarchical as well but that's a big difference, we would never approach the people at the top in the council . . . we become frightened by names and titles but generally in the voluntary sector, at least in my experience, the people are different than the private sector because they are doing it for a different reason, there is a different ethos about it. It's not the type of job you do for the salary at the end of the month, at least that's my experience of the few groups I've worked with. People are more down to earth.

A project manager of a smaller group concerned with drug abuse victims put it this way:

It's a lot more personal . . . The best thing is that I am in close contact with everybody. I get to know everything that goes on. Everything is so laid back. Last week my daughter was ill, she had to go to hospital, and I couldn't get in to open the office . . . I was two hours late, but no one condemned me for that. People understand. I put a note on the door and said we would be closed for the morning. Can you imagine doing that in a business? They'd be more concerned with the money they were losing.

An officer with a community housing association suggested:

It's a much easier working environment. I saw a real difference when I first came here, I worked in the council and then for Vauxhall, it was all money orientated and it was the same with the staff, you feel as if you are a person here whereas in the council before, I felt like a number. If you have problems it's much easier, it's a nice atmosphere. For example, if you are going to the doctor or the dentist, in the other company I used to have to work through my lunch-break to cover for that but here you can have time off to go. It makes a difference because you don't grab every half an hour you can, in fact you give more, and you can work over. If there's a problem you can ring up and say, 'Look this has happened' and it's not 'Well when are you coming in', it's more 'Can we do anything to help?' You give of yourself and here they seem to respect that. It also spills over into our dealings with the tenants.

A manager of a local voluntary group with a national remit commented that:

> Basically you are 'people orientated' in the voluntary sector whereas in business, local authority, and even the health authority you are concerned with numbers and how many you saw, how many people did you take care of today at the benefit office, everybody's got a number to their names. We do not have numbers, we are people orientated. There is no pressure on us, we will try to help other people, we will try to bring quality back to their life. It is very much [more] relaxed and I've got to say from working in different places the staff are very much nicer . . . because [you] are not pushed, you are not under pressure, we are under pressure sometimes when we have to get a bid in but as a whole you are not like that. You are not contained in a little box, you know, you can go out of these boundaries, it's very, very different very, very relaxed.

Finally, a director of a larger umbrella organization suggested the main difference was the freedom to manœuvre and implement various policies:

> Working for a statutory body you are constrained to work in your specialist fields, like I was a legal officer, doing case work, preparing cases for a number of years. Then I was their Policy Officer . . . but there were a lot more ideas that I wanted to explore. Here I can actually implement, and develop ideas . . . there's so much we can do here. I started off working for [an overseas company] in the buying office, so I've worked in a private sector before. It's not as satisfying. The private sector has its own limitations and is concerned with market forces, here I'm free to a large extent to try new things and explore new ideas that will ultimately benefit others.

These quotations seem to uphold some fundamental ideas about civil society. There is the perception amongst those interviewed that groups within civil society do operate at a different level from both the market and the state. Terms such as 'personal', 'informal', 'close contact' and 'viewed as a person not a number' are used to describe the approachability of members within groups and develop the idea that groups of this nature are interested in people (albeit in these cases people belonging to their individual groups), rather than profit or power. The reciprocal nature of civil society (so favoured by Putnam, 2001) is high-lighted in the view that giving of yourself is repaid through the gaining of respect from others around you. Money is not the driv-ing force for individuals within such groups. Indeed, it is 'not the type of job you do for the salary at the end of the month'. Rather, the driving force is described by the last comment, in terms of the 'satisfaction' gained, not from the accumulation of profit, but from the 'freedom' to 'explore new ideas that will ultimately benefit others.' A similar point was made by an earlier respondent in that satisfaction came from seeing the youths in his care grow and develop rather than from monetary gain. The effects of this way of working are not limited to individuals within these groups. The comments made by one respondent highlight that working in this way 'spills over' into the ways individuals deal with others.

It becomes apparent that the general consensus amongst those interviewed is that that there is a fundamental difference in both the aims and methods, or ways of working, of civil society groups. However, there is evidence to suggest that the ethical underpin-nings of civil society are under threat. The ethos of helping others, the idea of one individual doing something for the benefit of oth-ers or society more generally is central to the value system and ways of operating of many groups, yet interviews highlighted a tendency to focus on funding concerns. Groups have 'rebranded' or reworded their mission statements so as to secure funding from as wide a range of sources as possible. Funding was a central concern of formal groups whereas it did not feature highly in the priorities of informal groups and clubs, where the focus tended to be on membership and belonging, with an emphasis on both giv-ing and receiving.

Civil society is 'different' and it is this difference that makes civil society independent of the other spheres within society. This is not to suggest, however, that civil society is separate from the state or market in any real sense. Historically, groups in the formal voluntary sector have well-established links within the state appa-ratus, many being closely linked with local authorities. Many not-for-profit businesses and cooperatives operate by market rules and recent government initiatives actively encourage business and civil society partnerships, especially when it comes to providing services.

REFERENCES

Almond, G. and Verba, S. (1965). *The Civic Culture* (Boston: Little Brown).

Balsom, D. (1999). *Wales Yearbook 2000* (Cardiff: HTV Cymru Wales).

Cohen, J. and Arato, A. (1992). *Civil Society and Political Theory* (London: Massachusetts Institute of Technology Press).

Dahrendorf, R. (1998). 'A precarious balance: economic opportunity, civil society, and political liberty', in A. Etzioni (ed.), *The Essential Communitarian Reader* (Oxford: Rowman & Littlefield).

Deakin, N. (2001). *In Search of Civil Society* (Basingstoke: Palgrave).

Dicks, B., Hall, T. and Pithouse, A. (2001). 'The National Assembly and the voluntary sector: an equal partnership?', in P. Chaney, T. Hall and A. Pithouse (eds), *New Governance – New Democracy?* (Cardiff: University of Wales Press).

Eberly, D. E. (2000). *The Essential Civil Society Reader: Classic Essays in the American Civil Society Debate* (Oxford: Rowman & Littlefield).

Etzioni, A. (ed.) (1998). *The Essential Communitarian Reader* (Oxford: Rowman & Littlefield).

Finnegan, R. (1989). *The Hidden Musicians* (Cambridge: Cambridge University Press).

Francis, H. and Smith, D. (1998). *The Fed: A History of the South Wales Miners in the Twentieth Century* (Cardiff: University of Wales Press).

Fukuyama, F. (1995). *Trust: The Social Virtues and the Creation of Prosperity* (New York: Free Press).

Fukuyama, F. (1999). *The Great Disruption: Human Nature and the Reconstitution of Social Order* (New York: Free Press).

Giddens, A. (1998). *The Third Way: The Renewal of Social Democracy* (Cambridge: Polity Press).

Giddens, A. (2000). *The Third Way and its Critics* (Cambridge: Polity Press).

Hirst, P. (1994). *Associative Democracy: New Forms of Economic and Social Governance* (Cambridge: Polity Press).

Jones, R. M. (1999). 'Social change in Wales since 1945', in D. Dunkerley and A. Thompson (eds), *Wales Today* (Cardiff: University of Wales Press).

Keane, J. (1998). *Civil Society* (Cambridge: Polity Press).

Lambert, R., Groom, B. and Parker, A. (1999). 'Undivided loyalties' (interview with Tony Blair), *Financial Times* (14 January).

Morgan, G. (1990). *Organizations in Society* (London: Macmillan).

Morgan, R. (2000). *Variable Geometry UK* (Cardiff: Institute of Welsh Affairs).

Osmond, J. (1998a). *New Politics in Wales* (London: Charter 88).

Osmond, J. (1998b). 'Introduction', in J. Osmond (ed.), *The National Assembly Agenda: A Handbook for the First Four Years* (Cardiff: Institute of Welsh Affairs).

Putnam, R. D. (2001). *Bowling Alone: The Collapse and Revival of American Community* (London: Schuster & Schuster).

Salamon, L. and Anheir, H. (1997). *Defining the Nonprofit Sector: A Cross-National Analysis* (Manchester: Manchester University Press).

Seligman, A. (1997). *The Problem of Trust* (Princeton: Princeton University Press).

WCVA (1999). *Annual Report 1997/1998* (Caerphilly: Wales Council for Voluntary Action).

AT THE HEART OF THINGS

Peter Stead

The historian Gwyn A. Williams memorably asserted that 'Wales has always been now' and that 'the Welsh, as a people, have lived by making and remaking themselves in generation after generation, usually against the odds'. Nevertheless, as Wales sets out at the start of a new century to rebuild its economy, and perhaps even its society, it is as well to remind ourselves of the genuine excitement experienced by many of those who lived through the great industrial revolution of the late eighteenth and early nineteenth centuries. Today our hyped-up language often accompanies shallow achievements, but in that heroic era colourful language reflected a real sense of impending transformation and of potential fortunes. In 1840 Captain W. H. Smyth, the dockmaster at Cardiff, published a volume with the indulgent but precise, instructive and intriguing title *Nautical Observations on the Port and Maritime Vicinity of Cardiff, With Occasional Strictures on the Ninth Report of the Taff Railway Directors; and Some General Remarks on the Commerce of Glamorganshire*. Smyth's main aim was to warn against the dangers of any developments that would threaten the prosperity of his own docks, but he could not resist beginning his book with enthusiastic speculation regarding the true extent of 'treasure existing in this vicinity'. He was clearly enchanted by what he referred to as 'the value of the Glamorgan District'.

As Smyth did his calculations with regard to the fortunes to be made from the district's minerals he could only conclude that he was looking at a subject that was indeed a 'matter for meditation'. It was interesting that he thought of 'the treasure' as belonging to 'Glamorgan': the arrival of industry had given new life to the historic designation. Little is known of the native prince called Morgan but the notion that this land, or *gwlad,* should carry his name was accepted by the Normans and their royal descendants. Crucially, in 1536 Glamorgan became a shire as part of the Tudor Act of Union and thereafter landowners, magistrates and administrators gave the county a distinctive social identity. An intellectual flourishing in the eighteenth century emphasized the importance of the area within the Welsh context, but it was the exploitation of mineral wealth in the industrial revolution that transformed the significance of 'the Glamorgan hill district' and made contemporaries realize that it was at the heart of the nation.

Industrialists developed a great pride in this newly wealthy, populous and dramatically modernizing county, and it was that pride which gave identity and confidence to many institutions set up to cater for the new industrial society. Perhaps that nineteenth-century sense of Glamorgan's destiny was to be best expressed by the Glamorgan County Council (1889–1974) which, under the control first of landowners and then of working-class representatives, always regarded itself as a pioneering authority in British terms. The Glamorgan Constabulary (1839–1969) in its time became notorious for its role in containing the disorder arising out of trade union militancy, but its personnel chose rather to take pride in the height and military bearing of its officers and the distinctiveness of its Prussian helmets. Until the advent of the University of Glamorgan it was undoubtedly the Glamorgan County Cricket Club (founded in 1888) which had best kept alive that sense of a dynamic district as defined by Captain Smyth.

It is worth looking more closely at Smyth's 1840 'meditation' on the Glamorgan district, for he was keen to stress that ultimately these 'teeming mines' would greatly benefit 'the development of men's minds' and contribute to the 'progress of moral perfection'. He was in little doubt that 'the degree of civilization attained by any nation may be ascertained by the quantity of iron it consumes'. His district was clearly at the cutting edge of universal progress. But how could one account for this 'bountiful provision of nature'? It was, of course, all a matter of 'Providence': clearly this was the force responsible for 'ordaining the universal deluge' that had led to the formation of coal.

The town of Pontypridd, freshly named by a postmaster in 1856, was to develop an identity more closely influenced by the logic and rhetoric of Smyth than any town in Glamorgan other than Cardiff itself. Not only was it one of the county's historic market towns; it was regarded as the unofficial capital of the hill district, for it had important courthouses and was the focal point of the East Glamorgan parliamentary constituency. When I first encountered the town in the 1940s I was struck immediately by its own sense of significance; it comfortably filled its valley setting and seemed to constitute a natural gateway to a hinterland of its own choosing. As it happened, it was the notion of providence that came into my own mind, for as a regular traveller between

Cardiff and Merthyr I always greeted Pontypridd as a very welcome halfway point. My family at Merthyr had always regarded their town as the most important in Wales and I had never been allowed to forget the story of its vital role in the industrial revolution. I had therefore always known that the twenty-four miles between the works at Merthyr and the docks that the marquess of Bute had built at Cardiff constituted the most significant strip of land in Wales, if not the United Kingdom as a whole. Surely it had taken a formidable power to decide that the town I had been taught to call Ponty should lie exactly twelve miles between the twin poles of civilization as my family understood it.

Much of the romance of those childhood journeys could be explained by the fact that we travelled by rail, with the power being provided by magnificent steam locomotives whose numbers I eagerly collected. In this respect, too, providence had played a part, for it had chosen to make Ponty railway station a landmark that would thrill any child. As I looked out at a platform that curved away in both directions it would once more be explained that we were standing at 'the longest railway platform in the world'. Later I looked up the facts. That platform was almost a third of a mile long, and as recently as the 1920s a train had gone through the station every two minutes carrying some 10,000 passengers daily, not to mention thousands of tons of coal. All this traffic was carried on some two dozen lines controlled from a signal box in which there were 250 levers. In one striking photograph taken in 1927 from a street above the station the whole structure looks like a medieval fortification encircling an old town. Ponty, for me, has never lost the significance that the nineteenth-century railway bestowed.

It was just over a decade later and whilst I was an undergraduate that my family went to live in Pontypridd. My visits home focused on the heart of the town where the busy street market and market hall confirmed the town's status as a capital of the Valleys, as did the impressive church, the large police station (the most important in the county apart from the headquarters at Bridgend), the three cinemas, a theatre and a department store, albeit one owned by the Ynysybwl Industrial Cooperative Society which, it turned out, was to be my vacation employer. But my fullest sense of the town came when, with book in hand, I walked across to the Graig and then up to a spot where I could sit and look across the whole valley. What struck me immediately was the beauty of the setting. Undoubtedly this was an urban society: the smoke, the large works, the countless chapels, the trains and, perhaps above all, the cries of the newspaper boys, left one in no doubt of that. But above the houses and through the flocks of racing pigeons I could see the lovely green hills, the farms and the woods. Soon I came across Benjamin Heath Malkin's famous early nineteenth-century description of this precise spot where the Rhondda flows into the Taff and where William Edwards had built his 'stupendous bridge'. For Malkin 'the ampitheatre of hills' with 'the luxuriance of hanging woods' combined 'to make up as pleasurable a scene as the traveller could wish for'.

For the first time I was struck by the dramatic singularity of the valley of the Taff. South of Merthyr, as the travel writer Brian Dicks was to put it, the Taff ran through 'a pronounced and narrow defile'. To my eye this has never ceased to be a beautiful valley and one still imagines the salmon-rich river running swiftly between the low hills. Alongside the river was constructed the Glamorgan Canal and then the tramroad from Merthyr to Abercynon which carried the world's first steam locomotive designed by Richard Trevithick. However, it was the Taff Vale Railway, built by Isambard Kingdom Brunel and opened in 1841, that did most to transform this valley and to secure its place in British industrial history. Historians have stressed that the construction of the line was comparatively easy as it simply followed the river. Remarkably, no tunnels were required, although stone viaducts had to be built at Quakers Yard and across the Rhondda river at Pontypridd. The greatest difficulty occurred at Abercynon where a sharp incline meant that Brunel had to resort to cables and winding engines rather than locomotives. Only in 1864 did a new track enable locos, usually with the aid of bankers, to ascend the 1-in-40 gradient. This gradient came to the nation's attention during the famous Taff Vale dispute of 1900–1 when strikers tampered with the track and then watched blackleg drivers fail to negotiate the ascent. The great legal dispute that arose out of this strike and the famous judgment against the railway servants secured the Taff Vale Railway its place in history. Hitherto the TVR had been known chiefly for its remarkably high profits but it was (according to D. S. M.

Barrie) its 'unyielding spirit' in the long legal battle in which 'it gave scant quarter and asked none' that wrote it into the annals. Undoubtedly its fierce attitude and the subsequent judgment in its favour did much to guarantee the survival of the infant Labour Party following the election of Keir Hardie at Merthyr in 1900.

The great mineral wealth of Glamorgan ensured a railway mania and inevitably the TVR did not have things all its own way. In particular it had to share Pontypridd with the Barry Railway Company whose hugely profitable line came down the Rhondda Valley and ran via Maesycoed and a tunnel under the Graig to Trefforest where there was a junction with the TVR. By the 1960s the Barry line had long gone but I loved to walk its old route and to think back to those fierce days of competition. As things stand today the University of Glamorgan is well served by rail, but one cannot help thinking that the campus would be world-famous if the Barry line were still open. Bridging the line as it comes out of the Graig tunnel, the Gallery Restaurant would be a spectacular railway station. There are marvellous photos of the old Barry station at Pontypridd which stood at the other end of the tunnel. The story told is that every week the TVR manager would send his daughter to the Graig to buy a return ticket to Cardiff so that he could check the number to see how many tickets his rival had sold.

Sitting on the Graig in the 1960s I would imagine all those trains of a previous era passing through Ponty and carrying thousands of workers, mostly miners and their families, to days out at the seaside or to sporting fixtures, religious meetings or trade union and political rallies. When I travelled by rail myself it was the crowded trains on rugby international days that most fully evoked the old times; but there was one other particular incident that momentarily brought the past alive for me. On one journey two old men sat facing each other silently on a nearby seat until one of them opened a copy of a journal called *The Freethinker*; the other's face lit up and immediately they plunged into a discussion of their shared humanist views. Without difficulty I could imagine previous generations of Marxists or Unitarians discovering each other in the same way. Ideas, like coal, had always travelled this way.

Captain Smyth had been spot on, for the exploitation of Glamorgan's minerals had indeed encouraged the development of men's minds. From my side of the valley I would look across to the Common and the legendary Rocking Stone made famous in the nineteenth century by William Price and other so-called Druids. In her wonderful photographs Patricia Aithie has caught precisely the combination of cloud and light that suggests this might have been a magical place. The War Memorial stands as a reminder of a subsequent era that was less innocent. I will always associate the Common with the labour leader Ben Tillett who in 1893 came here to address a rally of 25,000 miners and to urge them to cast aside 'patriotism and cant' and 'to organise'. As things stood 'the body of Welshmen' were 'a mere rabble' deluded by a 'sham' primitive trade unionism. His challenging contention was that 'wages must determine prices, and an average standard of living must determine wages'. The miners followed Tillett's advice and formed a full-blooded union. In 1910 lodges of that union in the Rhondda and Aberdare Valleys forced their struggle up a notch and public order was threatened; photographs taken at that time of police reinforcements crowding the streets of Pontypridd highlighted the town's strategic importance. In that year the militant miners' leader stood for Labour in the East Glamorgan constituency but attracted only half as many votes as the sitting Liberal businessman. It took a war and redistribution to open the door for Labour. In 1922 T. I. Mardy Jones, a former miner whom Ruskin College had made into an economist, won the Pontypridd seat for Labour and from that time on the question of the town's political identity has never been an issue. Every Sunday in the 1960s we would see Arthur Pearson, the man who had represented the town for as long as anybody could remember, walking to chapel. I looked up his biographical details and found that prior to 1938 he had worked for twenty-five years in the chainworks that stood in the centre of Pontypridd and had served for seventeen years on Glamorgan County Council.

As I went to chapel every Sunday I was very conscious that I was witnessing the end of a custom that had once dominated the town. On every corner there stood an impressive place of worship but already one could sense the eerie emptiness. In a marvellous autobiography, *Days of Absence*, the Pontypridd-born writer Alun Richards conveys how much the chapel had meant to his grandmother. He was made to serve his religious apprenticeship but like so many of his contemporaries, he was far more aware of the ideas being outlined in an outstanding grammar school and by the diversions of a vibrant popular culture. After the service at my Baptist chapel near the Old Bridge I would walk down High Street with the minister. Invariably we would meet the minister of my mother's Welsh Independent chapel and the ensuing conversation would always end with a precise report on how many worshippers there had been in the respective congregations. We were consciously recording history. Today what was my chapel is now a museum and the pulpit from which I preached my first and last sermons is a prize exhibit therein. In the most stunning photograph ever taken of Pontypridd, Patricia Aithie looks northwards from the Old Bridge and captures the soft tranquillity of this stretch of the Taff; a beautifully proportioned chapel appropriately completes the idyll. A caption explains that Eglwys Bach is now a doctor's surgery.

Even at the time I knew that popular culture had won the battle for my soul. Notwithstanding the ecclesiastical architects, it seemed to me that the County Cinema was the most dominant building in town, although in honesty I preferred the White Palace where I was so impressed by Kirk Douglas and Tony Curtis in *The Vikings* that I went back several times, every time returning home up the path to Maesycoed humming Mario Nascimbene's glorious theme tune and imagining myself dancing along the oars. Meanwhile there were other attractions on offer in Ynysyngharad Park, a venue that had attracted me from childhood. Who could resist a park that one entered by crossing a bridge, let alone one which afforded a view of the confluence of the Taff and the Rhondda? The town owes this magnificent facility largely to the Brown and Lenox company, the owners of the chainworks which lies just a short distance away and which for most of Pontypridd's industrial history dominated the town. As I walk in the park I recall H. V. Morton's account of his visit to the works in 1931. He was enchanted to find a foundry that had hardly changed since the early days of the industrial revolution and which had made the Royal Navy's anchors and cables for almost as long. Morton might have added that, in one of the most famous photographs of the nineteenth century, Isambard Kingdom Brunel smokes his cigar as he nonchalantly stands in front of huge Pontypridd-made chains. What did strike Morton, however, was that making the links for the chains was difficult and exhausting; 'after every link the gang take a breather. They wash their hands, necks and faces. They take a step outside the factory and breathe the air.' I wonder if a worker once said, 'Wouldn't it be nice to have a park here?'

I went to the park to watch rugby, for it was here that Ponty played before they went upmarket and moved to the new ground at Sardis Road in 1971. There had been great players at Ponty. Amongst the crowd there would be recollections of a great post-war outside-half Glyn Davies (later to be lovingly eulogized by Alun Richards) and the tough forward Russell Robins who had gone to South Africa with the Lions in 1955. There were also great days to come, but in the early 1960s there was a pleasant informal-ity about rugby in Ponty and one was always a little surprised to see visiting stars run onto the field. After a match we would stroll up to the clubhouse, commenting on how Bob Penberthy had won every lineout or arguing about how many tries Tony Davies had scored that season. We also went to the park to see Gla-morgan play county cricket, and perhaps on these days more than any others we felt that we were living in a county town. I recall that during one match against a Sussex side bristling with current Test stars I suddenly experienced an enormous satisfaction and congratulated myself for being able to watch cricket there at the heart of things. It was a delightful sylvan setting and I was not at all surprised that the Middlesex and England spinner Fred Titmus described it as one of the loveliest grounds on the county circuit.

Of course there were days in Pontypridd that were far from lovely. However, even bad weather brought consolation. From my vantage point in Maesycoed the slate roofs of Pwllgwaun looked magnificent in the rain, and there was something atmos-pheric and Dickensian about those misty days when one could not see across the valley but could hear clearer than usual the diesel multiple-unit heading off for Porth. South Wales romantic I might have been, but tears would come to my eyes when the Car-diff Central announcer with a Caribbean accent thanked us all for 'travelling on the Valley lines'. I wanted others to share my enthu-siasm and as a lecturer at Swansea University I introduced a 'Valleys Tour' that to my amazement became something of a cult event, even surviving the passing of the course of which it formed a part. Needless to say, it always rained on those days, but as we went up the Afan Valley (noting Richard Burton's birthplace) and then over the Bwlch, this only contributed to the sense that we were entering a world apart.

On the 'Valleys Tour' students were shown Tonypandy, Clydach Vale, Maerdy, Aberdare, Aberfan, Dowlais, the Bevan Monument above Tredegar and Ebbw Vale. It was hoped that they would end the day with some sense of how the mineral wealth of the Glamorgan District had created a distinct urban culture, one that had shaped the political values of the nation as a whole. Over the years, however, the whole tone of the day changed and I found myself talking less about Keir Hardie, Noah Ablett and Aneurin Bevan and more about what lay before our eyes, things such as boarded-up shops, whole streets being up for sale and the profusion of satellite dishes. My rhetoric became more hollow with the years, and it was with some bitterness that I realized that I had been using the convenient and sanitized phrase of 'de-industrialization' as a let-out. All the news from the Valleys now concerned drugs, crime, murder and arson. Every statistic depressed. At one moment we were told the society in Europe that most closely resembled the County of Mid Glamorgan (1974–96) was that of Sicily, but it was not long before the figures suggested that this was perhaps the most deprived community in the European Union. The one thing I did not have to explain to students was that we were looking at the worst housing stock in the country. I had often thought of the hunger marchers in the 1930s walking through affluent shires and suburbs on their way to Westminster. In truth, at the end of the twentieth century that same journey was even more dramatic and dispiriting. Was it time to march again or were there more positive steps to be taken?

As far as the landscape is concerned, the greatest change has been the construction of new roads. The old roads were a hell and I often think of those Merthyr steelworkers like my uncle who travelled a round trip of 50 miles every day to work in the Dowlais works in Cardiff. The new roads, built in the main to attract new industry, essentially serve to suburbanize; private motorists just become caught up in a patchwork quilt of urban sprawl that provides motorways, shopping malls, leisure facilities and other attractions wherever planners find convenient. Shooting up or down the new roads in the Welsh valleys today one sometimes glimpses a row of houses and finds difficulty in recalling what the village, or even town, used to be called. Pontypridd has suffered particularly badly in this respect. Motorists from the Rhondda and Merthyr now pass quickly through the town without a moment's thought. Before the carve-up, not only did Ponty look like a county town nestling around its distinguished and steepled parish church, but in a certain light the view from the Common put one in mind of Heidelberg. The roads are a standing invitation for the citizens of the Valleys to avail themselves of a wider world. What, one has to ask, happens to the dormer communities left behind?

In the Valleys of south Wales nostalgia is inevitable; the mere mention of names, whether it be of villages, pits, chapels, choirs, coal and railway companies or even individual boxers or politicians, sweeps one up into a sense of history. Today, however, there is excitement anew as the fight-back begins. Most encouraging is the enhanced awareness of the Valleys as a distinct area, a phenomenon created in part by the broadcasters working for BBC Wales, HTV and S4C and encouraged by a new political dispensation involving a National Assembly and a bewildering local government reorganization in which Labour has had to look to its laurels. One positive development is a new sense of the Valleys as a distinct and remarkably beautiful landscape. Only very slowly is the rest of the country catching up with our well-kept secret: this is one of the best walking areas in the whole of Britain. I have heard some industrialists denounce the significance of Heritage, but clearly it is a dimension that the Valleys must deploy skilfully. The Taff Trail and the Heritage Centre are a start, but I think we are still too restrained and formal in our presentation of the past; if we are prepared to learn from the Americans, for example, we can offer both young people and tourists some notion of the commercial and human dramas played out in such historic tracts as the valley of the Taff.

We live in a culture in which individuals are encouraged to avail themselves of a bewildering and truly global range of musical and technological opportunities. Only the middle-aged can recall the days when fulfilment came from a participation in communal activities that were essentially local. It was the intensity engendered in choirs, bands, theatre groups and even cinema audiences that was the hallmark of Valleys life. The phenomenon lasted longest in rugby, initially because of a wonderful flowering of the national game in the 1970s, something occasioned by the prosperity of the 1960s and the vitality of schools. More recently rugby passions have reflected the need for a new generation to forge some kind of regional identity as an alternative to dominant English modes. The resurgence of Pontypridd Rugby Club in the thirty years since it moved to Sardis Road (and in particular its keen rivalry with the fashionable Cardiff RFC) has perhaps been the clearest statement that there is life in the Valleys and that we are not yet a totally coastal culture. As the twentieth century ended Neil Jenkins, the British Lions, Wales and erstwhile Pontypridd outside-half, became an iconic figure for the whole of Wales but in particular for the Valleys heartland. He was identified by BBC Wales as a 'working-class hero', the perfect example of the skill, determination and application needed for a Valleys youth to succeed.

The success and fulfilment of individual lives is the goal and has become the key to Valleys life; hence the emphasis on lifelong learning and the arts. The new priorities are nicely reflected in the fact that in 2002 the MP and the AM for Pontypridd held arts and education portfolios in their respective governments. All the indications are that the young people of south Wales have a vitality that needs to be expressed in music, acting and other public activities. It may well be that the drama of our history has determined that essentially we will be entertainers. There is a potential in the Valleys and I sense it still every time I take the train north from Cardiff. I love that view of the river with its herons and cormorants near Castell Coch, the fortress that protects the incredibly narrow entrance to the hill district. I like to recall that Rhodri Morgan came from Radyr, that Bleddyn Williams, the greatest Welsh centre, was born in Taff's Well, that Daniel Evans and many other great actors were taught at Rhydfelen and that Tom Jones, the most famous of all Welsh entertainers, started out in Trefforest. To travel up the Taff is indeed to be reminded of the wealth of 'the Glamorgan District' and, of course, these seams are far from exhausted.

REGENERATION, WALES
AND CULTURE

Dai Smith

Culture is one of the two or three most complicated words in the
English language . . . The complex argument is about the relations
between general human development and a particular way of life,
and between both and the works and priorities of art and
intelligence . . . It signifies that virtually all the hostility has been
connected with uses involving claims to superior knowledge and
distinctions between 'high' art (*culture*) and popular art and
entertainment.

(Raymond Williams, *Keywords*)

Some day under the impulse of collective action, we shall enfran-
chise the artists, by giving them our public buildings to work
upon: our bridges, our housing estates, our offices, our industrial
canteens, our factories and the municipal buildings where we
house our civic activities . . . it is tiresome to listen to the diatribes
of some modern art critics who bemoan the passing of the rich
patron as though this must mean the decline of art whereas it could
mean its emancipation, if the artists were restored to their proper
relationship with civic life.

(Aneurin Bevan, 1948)

T he regeneration benefits of a cultural policy – by government, local authority or private benefactor – are now legion
and obvious. From Merseyside to Tyneside, from Cornwall to
Glasgow, from Cardiff Bay to New York City, we can measure it
in visitor numbers, tourist dollars and civic pride. Whether it is
Rhondda Heritage Park or British Museum or DisneyWorld, the
cultural wrapper and the cultural object if you like, there is a connected success. And it extends, of course, to fine arts and music
and performance, in word and body, and festival. There is still a
debate to be had about this – over its quality and its effects – but,
nowadays, when the public hears the word culture it instinctively
knows it can reach for both the 'penny and the bun'.

In a deeper sense this is also because this aspect of culture has
been shrunk dried: just add the water of consumption to see it
expand into a fast food nutrient. The sustainable nourishment of a
culture we actually produce and have been made by is not so easy
to find. The ramifications of that meaning of culture, for societies
intent on being themselves meaningful, will be the burden of this
chapter so, just for now, I will park the culture bit of my title's
trinity and approach the stalled vehicle by another route, one

where it has become axiomatic to exhale the words regeneration and Wales in the same sighing breath. Time, I suggest, to breathe in again and fill the lungs with the fresher thought of how culture, as more than a mere policy requirement and a commercial spin-off, might yet become the unique deliverer of Wales's specific twenty-first-century needs.

Almost by definition we are required to know what 'Wales' is before we can apply the universal balm of 'regeneration'. Perhaps it is because we continue to assume (or rather presume) that such a definition is easy that we continue to be surprised that the magic properties of regeneration have been only haphazardly effective. Questions of civic governance, and its value, across a national unit that is more a geographical soundbite than a truly unified entity will continue to require the most profound speculation about the balance between a distended society of communities and the over-weening (necessary?) power of a growing capital presence. Will Caerdydd become the Wales we cannot otherwise inhabit together? Will Cymru accept the Cardiff which will dominate its future? Ireland now is a young, vibrant, close-packed nation and its real name is Dublin. The concept of Wales is more fluid than ever. The reality of Wales is as recalcitrant as ever. Nor will such issues subside by displacement – as in: resolution will occur when the fudge between a Welsh Assembly government and Westminster is settled in favour of greater devolved powers *or* bilingualism becomes a happy norm *or* Bangor is reached more quickly than Battersea *or* the Labour Party remembers its History is the key to its Future *or* political journalism in Wales acquires a brain cell or two which are not corroded with the lifetime's bile of the second-rate mind. Some things are, indeed, too much to hope for and some things will not come about by wishing they were so.

From this perspective, the historical viewfinder is absolutely a counter to nostalgia, that love-sick yearning for a corner that is never turned into a world that never can be. We need to turn away from the present, that always passing moment where the fixative of nostalgia really lies, and ruthlessly reassert the only ongoing process in the lives of human beings, which is the shaping of the actual future by the unfolding of experience in our past. And the connection between them is what we mean, in all its famous complexity, by the word 'culture'.

Or, let us simplify by imagining such lived culture in the more three-dimensional terms of an environment, a built or historic environment if you like, and contemplate how mindlessly we have cleansed parts of Wales of the substance and shapes in our daily lives that were once invested with meaning. Material things do matter and the more local and personal they are or have been, the more they have mattered to us. This is why, surely, immoveable mountains or unstoppable rivers or landmark buildings inhabit both popular perception and any aesthetic culture that seeks to express any particularized imagery. We cannot envisage Wales as flat. We may wish it to be tolerant. We cannot make it oil-rich. We may seek to maximize its talents. We should not glorify its history. We cannot regenerate a country as that specific country without acknowledging its past. And so on.

What then matters, it seems to me, is building *anew* so that the texture of that vanished historic environment is captured again, in its detail, but in *other forms* of retention. A landscape into a mindscape. And, if possible, fresh building of purpose.

Take a building like the Cwmaman Workmen's Institute in the Cynon Valley, not so much restored as reconfigured within its own identity, for fresh, yet connected, purpose. Connected because it was built, as most of the institutes and libraries across the coalfield were, to encapsulate, enshrine almost, the way in which localities like its valley, mere aggregations of people assembled for work had, in a few short decades, made themselves into congregations intent, through religion, politics, family life, voluntary societies and the rest, on being communities.

They had not possessed a 'historic environment' other than an immemorial landscape. They imbued the landscape with their mindset. Five pits were sunk in that small valley from the late 1840s to the 1870s, and hence population, and thence the financing and building of the institute – rebuilt, after a fire, in 1907 and by 1914 with a hall for concerts, lectures, public meetings, a library, a newspaper reading room, a billiard room, for boys as well as men, two bathrooms, a gymnasium, changing facilities for sports, and rooms for music practice and drama. And a mile down the road in Aberaman the community built an even bigger one – with an underground swimming pool!

It is the *detail* which scorns mere nostalgia. There, in

Cwmaman, where The Stereophonics make music whose international echo is unimaginable without that historical sounding
chamber, one of Wales's greatest twentieth-century poets and
short-story writers was born in 1915. When Dylan Thomas, born a
year before Alun Lewis, told the world about the Valleys, in a
famous prose piece in 1944, the year of Lewis's death, it was Alun
Lewis's poem 'The Mountain over Aberdare' that Thomas rather
lamely paraphrased on the BBC's Home Service.

But Alun Lewis knew *his* historic environment, precisely
Cwmaman, in ways Thomas did not, and it is in detail that Lewis,
in the late 1930s, linked people to what they had made and been
shaped by, as he looked down and over Cwmaman, and in an
early draft of his famous poem, named names with the precision
of local knowledge:

> To note precisely all I know
> From this high mountain ledge:
> The drab streets backed across the Cwm,
> Red ruck of rails, abandoned shaft,
> Grey Hebron in a rigid cramp,
> White cheapjack picture-house, the Church
> An old sow stretched beside the stream,
> My uncle's house in Milton Street,
> Black gardens row on row
> Old thorntrees stunted by the wind,
> The new building of the Labour Exchange:
> All moving me more, oh much more,
> Than the pigeons clearing and furling
> And all traditional beauty . . .
> Deliberately to understate
> To pare down to the quick
> Reality: to be
> In love articulate.

To be in love, articulate – which is what, I believe, we are when we
are, historically but as contemporaries, in sync with our environment and possessed of our culture.

This does not imply an unchanging envelope of existence. It
does propose a visceral awareness as being the warm counterpart
of that colder consciousness which allows us to have collective
purposes if we are to have, to quote our own National Assembly

policy document, 'A Culture in Common', which is, of course, a phrase from Raymond Williams.

The collective institutions of this society – voluntary, political, religious, sporting, etc. – no longer impact on individual lives or, at least, not in the same and shared way. The one(s) that now do are educational (to the age of sixteen) and occasional (the ones that are being generated or created anew out of choice: and these can be idealistic, altruistic, creative or mindless, even threatening and socially reprehensible to the point of danger). The University of Glamorgan, in the heart of this particular world, is, therefore, uniquely placed to serve as active exemplum (for individuals) and potential beacon (for a society). Our location is the locus of our educational energy. Strength of purpose and of delivery is our 'unique selling point'. Just as the University of Wales was, at its best, a nineteenth-century creation for the last century, so we can be a twentieth-century creation with this century in mind. We can lead on the concept of a university integrated into every educational and cultural level of its surrounding society – a resource in partnership with other providers but one uniquely equipped to raise expectations, set goals, be assured in quality and excellence *and* not stand aside or be aloof. We then become *the* entrepreneurial wealth creator *par excellence* by presenting ourselves to this society as its last best hope for a collective – and so community-building – solution. The implication of all this is that we take our current best practice and put it through a step change of ambition and delivery.

Culture, in these circumstances, becomes the key driver of social and economic regeneration. A society that possesses 'culture' as its texture can receive and hold material and structural forms of assistance. This texturing involves recognition and dissemination of achievement in order to build ambition and aspiration – Regenerate only in order to Generate. The University of Glamorgan, engaged as it will be with a range of other core activities and in widening areas, can become the institutional hub of a culture network across the Valleys.

It is axiomatic that the University signals its essence as a university since it is that assured stance which is the hallmark of our educational promise and our social potential. However, in delivering this widening-access agenda the University of Glamorgan

has become aware that it fails to reach the most excluded populations. We argue that policies and initiatives that push learning
miss those people who are already educationally disaffected, who
look at a campus with a sense of fear or even hatred, and who
have no confidence in their abilities to learn. A comprehensive
learning strategy for the Valleys has to move outside the normal
educational boundaries. All of the current work on increasing
access and widening participation must continue to consolidate
and expand. We have to be aware, however, that the current basket of policy and provision has a loose weave; it does not hold all
of the potential learners. We must reach into communities to
those who most need support but are least likely to present themselves for it.

We need to reflect on those linkages in our contemporary
Wales, between the acceptance of poverty as material fact and the
need to marshal the forces of imagination to defeat it root and
branch. There is a trinity of poverties to consider: poverty of experience; poverty of aspiration; poverty of imagination.

POVERTY OF EXPERIENCE

We surely do not need to linger overlong on any still-standing dis-
agreement about absolute poverty as it affects, even today, far too
many of our fellow citizens. Even in *this* Wales it has not been
eradicated but it has been moved into ghettos and amongst the
dispossessed, the single, the old, the young. There are, of course,
gradations, but I would still argue that it is, in what is now a classic sense since the 1909 Commission into Poverty, that rolling
stone for the subsequent welfare state, absolute. Absolute not in
the constant sense of hunger and certainly not starvation, but
absolute in the sense that certain citizens living in certain places
live closer and continuously to the displacements of poor living –
crime, drugs, a crumbling social fabric, a private struggle for
cleanliness and respectability, an aura of low expectation that follows from recurring unemployment, low pay, family breakdown,
peer pressure on the young to court failure rather than whatever
society may mean by success.

Alleviation of such poverty for individuals is not, and cannot
be, eradication of this social evil. From the University of Glamorgan, Professor David Adamson has eloquently argued

recently that, in a negative sense, such eradication could only follow on the intellectual acceptance that this material poverty is
inextricably connected to class division, corporate wealth and the
lack of progressive taxation policies to drive redistribution. In a
positive sense, he further suggests that community action via
community ownership of both problem and solution will, in
time, prove an irresistible political force for change.

It is to how that might be effected that I now turn, for the
word we are required to employ here is not 'absolute' but 'relative'. Relative deprivation was the term coined by the sociologist,
W. G. Runciman, in the 1960s, to express how the perception of
basic needs had changed. And that the lack of particular attributes
– access to widespread social goods, from consumer durables to
educational advantages, from affordable holidays to availability of
the arts, and so on – was also a key definer of being poor.

So material poverty elides inexorably into the kind of softer
focus deprivation, though none the less real, which defines social
exclusion in the manner that lets us know, instinctively, here
today, who is poor and who is not, what is an enforced choosing
of diet and dress, and what is proper choice, what prevents full
cultural succour and what ensures a recycling of deprivation, for
some, from generation to generation. Is there a trip switch for this
poverty trap?

POVERTY OF ASPIRATION

This *can* be worked on as well. And, indeed, I think the track
record in Wales, in both the voluntary and public sector, is pretty
admirable. I think we do have, amongst our local authorities and
the wider field of community education, sensitive and sensible
policies that are eliciting demand for as well as consumption of
those wider social goods. The learning outcomes that are being
made integral to Communities First programmes are surely of the
essence if sustainable social development is to be delivered. Economic support and entrepreneurial spin – social and economic
regeneration – require, not as an incidental, but as a core platform, the catalyst of culture. What we should mean by this is that
past achievements from within those communities can be so con-
veyed in the present as to help contemporary aspiration towards
future ambition for achievement. We could spend a long time

tabulating how our industrial communities, from Brymbo to Bed-was, from Gwent to Gowerton, had their self-worth dumped upon, along with material destruction some two decades ago, but suffice to say that a revitalized sense of culture is not an incidental luxury in community regeneration – it is the very key we seek.

Consider the once unformed maelstrom of industrial Victorian Wales and the lesson of its legacy as expressed by Professor Ieuan Gwynedd Jones in *Communities* (1987):

> The eisteddfod, the chapel, the friendly society, the pub were gen-uinely the creations of a working class culture providing for itself by itself and with a breathtaking confidence taking over the cul-tural-literacy role of an aristocracy . . . communities such as were these, existing sometimes on the very edges of survival, threatened with the degradation of excessive labour, plagued by endemic sickness, knowing poverty . . . need above all self-confidence. Community for them is not some kind of product of conditions – it is the condition of existence.

The self-confidence was the by-product of cultural aspiration; to give it three-dimensional shape they needed a flight of fancy.

POVERTY OF IMAGINATION

This is, I believe, the greatest shackle we have on our well-mean-ing efforts, to devise a policy agenda that can stifle the poverty of experience and nurture aspiration. We are simply not bold enough, often enough, to think outside the comfort of our boxes – administrative, educational, governmental, environmental, architectural, local and global. To be imaginative in this context is to be holistic; to refuse the public separation of functions which are, in individuated private lives, lived as a whole. That is what a culture is – a whole way of life. Living in poverty is to be denied that wholeness. It may present itself as poor health or educational slippage at thirteen or sixteen or twenty-five but, at root, it is being unable to shatter the glass wall where you can look but you better not touch, boy.

There are no panaceas to offer. If there were a ready-made for-mula we would be marketing it. But we can say that, for Wales, it is about making connections in a society more fragmented – geo-graphically, historically, socially – than we sometimes *care* to say. But those connections have to be made not just at a national level of rhetoric – a faster link from north to south, a pan-Wales governance, a culture in common – but also at the *local* level where the universe begins from where you are.

The process is of identity – who you are and why – of discovery – in which wider context you are situated to grow – and of creation – what you make and think of all this, in many forms, in order to be liberated. It is the case, of course, that this species of cultural consciousness is most urgent in those places where poverty and social exclusion have shut memory and hope out.

There are already many initiatives, and one such which the Welsh Assembly government is supporting will be the University's plan to pilot the opening of 'Gates' in the south Wales Valleys: gates which, in buildings and personnel, will act as spokes to a University's hub but where the emphasis will be on learning through cultural activity in order to raise the capacity of communities, not just individuals. What will be on offer will be permanent, not a tap to turn on or off or a ladder to climb. We have the opportunity to make a great experiment work, maybe a once-in-a-lifetime opportunity.

In Trevor Griffiths's award-winning play about Nye Bevan, in his centenary year, 1997, *Food for Ravens*, Nye is speaking to a Boy, his past and his future presence, as he himself approaches the end of life.

> NYE: Once I asked a simple question: what do we put in place of fear?
>
> *He opens his eyes, smiles, watches the still-watching boy.*
>
> . . . If we let ourselves believe that reading and writing and painting and song and play and pleasuring and imagining and good food, good wine, good clothes and good health are the toff's turf, boy, haven't we lost the battle already? They're ours. Human birthright. All right?
>
> *The boy frowns, screws up his eyes.*
>
> BOY: How about sums?
>
> NYE: Sums too.
>
> BOY: So I can be a toff, can I?
>
> NYE: Aye. So long as you remember. Everything comes off the point of a pick.

The University's current practice and the experience of community regeneration organizations have pointed clearly to the role of cultural activities in informal learning and capacity development. There are of course many ways by which to interpret cultural values and cultural relevance. We argue that culture, as a word and a concept, unlocks the door into a world of participation in learning which is attractive and characterized by anticipation, enjoyment, interest, relevance and entertainment. The education baggage of classroom, teaching and assessment – along with potential corollaries of control, boredom and failure – is left at the doorway. An educational settlement that is typified through cultural priorities has an air of excitement, and it is constantly saying things about communities and their people. In order to support cultural production participants have to develop methods, experiences and perspectives from many different sources. This is the bridge between learning and culture, where education is not the destination but is an attractive and desirable means to an end.

The issue is how to make successful past practice relevant to our own contemporary circumstance. Thus, the 'Gates' is more akin to a workshop, exhibition and festival, as compared with the more usual classroom or outreach centre. It is, however, more than just a place. We can view such a development as offering links and portals to specialist expertise and huge resources located elsewhere – especially a university campus. For this reason we use the term *gate* to refer to both a physical entity and a means of travelling into other worlds.

We cannot do or affect everything, but we can be the best example of cultural practice by making it a natural part of all our core purposes. It can allow us, everywhere and in every way, to connect to the contemporary society by sharing cultural achievement (past and present) as a key signifier of current worth. By helping sustain a culture that aspires to go forward through education to employability and entrepreneurship, we provide *the* building block for a civic society. At the very least it can make the Valleys a more obviously welcoming and pleasant place to live and work. At its best, the culture project can make the Valleys future places for future people. Again.